WHITE BUTTERFLIES

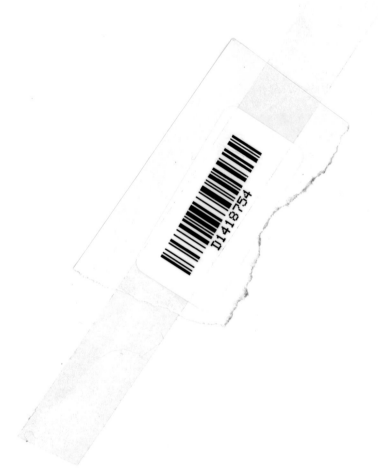

WHITE BUTTERFLIES

COLIN McPHEDRAN

PANDANUS BOOKS
Research School of Pacific and Asian Studies
THE AUSTRALIAN NATIONAL UNIVERSITY

Cover: Photograph of Colin McPhedran aged 13 in Calcutta.

© Pandanus Books 2002

Typeset in Goudy 10.5pt on 13.25pt by Pandanus Books and printed on Glopague 110gsm by Pirie Printers, Canberra, phone 02 6280 5410.

National Library of Australia Cataloguing-in-Publication entry

McPhedran, Colin.
        White butterflies.

        ISBN 1 74076 017 4.

        1. McPhedran, Colin. 2. Refugees — Australia — Biography.
        3. Refugees — Burma — Biography. I. Title.

325.21095910994

Editorial enquiries please contact Pandanus Books on 02 6125 3269

Published by Pandanus Books, Research School of Pacific and Asian Studies, The Australian National University, Canberra ACT 0200 Australia

Pandanus Books are distributed by UNIREPS, University of New South Wales, Sydney NSW 2052 Phone 02 9664 0999 Fax 02 9664 5420

Editors: Verona Burgess and Julie Stokes
Production: Ian Templeman, Duncan Beard and Emily Brissenden

With fond memories of Laurel, and to my dear family:
Cheryl, Ian, Shaun, Lynne and Jane,
who might well say, 'About time!'

ACKNOWLEDGEMENTS

Writing down this register of events in their order of time has caused me some anguish. What helped me cope were the memories of the span of good times which preceded and succeeded the sad times.

There were moments in my struggle to pull myself out of the quagmire of depression when I would 'fog up'. Unlocking and revisiting events of the past led me to experience flashes of sadness, but also to experience sheer joy.

I once heard a speaker describe life as a craft. That being so, I believe I have served my apprenticeship, enjoyed the process and earned a certificate of trade.

Along the way I was assisted by some fine tutors: the gentle and kind Indians who nurtured me, the Christian family who fostered me, the burly Scottish tea-planter who pulled me from the mud on the trail and would not let me give up and die, and my mother, whose love has enveloped me throughout the years.

There are many people who have helped me in the publication of this account of my life. I would like to acknowledge a few of them: my daughter-in-law Verona Burgess whose editing made it happen; Penelope Layland for her fine-tooth comb; Anthony Hill for his writer's eye; the late Ron McKie whose idea it was; Kay Jones and Joanna Gash for the typewriter and the hospitality; Dora Burgess, Jenny Corvini, Mac Cott, Olivia Kent and John Knight for their feedback and my brother Donald who filled in some gaps; and Ian Templeman and the team from Pandanus Books, Emily Brissenden, Duncan Beard, Ann Andrews, Julie Stokes and Peter Fuller, who believed in it.

Colin McPhedran

CONTENTS

Part I: The Trek

Part II: Mother India

Part III: East to West

I

THE TREK

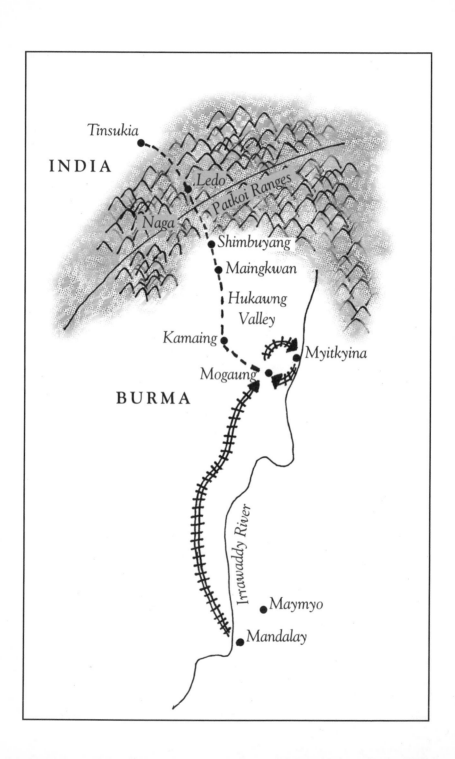

Chapter 1

THE BEGINNING,
OR WAS IT THE END?

I remember the moment. We had disposed hungrily of our school breakfast of porridge and limp toast thinly coated with Palmboter, a dairy substitute made from palm oil. We waited silently for the white-sheeted Brother of the Sacred Heart Order to finish his meal.

It was December 1941.

Brother Fulbert sat on a dais at the end of the refectory eating his traditional breakfast of German sausages and fried eggs. Then he mopped his tobacco-stained moustache and beard and looked up.

In a gargling voice, typical of the German brothers at St Paul's, he announced, 'All students are summoned to the courtyard for an important announcement by the principal Father.'

I turned to my closest friends, a Burmese boy named Alfie and an Indian Muslim called Huq, who shared my misery at boarding school in Rangoon.

'What's this all about?'

They shrugged their shoulders. It was not unusual for the principal to appear on the balcony to address the school. He loved the sound of his own voice. The dining room emptied and we took up our positions to march in Indian file to the courtyard. One thousand thoroughly bored students stood, eyes fixed on the head in front, and waited for the proclamation from on high. I looked about and noticed a few of the favoured boys — the teachers' pets who sneaked about the school gathering information on the rest of us — looking upwards in anticipation of a stimulating announcement from the principal master.

It seemed an eternity before he strode out on to the balcony. The proceedings began with everyone chanting the customary, 'In the name of the Father...' and crossing our chests. He talked about the dedication of the brothers and teachers, then rambled on about the war.

'You are all aware that the war being waged in the peninsula south of the country has taken a turn for the worse. Now we are informed by the military authorities of the threat of a Japanese invasion of Burma, and the probability of air raids over Rangoon.'

This grabbed our attention. We all knew that the Japanese had bombed Pearl Harbour, in Hawaii, on 7 December. Two days later, the pride of the British navy, the battleships *Prince of Wales* and *Repulse*, had been sunk in the Straits of Malacca, off Singapore.

'In view of the present situation,' he said, 'we have decided to close the school. Your families have been informed.'

A huge cheer arose, but I couldn't help glancing quickly in the direction of the favoured boys. I nudged Alfie.

'I get the impression they aren't displaying quite the same enthusiasm as the rest of us,' I whispered.

Then I realised that this meant the end of my worst experience of schooling. The world was being torn apart but I, aged 11, was simply overwhelmed with the joy of escaping St Paul's and going home.

The school was known to every school pupil in Burma as the '*chota* [small] gaol'. It was strict and regimented like an army barrack. The slightest freedom of speech or action was never tolerated. The rules seemed designed to produce zombies. The school also pandered to wealthy parents, with boarders segregated into three distinct classes.

My older brother Robert and I were first-class boarders, the privileged ones with separate dormitories and dining rooms. The meals were of poor quality and anybody who complained was spoken to sternly. I felt sorry for the boys who were less fortunate than we were. Boys in the second and third classes often had to put up with eating our leftovers. They pleaded with us to eat everything in our dining room.

'We're so tired of being fed on stale bread and reconstituted curries. If you eat all yours, they might give us something fresh.'

The most loathsome aspect of St Paul's was the ritual of the morning bath time. The ablutions block was a long tin shed with a concrete floor. In the middle, a trough full of cold water stretched from one end to another. Each boy was supplied with a tin bucket.

Every morning, even in the coldest weather, we had to line up naked and at the sound of a whistle from the priest overseeing all the naked boys, we dipped into the water and wet ourselves. Another whistle and we had to stop and soap our bodies. The last whistle permitted us to dip into the trough and wash the soap off. Any boy going beyond the whistle was punished. It was a ridiculous and cruel ritual, and we were helpless. The priest in charge leered at our naked bodies as he regulated every movement by the whistle.

Our class mistress was an Anglo–Indian lay teacher called Miss Stevens. She had a sharp tongue and I was often the victim of her broadsides. I suffered her barbed criticisms of my work, but most of the time I let them go over my head and drifted along with my schoolwork.

Having two good friends in Alfie and Huq made my life just bearable. Boredom overwhelmed me most of the time. The only time I was happy was in the playground.

My brother Robert was an adaptable person and had settled in to the school much better than I. He seldom complained. He was a top student and the family was justifiably proud of him, as was the school. Since the exams in the higher grades were public, the Protestant and Catholic schools competed to produce the brightest students. Robert was a prize as far as the Catholics were concerned and they showed him special attention. The fuss did not concern him at all. He did what he had to do.

One day when he returned from a public scholarship exam I asked, 'What was it like?'

'It was as easy as pissing off a bridge,' he told me and my awed friends. He did not mean to brag, but he did truly find school lessons easy and interesting. Robert was held in high esteem by the priests.

'Why can't you be more like your brother?' they asked me.

I did not like the constant comparisons, but I was never jealous of Robert's achievements. I was proud of him and looked up to him.

We dispersed enthusiastically, without waiting for instructions from the grim-faced wardens who had lorded it over our very souls. As the three of us walked back to the dormitory together I had a premonition that our lives would change forever. Yet I would have laughed in disbelief had anyone told me that the day's events would lead me to live my adult life and raise a family in Australia, a country I knew only as part of a geography lesson.

I did not think about the fact that history was being made or what the war meant for our country. My spirit rallied. I would soon be reunited with the person I loved most — my mother — and the many friends I had been forced to leave behind in Central Burma when my father had decided arbitrarily to move Robert and me away from our mother's influence to the strict jurisdiction of a Catholic boarding school.

Born in September 1930, I was just 11 years and three months old when the school closed down. I had been at St Paul's for just over a year.

We were an Anglo–Burmese family. Our father, Archie, was a Scot who had come to Burma in the 1920s with the Shell Burmah Oil Company. Soon afterwards he married my mother, Daw Ni, a young, educated woman from a scholarly and well-regarded Burmese family whom he had met through the strict Plymouth Brethren church, to which they both belonged.

At first the family had lived in Insein, a suburb out of Rangoon, in the south of Burma. The oil company frowned on European employees who had native wives and families and did not permit them to share the company houses at Syriam. This was the company's base across the river from Rangoon, where there was a huge oil refinery.

Donald was the eldest child. Ethel was second, Robert third and I was the youngest. After I was born the family moved to Maymyo, a hill town about 3000 feet above sea level in Central Burma, not far from the old capital of Mandalay.

Maymyo was the summer seat of government, an affluent hill station where the British governor and his officials went to escape the heat of Rangoon summers.

Jamshed Villa, the house our father bought in Maymyo, had once been the summer residence of an Indian industrialist, Tata, whose business was based in the Indian city of Jamshedpur.

It was a comfortable brick dwelling, surrounded by beautiful gardens and with a sweeping curved driveway. There was a big oak tree at the front, and purple bougainvillea trailed over a shelter a little way from the house. Canna lilies, African daisies and Arum lilies grew like wildfire, and I remember dahlias flowering every year. My mother's pride and joy was her rose garden, where she cultivated many species. She always said, 'I love roses the best.'

My father remained living and working in the south. He travelled the 400 miles to the Shan States several times a year to see us. We visited him in Rangoon at least once a year. The arrangement did not seem to worry my mother and I never questioned it.

'I prefer to be away from the social scene,' she always said. 'I am content to raise my family with the country people of my home province.'

Before marrying my father, she had graduated in Arts at the University of Calcutta. Pushed to decide on a career by her two cousins, one a lawyer and another an academic at the University of Rangoon, she had chosen to go into education and, as she put it, to 'help the masses'.

She thus followed in the footsteps of her forebears, the Mon tribe, who for centuries had been the educators in Burma. Although she gave up her job with the Department of Education when Donald was born, she never really stopped teaching. In her spare moments she gave English lessons to her servants' children and those of her less well-off relatives.

My father, on the other hand, never stopped learning. He was a compulsive student of languages and spoke and wrote in many. It was in expressing himself in the spoken Burmese that he had the greatest difficulty. Whenever he spoke at a Gospel service in the native tongue, even I had a problem grasping everything he said. It was no fault of his that the burring speech of a Scot did not suit the soft tonal sounds of Burmese. Their most pronounced consonant, 'R', does not feature in the Burmese alphabet.

'If you had been born a Welshman, we would all understand you better!' my mother used to say.

He was single-minded and loved setting benchmarks in achievement for those around him, but whether he set the same standards for himself was another matter. Early on he had mapped out the future careers of his children and he kept closely in touch with our development by correspondence.

'Och, Donald will become a doctor,' he used to tell people. 'Ethel will go into education and Robert will join the Foreign Office.'

I had been left out of the calculations until I grew older.

———

My mother travelled the 400 miles down to Rangoon to accompany us safely home from school. She looked young and beautiful as she stepped out of the oil company car and greeted Robert and me with tears in her eyes. She tossed back her long black hair.

'I'll never let you children go again,' she said as she hugged us.

She added afterwards, 'Apay [father] couldn't come to see you off. He has a pressing engagement.'

Ethel's boarding school in Rangoon, the Diocesan girls' school, had also closed down. She did not travel with us by train, because a young man who was sweet on her had offered to drive her home to Maymyo. He was a young cadet officer called Noel whom she had met in Maymyo. His family too were Anglo–Burmese, very nice people. He was Ethel's first boyfriend and the arrangement to drive her home was made without my father's knowledge.

When he found out a day or so later, he was furious. He wrote sternly to my mother in Maymyo.

'Ethel is not to see Noel again. His family is unsuitable.'

I remember Ethel crying her heart out.

'Why would he say that?' she kept saying.

We spent the night with our relations in Rangoon and caught the morning train to Maymyo. The train was packed with people fleeing the impending attacks by Japanese planes. This was the first time I had seen refugees and it never occurred to me that I might become one myself. Observing their sense of urgency gave me my first inkling that the situation in Rangoon was truly ominous, but I barely noticed it in my eagerness to get home. My mother was brimming with happiness, and so was I.

Our reserved compartment was roomy and comfortable. Before the train departed, Mother felt sorry for the poor passengers fighting for a place on the train. She spotted two women with young children on the platform trying to get on board. One, carrying a baby, was barely more than a child herself.

My mother leant out of the window and said in Burmese, 'Where are you going?'

'To the country, to get away from the bombs,' the older one replied.

'Well then, we have plenty of room. We would be delighted if you would join us.'

They did.

The baby was crying and restless and the young mother did not seem to know what to do.

My mother gently said, 'Perhaps you would like to feed your baby.'

Straight away, like an obedient child, the young girl pulled out a breast and gave it to the baby, who drank happily and then fell fast asleep.

After that we all travelled comfortably together. They got out somewhere in Central Burma and we went on to Maymyo.

We arrived at night and were greeted by a host of my mother's servants and their friends. They were overjoyed to have us back in town.

'We have all missed you very much!' our cook said with a broad smile, and added quietly, 'But not as much as your mother did.'

The first air raid hit Rangoon at 10 am on 23 December, within days of our departure. Seventy Japanese bombers attacked the airport, the docks and the city. The school building survived the war.

Chapter 2
MAYMYO

'*S*ince the schools in the Shan States have not closed,' my mother said, 'I have enrolled you in your old school, to start when the new term begins.'

In the meantime, I was back in my beloved Maymyo and our house came alive. Friends flocked back and the holidays were full of adventure.

The Japanese army was winning every battle against the British and Indian troops, but it meant very little to me. I was just a happy lad who had returned home at long last.

The British had built government offices and stately homes for themselves in Maymyo. The town was also a fashionable summer retreat for rich Burmese and Indian families. The British had established beautiful botanical gardens and the well-to-do part of the town was set in gentle, rolling green hills.

Our house was in Circular Road on the edge of the jungle. Occasionally tigers prowled right inside our back garden. They helped themselves to our dogs on more than one occasion, much to Robert's distress.

The familiar surroundings and faces I loved and had missed so much were all there. Everything moved along comfortably, despite the gloomy news from the war front. The garden looked beautiful. The Japanese cherry trees lining our driveway were blossoming and soon there was a massed backdrop of pink. Even the animals seemed happy to have us back. The ducks, geese and chickens were all getting fat and the ponies had been well groomed and fed.

Robert's favourites were Molly and her foal, Cross Bun, who had been born on Good Friday. Robert, who was 13, and Ethel, 16, were both keen riders.

Picnics were the order of the day and we took trips with our friends to Anisakan, Elephants Falls and many other favourite spots. Our cousins on our mother's side, the Thwins, were staying with us and every room in our house was full.

The Thwins came from Namtu, a mining town on the Chinese border. Their father was the district commissioner of police and active in the fight against the opium traders. Uncle Thwin was my mother's only brother and she educated his seven children, one after another. Whoever was of the right age would come and live with us. She taught them to read and write English well enough to gain entry to an excellent English-language school, St Michael's. She also taught them music, and they became a fine bunch of musicians. Ethel, too, had remarkable musical talent. I remember her as a young girl of 10 or 12 sitting beside my mother at our old German walnut piano, the candle holders swung out to light the music for their duets.

Another favourite spot was the Goteik Gorge. The bridge across it was reputedly the highest rail bridge in the world and was on the rail link to the Chinese border. Viewed from the caves below, the trains appeared like tiny toys as they slowly crawled overhead.

In the markets the familiar shopkeepers were delighted to see the family back in town. The old Indian rice-seller was still there, sitting cross-legged and beaming at his customers. He was very fat and never seemed to move from his position among the bags of rice. Buying rice is an art.

'Smell this one, Memsahib, this is very special,' he would say to my mother in Hindustani, offering her handfuls of the different types of rice he had on display in big, open sacks. She would put the grains to her nose thoughtfully before making her purchase.

'Always smell the rice before buying it. The older the rice, the better the quality,' she had told me ever since I could remember.

Home was a short distance away but we always rode in a horse-drawn carriage. Fights would break out frequently among the drivers, to see who could win my mother's business.

Yet the appearance of normality around the town was deceptive. People in the streets whispered to one another.

'The authorities know more than they are telling us,' the vendors in the markets would tell my mother, while I listened in.

Rangoon was still being bombed; in the pattern adopted by the Japanese, their planes flew in from the East out of the mid-morning sun and razed the dock area. Rumours abounded.

'Hundreds have been killed,' one man said.

'No, thousands,' said another.

'The Japanese are using a new type of bomb called the anti-personnel bomb,' Robert told me one day. 'It's designed to blast on a low parallel plane in relation to the ground and maim or kill people rather than destroy buildings.'

At the same time the Japanese land army began its push across the Burmese border with Siam (now Thailand).

Yet radio broadcasts claiming that Burma was well prepared for hostilities were constantly beamed over the air.

We did not know it, but the Japanese had a four-pronged invasion plan. One force was to capture Rangoon and proceed west towards India. The second would take the central route to India, via Mandalay. A third would secure the north and the fourth would cut the crucial Burma Road supply route to China.

Because the battle lines were 400 miles away, our town carried on more or less as usual. More troops were evident, but school, once term began, went on as normal. Some of the European students and teachers left for India but many remained.

'The Japanese will be turned back,' they said confidently.

Army manoeuvres were stepped up and Indian artillery units moved into town. Field guns being towed behind army lorries were a common sight in the streets.

Then one day my mother called us together.

'We are going to have a shelter built in the back garden in case of air raids,' she said. 'I expect we will never have to use it, but it is better to be prepared, just in case.'

We watched while a huge hole was dug on the boundary of our property and covered with logs on which tons of soil were deposited. The inside was lined with bamboo mats and seats to accommodate about 20 people in reasonable comfort.

The two Japanese families in town had slipped away. Mr Fujo, a photographer, had been an intimate friend of our family for years. He was a refined gentleman who loved classical music. Whenever his family came over for a meal he brought his violin, and my mother on the piano and Fujo on the violin entertained us for hours. He was never without a smile, and always took his leave by bowing to everyone present.

The university in Rangoon had closed when the city was bombed and my eldest brother Donald, who was 18, returned to Maymyo. My mother was overjoyed to see him. He enlisted in the army auxiliary corps and spent his time training to be a soldier. More and more army people visited our home. Some were on leave from the front and others were officers in training at the army school of jungle warfare. Some Chinese officers came around to relax and enjoy a game of tennis or just listen to music. The British Club was as well patronised and as lively as it had been in pre-war times. To see the members trooping in dressed in evening attire, anyone would have thought that the war was in Europe and not right here on our doorstep.

The convoys of trucks to China continued; the authorities were working feverishly to keep the Burma–China road open. The Japanese had not yet cut this crucial north–south road but people said its closure was imminent. The long convoys of trucks in the hands of the worst drivers in the world, Chinese peasants, were being bombed unmercifully by Japanese planes on the roads to Lower Burma. The Japanese had broken out of the south-eastern front and were pushing ahead to cut the main route to China.

The news became all bad. The British dominance of the East seemed to be crumbling. Despite Mother's optimism, it was becoming clear that the Japanese were gaining the upper hand and were intent on driving Britain out of its colonial possessions.

The bombing of Rangoon had sparked a mass exodus. All manner of transport brought thousands who fled from the city to the relative safety of northern Burma. Some, native labourers of Indian descent, made the journey north on foot. Many changed course and headed west to their homeland, following the route through Lower Assam. Others flooded into our affluent town of Maymyo.

Overnight, the town filled to bursting point. Thatched buildings sprang up to house the refugees and tent cities sprouted to shelter the large influx of Chinese troops en route to the front lines a few hundred miles south.

When school holidays came again many boarders returned to their homes in other parts of the country but our family's social scene continued. There had always been a heavy military presence in the town and many sporting events were still held. The upper crust played polo, the middle class indulged in that so British game of cricket and the locals crowded to the football matches. If the war was at our doorstep, and it was, there was little sign of its intruding upon the normal activities of the town. There was a lot of military movement, but the townsfolk had accepted that the vehicles were part of a build-up of supplies to China via the Burma Road. This was as a result of an undertaking by the Americans to supply Chiang Kai Shek in his war against the Japanese, which had been going on long before Japan invaded Burma.

Reluctantly, my mother called the servants and us children together.

'We must prepare the house for air raids,' she said. 'The air-raid shelter is ready, but the house needs some attention.'

We all joined in and cut newspapers into strips. It was quite fun. With the aid of a rice-gruel paste, we criss-crossed all the window panes with the strips of paper. We hung up black-out sheets, too.

Despite the air raids in lower Burma, the radio news bulletins always concluded with an assurance.

'Reinforcements are on their way and the Japanese will be driven back.'

The talk around the markets, though, was that a lot of towns were being destroyed and casualties were high. Rumours abounded that Mandalay, the second largest city in Burma, was targeted for bombing.

Maymyo is 3000 or more feet above sea level and at certain points along the trunk road it was possible to see the plain and the Irrawaddy River on which Mandalay sprawled.

Donald, who was the only one old enough to drive, pulled Robert and me aside one day.

'Why don't we drive down to a vantage point with a good view of Mandalay, to see the bombing of the city?'

We thought it was a brilliant idea but we did not dare let our mother get wind of our plan.

Not being privy to Japanese intelligence, we could hardly know when the attacks would take place. With a few of our friends we drove the few miles on many occasions, but never at the right time to see the bombing. We were disappointed.

I was a fairly keen cricketer and one day a master at our school, who lived in the town, came to see me.

'Would you like to play a match against a team from the British soldiers in town?' he asked.

'I'd love to,' I said.

It was a delightful winter's day, cloudless and mild. The match progressed for a while and then it was my turn to take the crease. I remember facing the bowler, an Indian officer and the only native on the British team. He wore a turban and was obviously a Sikh. Every time he bowled and I received, he would jump up in the air, as if to say, 'Nearly got you!' He did not manage to get me out and the memory of that match remains, because it was the last time I played a game of cricket in Burma.

At the end of the over, we heard the sound of air-raid sirens and up in the sky to the east at about 8,000 to 10,000 feet there appeared the grey outline of an aircraft formation. We ran for shelter in the open trenches that had only recently been dug around the school. In a moment I heard the thudding of bombs as they hit the other end of town near the army barracks. The town was defenceless. It was all over in a matter of moments. The game was abandoned. The army cricketers rushed off in their vehicles, no doubt back to barracks. It was my first experience of an air raid and when I reached home my mother, who was almost out of her mind, gave me a huge hug.

'Thank God you're safe!'

With the help of our servants she set about taking further measures to protect the house.

'We must stock the underground shelter with tinned food and blankets in case we are forced to stay there for long periods,' she explained.

Most of our pet dogs had disappeared during the raid and were now gradually returning home. Robert, who collected strays, was thrilled to see them. During the next few days Mandalay was bombed again and a big part of the wooden city was destroyed. Days went by and certain goods were in short supply. Petrol was becoming hard to procure and it became difficult to keep civilian vehicles on the road.

The Burma Road had always been regarded as one of the most dangerous highways in the world. The mountain sections were narrow with many hairpin bends. During our trips around the countryside we saw a lot of army vehicles crashed in the ravines. The convoys of army trucks from Rangoon to China were driven by inexperienced Chinese drivers.

Donald hatched another plan.

'Let's drive to the crash sites at night and loot the drums of fuel that lots of the trucks were taking to China,' he said.

We younger boys were all in favour of another adventure. This time we had a lot of success and spread the petrol among our friends. It was fun, except when we came across a corpse or two, victims of the crash. Then it was not quite such fun. During one of these night manoeuvres, I sat on a twelve-gallon drum of petrol in the back of the jeep. The petrol was sloshing about through a badly sealed cap. Back home, I spent the night in agony. The petrol had burned the skin on my behind and turned my rump raw. I received no pity from my mother.

'There is nothing you can do about it other than sit in a bath of cold water to cool down,' she said. 'Naughty deeds invite sore backsides.'

Our town was bombed on many days, always at sunrise. News from the front line was not encouraging. Yet Mother always appeared optimistic.

'I have complete faith in the Allies and in God,' she would say.

Word had reached her that our father had evacuated from Rangoon after it fell to the Japanese and had found a safe passage to Calcutta. She was immensely cheered by the news.

More Chinese troops poured into Burma and passed through Maymyo on their way to the war zone. High-ranking officers from the British, American and Chinese forces constantly came to our home to be entertained. The Japanese were advancing rapidly, yet the radio propagandists poured out assurances. What did surprise me was our town's lack of defence against the constant air attacks. The bombers seemed to come and go as they pleased. Gradually the flow of military visitors wound down. There was an air of deep concern at home and among our close friends.

More locals visited us now for prayer meetings in our large drawing room. This was another signal that things were not good.

Then, one day, Donald made an announcement.

'I have volunteered and have been accepted by the American forces,' he said.

When the day arrived for him to catch the train to headquarters, everyone went to the railway station to say goodbye. A large contingent of family, friends and servants came because of their enormous regard for my mother, who was known in this part of Burma as the 'Angel of Mercy'. This was because she would employ any new arrival who could tell a good 'sob' story.

Donald joined the other recruits on the train and the band played a song I shall always remember; it was *We'll Meet Again*. Mother wept as she embraced her oldest son for the last time.

———————

One of Mother's cousins, Dr Ba Maw, had been jailed for collaborating with the Japanese in July 1941. Ba Maw was a minister in the Colonial Government and had always hated the British. He had been a frequent visitor to our home before the war and had constantly raised the subject of home rule for the Burmese. It was a serious subject but I remember the discussions being friendly and fun.

Uncle Ba Maw frequently teased Mother.

'After all, you are married to the enemy,' he would say, and she would laugh and laugh.

Dr Ba Maw was to become the puppet Prime Minister of Burma during the Japanese occupation. He was one of the Burmese pro-Independence leaders who believed Japanese promises that Burma would be granted early independence if the Burmese helped them drive the British out. Another believer was General Aung San, father of Nobel Peace laureate Aung San Suu Kyi. A third associate was Ne Win, who became Burma's long-lasting dictator in 1962.

The hustle and bustle seemed to be dying down. Even the air-raid sirens sounded less frequently. There was a calmness about the town and the markets appeared normal. Then one day we children awoke to some news from our mother that came as a blow.

'The time has come to evacuate our home,' she said simply. 'I have decided that we must move north to Myitkyina, where we will be safe in a place where we can see out the war.'

In a flurry, she called the servants. They carted many of our possessions down to the air-raid shelter to be stored. An open truck arrived and Mother handed the house over to her trusted servants, whom she hoped would be able to take care of it until our return. The truck was to transport the family with other fleeing Eurasian families to Mandalay.

'Even though Mandalay is being bombed, we have to take the risk,' she said. 'It is the only point of departure for Myitkyina.'

Why did she decide to leave Maymyo when she had such a powerful relative on her side? Ba Maw had escaped from prison in March and was in hiding, but he had sent word to my mother that she should stay in Maymyo, where he said she would be safe.

'I know he means well, but I cannot agree with him,' she said quietly. In her view, Uncle Ba Maw was a weak man, a show-off. She would not have been surprised that he became a puppet for the Japanese.

'I cannot believe he will be able to exert any influence over the Japanese on our behalf,' she said.

She understood clearly from Uncle Ba Maw's message that the Japanese occupation of Maymyo was inevitable and imminent.

'As the wife of a British oil executive and the mother of four Anglo–Burmese children, I think the risk of staying in Maymyo is simply too great,' she said.

The Chinese officers who came to our house had discussed privately with her the shocking atrocities perpetrated by the Japanese soldiers during their occupation of China. Rape and murder had been commonplace.

'Anybody associated with the British regime is likely to become a prime target for Japanese retribution,' she said. 'My duty is to protect all of you children, and Ethel is especially vulnerable, because she is a girl and because she is so pretty.'

My mother also had her own network of contacts among the servants and the Chinese and Indian traders in the market. She had no shortage of information about the dire situation that would very likely face her family when the Japanese arrived, even though she had tried to keep her thoughts hidden from us children. She was right to be afraid. Within weeks, many Anglos in Burma were imprisoned in concentration camps and subjected to brutality from their Japanese conquerors.

Chapter 3
TO MYITKYINA

*I*t was a hairy ride. The truck driver was a British army recruit who seemed more preoccupied with having a good time than carrying the families safely down the mountain road to Mandalay. There were times when he drove dangerously close to the edge of the bitumen, and his negotiation of the hairpin bends was downright hazardous. We arrived in Mandalay after two to three hours of a horror ride. The driver took us to some government buildings in the centre of town.

'Everyone off!'

Mandalay seemed deserted, but this large building, which turned out to be the municipal offices, was teeming with confused people.

We scrambled for a square of space while Mother went looking for somebody with a bit of authority. She came across a couple of Burmese government officials who recognised her and took us to a vacant office. The high-ceilinged room, typical of colonial buildings, was to be our digs for the next few days. While it was imperative that one of us stay there to be informed of any developments, we snatched some moments to visit old friends who had stayed in the ancient city. Rumours of the Japanese advance circulated, amid turmoil and fear. There was talk that if we did not get the transport to the north, we would be captured.

Fortunately there was only one air raid during our stay and it was directed at the wharves on the river. We were camped with hundreds of families, mostly

Indians who had already experienced extreme hardship and privation during their trek from Rangoon. Nobody seemed to know what was going on, and if they knew, they were not going to tell. Whispers spread that a train would leave soon. Yet nobody could pinpoint the time of departure.

One of the officials, who was a friend of the family, arrived one morning with some news.

'You must get to the rail station quickly. There is a a possibility that an engine will be fired up and it will be the last train. It will be driven by volunteers.'

We arrived to find a group of men working on an engine and others coupling up some carriages. Our family chose the carriage nearest the engine and deposited our gear on the hard wooden seats of a third-class carriage. Suddenly Robert, who had been rather quiet up to this point, spoke up urgently.

'We should move to the middle of the train. If there is an air raid, the fighter bombers will attack the engine first and we will be exposed, sitting so close to the front.'

It was a valid point, but the train had already begun to fill up and any chance of finding another seat or even a spare inch of space had disappeared. We stayed where we were. It was to be our home for the next six days.

Eventually the train pulled out of the station and headed off in the direction of the Ava bridge, the only structure crossing the mighty Irrawaddy River. The bridge was a magnificent multi-spanned structure about a mile long. The train took us past towns that were once the capitals of ancient Burma, the Royal Kingdom of Burmese Kings.

'Why are we moving at a snail's pace?' I asked a man who was near us.

'To conserve fuel and to be in a position to stop if there is an air attack. The passengers travelling on the roofs of the carriages are our spotters.'

We arrived at the bridge and were confronted with a large contingent of soldiers.

'They're sappers — engineers — and they'll be blowing up the bridge after our train has crossed.'

We inched our way over for fear of setting off the charges. Just before we pulled into Sagaing, the town on the western side of the river, we heard an enormous explosion and knew the job had been done.

Forty years later, during my return visit to the bridge with my son and his wife, we drove up to one of the many pagodas to photograph the Ava bridge. A Buddhist monk in a nearby house spotted us.

'Come up for a chat!'

I went to meet him and he suddenly looked quite shocked. He came closer and said, 'I know you.'

I could hardly believe my eyes either. He was my old friend Alfie from St Paul's school, now the respected head monk, U. Endika. We embraced, much to the astonishment of my son.

Alfie's father had been a Chinese teak millionaire. During the years since our separation, Alfie had gone on to study engineering at the Massachusetts Institute of Technology in the United States. He had returned to his homeland after the war and one of his first assignments had been to repair the bridge.

'The bridge was only partly destroyed by the retreating British troops at the time of your crossing in 1942,' he said. 'Only one span collapsed.'

He even produced a photo of the class of '41 featuring two smiling larrikins.

'Being a small lad, I used to pay pocket money to your father to protect me,' Alfie told my son with a chuckle.

Our meeting was an unexpected and memorable reunion.

I have always been fascinated with train travel and, despite the obvious discomfort of the hard seats and the constant threat of attack, I was thoroughly enjoying myself. Robert and I were invited into the engine a few times and travelled with the stokers and driver. At the numerous stops we would go with other passengers to collect wood for the engine fire and also join the bucket brigade that was called upon to water the engine from waterways and rivers. Yes, it was fun, until one day the train screeched to a stop and, amid warnings of aircraft approaching, we scattered and sheltered in the deep drains adjacent to the tracks. Fortunately, nothing came of these attacks. Perhaps the Japanese planes were searching for troop movements; nonetheless it was a scary experience.

All along the way, the locals in the villages gathered to help the refugees with food and flowers. They were extremely kind and were aware that our group had been driven from our homes to seek shelter at a safe haven.

After days we arrived at the station in Mogaung, a bustling trading town in peacetime, on the route from the nearby jade mines to China. No longer was it a busy outpost. There were still many people about but it was obvious that they too were preparing for some form of attack.

North of Mogaung on the track to Myitkyina, which was our destination, we came across a derailed train that blocked our progress. We were told that word had got to Myitkyina and hopefully another train would come down the track and pick us up to complete the journey. As we approached the wrecked carriages the smell of dead bodies filled the air. Evidently the Japanese had struck the engine and strafed the soldiers in the carriages. We climbed all over the wreckage.

'Look here! Tins of food! Camouflaged oilskin raincoats! And oh, look, a gun!'

Robert had found an army 303 Lee Enfield rifle. He clutched it as if it were a prize.

'This will help protect us,' he said proudly.

The country was in a state of emergency, which meant that anybody could carry a weapon. Army revolvers were a common sight hanging from people's waists. Self-protection seemed paramount, but strangely there was not much aggression evident.

We waited in the hot sunshine. People sprawled all around the rail tracks. The younger children played about, some putting their ears to the tracks to pick up the sound of an approaching train. Very slowly a train came into view. The engine was pushing the few carriages. We all climbed aboard and started the short journey to Myitkyina.

The English translation of the Burmese word Myitkyina is 'near the large river', and so it is. It was built on the banks of the Irrawaddy River, which flows through the centre of Burma and splits the country in half. The eastern half borders on China down to Thailand and the western half nudges the Indian region of Assam. The river itself is navigable for almost its entire 1000-mile length and is the lifeblood of a country rich in agriculture and timber. Historically it is known to the locals as 'the cold river'. Unlike many rivers throughout the world that begin their flow from the trickle of a spring, the Irrawaddy is vast even at its headwaters. Like the Bramaputra in India, it is a product of the overflow of melting snow high in the Himalayas.

It was the end of our journey north. In normal times it may well have been an adventure in search of a river, since the train tracks followed the river and for the 400 miles of the trip never lost sight of its waters. But today was different. It was, we thought, the end of our flight from the advancing Japanese troops as they stormed north, driving the British out of one of their jewelled colonial outposts.

The hundreds of people who dragged themselves off the train gathered in small chattering groups for some time before heading off in all directions.

'Look at all the women and children. There are hardly any men, just a smattering of old ones,' I said to Robert.

Like the faithful Christian that she was, my mother asked for directions to the nearest church.

'I am confident we will find shelter with good Christian people until we know what we are going to do,' she said.

So Mother, Ethel, Robert and I walked along a quiet street in the direction we had been given. Like most Burmese provincial towns the streets were wide and clean. Shade trees lined the roads. In the south of Burma the streets are usually lined with exotic species, some tamarind and a lot of mango. They serve a dual purpose of providing shade and food. In Myitkyina, where the climate was cooler, bordering on the temperate, the trees were hardwood, with the occasional cherry or plum tree creating an avenue of cool colour.

We arrived at a teak bungalow. It was built on stilts, as in most country towns of Burma, to keep predators out of reach of the occupants. There was nobody home, so we rested in the shade beneath the building. Before long a middle-aged Burman and his wife arrived in horse-drawn carriage. They greeted us kindly.

'Do come in,' the lady said.

The pastor went closer to my mother and gave a start. 'I know you! Aren't you the lady who plays the church organ? I am sure we have met before!'

I was delighted to see my mother smile and hear her laugh. It seemed so long since she had shown any joy. The past few weeks had taken their toll and the burden of caring for us children must have been a heavy cross to bear. I was happy for her. After a fine meal the family joined in singing hymns around an old piano. Mother played tune after tune without being prompted for more. A prayer meeting followed and we children were ushered into a verandah room to spend the night.

On the following morning my mother and Ethel walked the short distance to the market. When they returned we gathered for lunch and Mother said, 'I have changed my mind about staying in Myitkyina. We will be leaving the parsonage today for a school nearby, where a government-sponsored camp has been set up for refugees.'

'Please, no,' the pastor said. 'We have plenty of room here. We would be delighted to have you stay and share our home, for as long as you wish.'

His wife agreed. 'Please do,' she said sincerely.

But my mother, while moved by their generosity, said no.

'Thank you, but I really feel it is best that we move to the camp, where we are more likely to hear news of further movements. People were saying today that the airfield is still usable and that some refugees may be able to secure seats on evacuating aircraft. It is too good an opportunity to miss the chance of getting to India.'

This was the first I had heard of our trying to get out of Burma altogether. Nothing seemed to make much sense, but I could see it was not the time to start asking questions.

We duly moved, and settled in with hundreds of people — mainly Indian refugees — at a school on the banks of the Irrawaddy River.

Strangely, we knew no-one. Our friends who had left Maymyo before us must have crossed into India on the Imphal route, 200 miles south, a road that connected Burma with India and had been constructed during peacetime to ferry native labour from India.

Rumours abounded as to what steps were being taken to move the refugees out and into India. Planes flew over every day but they were Japanese aircraft bombing parts of the town and the airfield. There was talk that some of the aeroplanes sent to pick up the refugees had been shot down. There were rumours also that the Japanese had broken through from the East, where they were engaged with troops of the Chinese army.

'It will be only a matter of days before they capture Myitkyina.'

Even as a young boy, I could believe that. It seemed there were no troops in the town capable of mounting any sort of defence. After a couple of days we were alerted to the arrival of a platoon of khaki-clad troops. Fear ran through the camp. The soldiers were dressed in tattered uniforms that looked rather like pictures of Japanese soldiers. And they were barefooted. Could they be Japanese?

This group of rabble could not speak Burmese or, if they did, they appeared not to want to communicate with the inmates of the camp. By the waving of hands and pointing they made it plain that they were about to commandeer the whole compound. Many of the Indian refugees became certain the new arrivals were a vanguard of Japanese troops and fled. It was some time before my mother found it safe to approach a soldier to speak with him. Mother had studied Asian languages at university. She spoke Cantonese and five other Oriental languages, including Japanese.

She told us what she had learnt.

'It seems these troops were attached to the 5th Chinese Army and were cut off from their retreat into China by the Japanese. They struck out to the west with a plan to move up the northern valley of Burma and link up with the southern Chinese army in the western province of Yunnan, but they could not get there.'

The new arrivals took over the camp and organised duties for the inmates. It was like an internment camp. Robert and I were assigned to fetch water from the river. It was not an arduous job and we combined our duties with some frolicking in the clean water.

My mother soon realised no information about refugee movements was coming through to the camp.

'I think we had better move out to the airfield. We might just manage to get a ride on a plane,' she said.

We set off from the school with our belongings strung across our backs and headed out to the airstrip, which was some miles from the township. It was a long walk that took us back past the residence of our friend the Baptist pastor and his wife.

'Please stay with us,' they said once again. 'We would be truly glad to have you here. Abandon any idea of leaving Burma. You will surely be safe here with us.'

But Mother spoke softly to the pastor.

'There has been so much talk of Japanese soldiers taking advantage of young women. I just cannot bear to put my daughter at risk. Besides, she is so European-looking that she would be especially vulnerable.'

The pastor nodded. He could see she was tormented at the thought of leaving her beloved people and country, but the well-being of her daughter was uppermost in her mind.

'I can well understand your concern,' he said. 'But remember, we are here if you change your mind.'

We arrived at the airfield late in the afternoon. The landing strip was in a shallow valley bed and ran from north to south. We perched on high ground on the perimeter and looked down on the hundreds of people, mostly Indians, crowded around the edge of the landing strip.

Robert said, 'I don't think we will ever have a chance of beating that crowd in boarding a flight!'

We camped in a clearing near a well, 100 yards or so from the landing strip. The rains were still some weeks away so we were quite happy to sleep beneath the stars. It was an uneventful night and, as darkness closed in, camp fires sprang up all around the airfield. A short time later the smell of spice from the Indian curries prepared by the women wafted across the higher ground where our small group was camped. Unusually, there was little chatter. People were tired, hungry and fearful. Even the children, who would in better times be scampering about before bedding down for the night, were unusually quiet.

Chapter 4

AT THE AIRSTRIP

The night passed without incident. I heard occasional gunfire, but it came from somewhere far away. The odd explosion also carried in the still night, but nobody took much notice.

At daybreak an early convoy of army vehicles raced onto the perimeter of the strip. Indian soldiers armed with rifles alighted.

'Move out of the way!' they shouted as they cleared a path through people sprawled on the ground, who were still hardly awake.

They proceeded on to the apron and began unloading the trucks.

'What's all the commotion about?' I asked Robert.

A car drove up and stopped alongside the trucks.

'A plane must be arriving to ship out some cargo,' he replied. 'Maybe even a few planes. Perhaps we'll have a chance of catching one out to India!'

Word spread that the passengers waiting on the strip included the Governor of Burma and some of his entourage.

Nobody was allowed near them. I had walked to the well to fetch some water when I heard the drone of aircraft engines. Imagining it to be a Japanese fighter bomber, I scurried back to the campsite. A plane came into view in the west, circled and came in to land. It was an RAF cargo plane. It turned around on landing and was waved up to the group of people on the strip. The side cargo door was facing us and we watched as the soldiers loaded the plane. The

Governor and his group climbed aboard, the door closed and the plane taxied to the far end of the strip to begin its take-off.

Our family was disappointed and angry. Robert could hardly believe it.

'The Governor has got away safely and we, along with thousands of poor Indian refugees, are left behind!' he said, desolate.

I did not feel abandoned, as he did. I felt furious.

'How dare those able-bodied people take a ride while Ama [Mother] and Ethel have been left behind?'

While we sat around and hoped another plane would arrive over the horizon, Robert said in a flat voice, 'This means the British are beaten.'

I was still angry, not only at those who had just left us behind, but at the system that treated everybody but the British as second-class citizens.

I recalled the many occasions when, even as a young boy, I had witnessed this discrimination. My mind flashed back just a few months to a day when our family had driven to the Royal Sailing Club for afternoon tea. My mother had been barred at the door, obliged to sit on the lawn outside while we, her children, were escorted in to be served tea. I had thought it was wrong.

'Why don't you protest?' I had asked my mother.

'It's the rule,' she had answered.

Some time later I had innocently brought the matter up with my father. He too said, but in an altogether different tone, 'That's the rule.'

I never forgot that incident and I never forgave my father.

Forty-five years on, during a visit to the same club as a dinner guest of the Burmese Minister for Tourism, I walked over to the edge of the verandah and urinated into the water below. My host, a good-natured fellow, was astonished. I told him the story.

'That's the tree where my mother sat so patiently waiting for us,' I concluded.

U Maungyi was a fine man with a sense of humour.

'Perhaps it would be a good idea if I proclaimed this hotel a Burmese-only hotel and banned Englishmen!'

But now it was May 1942, and we waited for another plane to arrive. There were rumours that the Japanese advance troops had entered the town a few miles away. We knew they had moved their front to the east to cut off the retreat of the Chinese army. They had planned to cut off the only road north from Myitkyina. This was the road we had been thinking of as one option for our escape, a rough track used in peacetime by Chinese jade smugglers who took gems from the region over the mountains into China. We were concerned.

'What if no more planes dare come in or if we are shot out of the sky?'
I asked Robert.

As we waited, we could hear clearly the distant sound of bombs exploding.
The airstrip was spared.

Robert said, 'The Japs are not stupid, they plan to capture the strip intact
and use it as a base to attack India and China.'

Three years down the track, almost to the day, the British 36th Division
and the Americans led by Lieutenant General Merrill captured the town of
Myitkyina only a few miles away, but were engaged in one of the bloodiest
battles of the campaign to dislodge a small garrison of Japanese from the strip.
The battle lasted for seven weeks. The Allies too had recognised the strategic
importance of this strip of flat land in the wild north of Burma. For them it was
a staging post for supplies from India for the forces in China. Hundreds of
planes were lost in this very dangerous air route over the Himalayan 'hump',
because of the weather and high mountains.

As the evening closed in, everyone had the time and the inclination to
chat and socialise quietly. I befriended a group camped near us and Robert and
I joined their family and talked about the events of that day and days past.

Like us, every one of them had left behind good times. And like us, all their
worldly possessions amounted to what they could carry on their backs.
I thought of the evenings at home during peacetime when sunset signalled the
start of being alive; of noise, music and the sound of bells. Here in Myitkyina it
was time to get together and talk, albeit quietly and with anxiety, about the
future. Despite the hardship, there seemed to be a strange air of optimism.
I was soon to learn that people somehow muster extra strength when the odds
seem hopelessly stacked against them.

The following day we were up and about very early. We had sat down to
discuss different escape plans during the night and had decided that, failing a
flight out, we would do it the hard way and walk to safety.

'There are two routes out of Burma, one to China in the north and the
other to the west and India,' Mother said. 'The northern trail is by far the
shortest, about 200 miles, and people say the physical features are
surmountable. There are high mountains to cross, but mostly they run north
and south. India, on the other hand, is much further away and the only
remaining trail leads through the Hukawng Valley.'

This, we knew, was an area of malarial swamps, a multitude of rivers and
inhabited by the feared headhunting Naga tribes.

We asked questions.

'What kind of reception might we receive in China or India?'

'Would we be herded into a remote camp to spend months, or even years, awaiting the outcome of hostilities?'

'Which of the two countries will be more receptive to refugees like us with no means of support?'

'I know from my own experience that India is likely to be more hospitable. I trust the Indian people more and, besides, China has already been under Japanese occupation. And your father is bound to have left messages for us in Calcutta,' Mother said, adding hastily, 'although, of course, I still feel confident that the British will win the day soon and we will be rescued.'

The last time any white person had walked the Indian route had been in 1927 when a group of British and Indian surveyors had set out to map an overland road to India. At that time many Indian labourers were being sent into Burma by the British for construction work. Transportation was by ship and the authorities were looking for an alternative route. Government reports, however, were not encouraging. The terrain was unsuitable for roads and the cost of building bridges to cross the myriad rivers that were subject to enormous flash flooding was not economic. A health department report also indicated that many workers would be lost through malaria and other tropical diseases. Finally the British Indian Steamship Company, which had the lucrative contract for transporting the natives from India by sea, lobbied the British government to abandon the plan for an overland road to India.

Our family took all this into account when we discussed the alternatives, but none of us could really envisage the difficulties. How could we? We were a well-to-do family who had never walked further than a few miles in our lives.

Another day arrived and hopes of a plane arriving to pick us up rose. At mid-morning when our family, along with thousands of other refugees, was busy preparing a meal, we heard the drone of an aircraft. Immediately there were shouts from the crowds; shouts of hope and joy that we might be rescued and flown out of the war zone.

'The plane could well be an enemy aircraft,' Robert cautioned.

He was mistaken. It was indeed a friendly plane and as it came into view we identified it.

'Look! It's just like the one that came yesterday!'

Indeed, it was a cargo plane similar to the one that had taken off with the remnants of the British Raj the previous day. The crowd surged on to the apron of the strip and waited for it to circle and land. Soldiers armed with rifles appeared from nowhere and took up positions at the point where the pilot would stop. There was much screaming and yelling as the armed men threatened to shoot anybody breaking rank.

As the plane came to a stop, the cargo hatch was thrown open and the soldiers formed up and proceeded to let people in. Families were separated in the rush and I saw small children sitting on the ground wailing for their mothers who seemingly had already entered the plane. It was nightmarish and despite the throb of the engines still running, the sound of human voices was deafening.

I looked up at the front of the plane and saw the pilot and his crew half out of the open window waving at the people to hurry along. The pilot, whom I could see clearly, was clothed in a singlet and he had a head of the reddest hair I had ever seen. He was just a youngster and the look of urgency on his face made me think that he was aware of some impending danger from the enemy, who were just a few miles east of the town.

My mother and sister were bundled aboard but a surly soldier barred Robert and me.

'Only women and children are allowed on,' he said.

There was no point in arguing with a madman armed with a rifle. So my brother and I waited to wave goodbye and signalled to my mother, who was still standing in the opened hatch.

'We will walk across the mountains and meet you in India,' we mouthed, and tried to convey the message in sign language.

She shook her head as if to say there was no way she would go without us and scrambled off the plane, pulling my sister with her. As she did so, she picked up a young child who seemed to be holding its arms out to somebody on the plane and lifted the crying toddler into the hatch-way.

It only took us a minute to realise that our hopes of getting on were dashed, so we regrouped and moved away from the milling mob and the stifling heat, back to our campsite about 150 yards from the strip on higher ground. In many ways it was a relief to get away from the dangers of a panicking crowd. We chatted while we watched the final closing of the plane's cargo hatch from our grandstand position.

The engines roared as the pilot made to move off with an overloaded plane. It moved slowly and turned to taxi to the far end of the strip. At this moment I was surprised to see two smaller planes at low level heading straight at the landing strip. Their engines could not be heard above the roar of the larger plane's engines.

'They're Japanese fighter bombers!' I shouted.

The faces of the two-man crew were plainly visible and the red ball of the rising sun painted on the fuselage stood out against the camouflaged body of the rest of the plane.

The bomber flew over the aircraft loaded with refugees at tree-top level, before banking and making another run at the bigger plane. It opened fire with all guns blazing and scored a direct hit which burst the tyres of the cargo plane, immobilised it and left it lurching on its side. The second fighter that followed close behind unloaded its bombs which hurtled down to explode directly on the stricken aircraft. We watched in horror as people fell out of the flaming wreck. There was nothing we could do but witness the slaughter.

The two planes flew back and forth for what seemed a long time, time enough for my brother Robert to display his anger by picking up his old Lee Enfield rifle and having a shot at the planes. I too fired a few rounds at the low-flying planes, until my mother screamed at us.

'Quick! Take shelter! The planes are attacking the people skirting the strip!'

At this point my mother, sister and brother jumped into the well nearby while I ran behind the only trees in sight. With the plane full of refugees in flames the Japanese aircraft moved off the direct flight and dropped a couple of bombs perilously close to us. I could feel the blast and watched the planes climb and head away. The other three came running over and gave me a dressing-down for exposing myself to the attack.

Mother put her arms around me and in a flash drew back and exclaimed, 'You've been wounded!'

I had sustained a wound on my right shoulder and a few minor shrapnel shots down the right side of my body.

'It's nothing serious,' I said.

I had not even felt it during the excitement of the attack. At that moment a middle-aged Anglo–Indian man came over and began to abuse Robert and me for shooting at the Japanese planes.

'Such stupid behaviour could have attracted the pilots and diverted their attention in this direction. We could have all been killed,' he said. He continued to berate us until he eyed Robert with his hands on the offending weapon.

The plane on the strip was still alight and clouds of smoke continued to pour out. People were screaming and bodies were scattered over the ground. There was nothing anyone could do. Nobody possessed any first-aid equipment, since we were all travelling with the barest essentials.

My mother was visibly saddened.

'This looks like the end. The strip has been damaged to such an extent that no plane could possibly land there safely now. Our only option now is to take the long walk back to the township, find a spot to spend the night and talk over our plans for the trek out.'

Hundreds of people joined the long line of desperately saddened families. I still remember the eerie quietness of the walk. Nobody seemed to utter a word and everybody seemed intent on just following the footsteps of those ahead. I don't recall the scenery or any of the landmarks along that eight to ten mile walk. Only once, late in the afternoon, did we break rank. A plane flew overhead and, suspecting it was a Japanese plane about to offload its cargo of bombs, the long line of weary walkers dived into the deep drains that are a feature of any town or village in tropical countries.

The road was treeless, which seemed unusual. Perhaps the adjoining land was cultivated for crops, hence the treelessness; I did not know. I did not want to know. I knew there was a long walk of hundreds of miles ahead, no matter what the decision was about the route. The makeshift bandages on my leg and shoulder were steeped in blood. The superficial wounds did not impede my walk, but the flies were having a feast and I wished the sun would soon set, encouraging them to rest somewhere else.

Chapter 5

THE WALK BEGINS

*T*he line of refugees headed straight for the railway station. It is a strange human trait that whenever people are lost, they head for a transport terminal — bus, rail or ferry. The place came alive. The long line of zombies changed into a mass of chattering people and there seemed to be a tinge of optimism in the air.

Our group settled down to prepare some food.

'There's water available over there, in the tanks along the rail tracks,' someone told us.

Very soon people were lighting fires to start cooking. In the meantime plans were afoot to get the engine that stood idly on the track fired up and hitched on to a few carriages. What would happen then, nobody seemed to know.

'Let's just get the train moving.'

Since Myitkyina was a rail head, the only direction we could possibly go was south, straight into the advancing Japanese troops.

Robert, despite the confusion and turmoil, remembered that the remaining trail into India began at Mogaung, some 40 miles south of Myitkyina.

'So it does seem logical for us to go south.'

By now there was no more talk of our trying to reach China. My mother had fixed her mind on India.

'Besides, the war won't last forever. The British will win soon, and we will be reunited as a family.'

Our train limped into Mogaung.

Nothing had changed since our earlier visit on our way north except that the bombed-out train that had blocked our passage then had been cleared. Mogaung railway station was deserted save for a few mangy dogs scurrying around in search of a feed. People alighted slowly. There was suddenly a distinct air of hopelessness about the passengers. Like us, most of them were weary of constant displacement. There were hundreds of very young children, mostly in the care of their mothers, it seemed. They were a quiet lot, bewildered perhaps.

Our group of four joined them and walked through the structure that served in peacetime as a ticket office. Many of the Indians spilled on to the street that led towards the more built-up area. We rested a while and I was surprised to see a few people still on the train.

They were mostly Anglo–Burmese families and a few Burmese.

'What's going on? Why are they still on the train?' Robert asked one of the engine-drivers.

'They are prepared to take their chances and travel south into the Japanese-occupied towns,' he said heavily. 'They think a bit of hostile treatment by the enemy is preferable to the long and dangerous walk over the mountains to India.'

He paused, then said, aside, to my mother, 'They have endured too much and the urge to get back to friends and relatives in occupied territory is irresistible.'

We said goodbye to those few brave ones.

Even before the train pulled out, I could hear the thud, thud, thud of field guns and bombs further to the south-east. Fifty years later, at a function in Perth, Australia, I came across one of the people whose family had decided to take their chance with the enemy. That particular family were educated Burmese people and they survived the war unscathed. Many of their Anglo–Burmese fellow travellers, however, would have ended up in dreadful internment camps.

We planned to move out the following day, along the route west through the Hukawng Valley.

'Before we go, we must find the Baptist church and the *Pongyi Chaung* [Buddhist monastery] to seek guidance,' my mother said.

In a surprisingly light-hearted manner she added, 'We will seek their help and advice on the physical path to India and, failing that, they might offer some guidance on that other "path" to spiritual joy.'

Even though everything around us seemed to be falling apart, my mother still displayed a ton of faith in the Almighty. I often wonder at the torment that must have been her lot as she struggled to make the right decisions for the safety of her children, keeping us together without much food or shelter, with the constant danger of bombing and the threat of being captured.

The Buddhist monks received us kindly and gave us food.

'Please reconsider your plans. It is a very treacherous journey. The monsoon is not far away and the rain comes down like a waterfall in the mountains.'

'Thank you for your kind thoughts, but I feel I have no choice but to set out towards India. I have to put my daughter's safety first. Besides, the war may not last much longer. I have faith that everything will work out for the best.'

Next we made contact with the Baptist pastor and his wife, who were delighted to see us. They fed us and talked late into the night. This pastor, too, had met my mother previously at a church convention. All the talk centred on our immediate welfare and the Christians took the same view as the Buddhists.

'Please, I beseech you, don't try to take your family over the mountains. There are so many obstacles: mountain crossings, waterways, the mosquito menace, monsoon rains and Naga headhunters.'

None of this swayed my mother. Deep in her thoughts were those stories of Japanese atrocities.

'My overriding duty is to protect my young daughter from being ravaged by the Japanese,' she repeated. It was her main theme and in her typical Burmese way she sought to explain their behaviour in terms of her own unshakeable faith in the power of learning and education.

'It is not that they are bad people, but they are unskilled.'

We gathered for prayer and spent a comfortable night with this truly Christian couple.

Very early the following morning they accompanied us for about a mile and set us on the road to India. It was 6 May 1942, the start of a journey that would take three and a half months to complete. It was a journey that claimed the lives of tens of thousands of men, women and children. General Joseph Stilwell of the US army (dubbed 'Vinegar Joe') travelled the same route in reverse, two years later, and described it as 'the path to Hell'. Stilwell had fled Burma at almost exactly the same time as us, but had travelled on the lower route to Imphal.

One week after we began the walk, unbeknownst of course to us, the Japanese commanders made contact with Uncle Ba Maw. Soon afterwards they met the other Burmese pro-Independence leaders in Maymyo, to canvass installing Ba Maw as chief administrator.

Monsoon clouds were building up in the west but the locals said the rains could still be a few weeks away. The road was dirt, like many that connect villages all over the north of Burma. Kamaing, approximately 30 miles away, was our destination the first day. The track ran along the valley of the Mogaung River, a tributary of the Irrawaddy.

Robert had arranged for each of us to carry a share of the goods.

'I'll take the rifle, the rice and the condensed milk. Colin, you carry the water bags and the tea. Mother and Ethel, you take the blankets and the change of clothes.'

We sat close together and Mother prayed. She felt better and said, 'Whatever happens to us, it will be the will of God.'

The track was flat and there was not much in the way of trees. I looked ahead and away in the distance I saw a streaming mass of people, our fellow refugees. They were all Indians as far as I could tell.

It was a wave of human movement, stretching as far as the eye could see. In front of us there were literally thousands of people; we brought up the rear.

Now I felt good, and thoughts of an adventurous journey played on my mind. We all handled the first few miles well. There was a lot of talk of what we could expect on the road ahead. Around mid-morning the sun became hot and we decided to take our first rest when a shady spot could be found. We ate a decent meal of rice and fried vegetables, washed down with tea, but wasted little time.

'We have to reach Kamaing before nightfall,' Robert said, urging us on.

In the mid-afternoon we came across the first casualties. Dead bodies began to appear along the way, mostly Indians who had probably been on the road for weeks, fleeing from the southern towns. Other groups sat about resting or nursing sick companions. I had not expected to be confronted with refugees giving up so early in the trek. My early thoughts of an adventure walk were soon dispelled. Japanese planes flew overhead and we scuttled off the track and lay in the deep trenches alongside, trenches that would carry the rains when the monsoon hit. The planes seemed to be targeting the refugees in the vanguard.

'Try not to look up at the skies all the time. It's slowing our progress. We have to keep up a good pace,' said Robert.

We were in grass country and he had learnt it was tiger territory.

'Camping out at night could be a hazard. We must average three to four miles an hour to reach Kamaing before dark tonight.'

The sun was setting when we passed some cropped fields.

'Look! We must be getting near a village or a township.'

A few miles further on there appeared the first cluster of thatched houses. We were entering Kamaing. The track improved and other paths appeared, heading in various directions. The place was almost deserted, which seemed strange. At the village well we inquired if there was a church. One of the local Chin people pointed in the direction of what seemed the village centre. Just off the main track and close to the river we saw a sign indicating a church. Adjoining the wooden hall was a residence in which the pastor lived. Mother walked through the gate into the compound and was met by a man who introduced himself.

'You are most welcome. Please come inside,' he said, ushering us into the residence.

We explained our mission.

'Well, then, you must stay with us for tonight at the very least. We have plenty of room. Please, make yourselves at home.'

'Let's leave *Ama* and Ethel to use the bathroom in the house and walk down to the river for a swim and a clean-up,' Robert suggested. We did, and felt much better for it.

The pastor and his wife were very kind. They talked about the work of the Christian missionaries in these far outposts and exchanged news with my mother about friends in the church.

The pastor said, 'No doubt you children are aware of the wonderful contribution your great-grandfather made in spreading the gospel throughout the country.'

We had always known that my mother's grandfather had translated the St James version of the Bible into Burmese. My mother brightened up.

'I always feel happy talking about the good times,' she said.

The pastor produced the Bible and took particular pride in pointing to our great-grandfather's name printed on the inside cover. He chose the Old Testament story of the first refugees, Moses leading his tribe out of bondage into the Promised Land. We sang hymns and Mother led the prayers. Again the pastor pleaded with us.

'Please, go no further on this treacherous journey. Ours is a small but strong Christian community and we would be delighted if you would live out the war with us.'

Again my mother explained her reasons for undertaking the hazardous trek.

'I am resolved that this is the right thing to do,' she finished.

With no destination targeted for the next day's walk, we did not leave until sunrise.

'The next section of the trail will pass some villages, but they are of no significance,' our host told us. 'The first hundred or so miles will be flat and the last large village before the mountains is Shimbuyang.'

The trail out of Kamaing led north but a few miles out turned directly west. We passed slow bullock carts hauled by bony oxen filled with families of Indians. Occasionally a battered truck loaded with noisy Chinese soldiers would speed by recklessly, as if being chased by an enemy. These soldiers were remnants of the Chinese 31st Army who had been cut off from the main group as they retreated into China.

It was a slow and hot walk. We were constantly alerted to Japanese fighters who, not content with having driven the might of the British army out of Burma, now enjoyed destroying the trail of hapless refugees as they walked west. We were past estimating distances and cast aside the goal of reaching a certain place by a certain time.

'I just wish it would get dark so we couldn't walk any further,' I said to Robert, and the others murmured their agreement.

This was a dangerous situation so early in the trek, a weakening of the spirit of survival. I was acutely aware of it, even at my age. But then I remembered that while we were 36 hours into the trek, we had really been on the trail for weeks, since leaving Maymyo. The sad sight of weeping people gathered in groups as they sat beside dead family members was beginning to awaken me to the realisation that we were indeed on a dangerous trail and that the days ahead would be filled with the sorrow of people parting from loved ones. Already, I could cope with seeing a bloated body, lying face-up, as if pleading to the gods for help.

The flood of refugees early on in the trek was slowing to a thin line of stragglers as many fell by the wayside, exhausted or dead. The flat bed of the Hukawng Valley stretched for miles and in the heat haze we longed for relief from the blazing sun, some shelter and a hiding place in case of an air raid. Terror gripped us whenever we heard the sound of planes. Everyone was preoccupied with an attack from above, and constantly looked up to the skies behind. Along the way we crossed some creek beds which had dried up since the last monsoons. Tiny puddles of water helped ease our sunburnt faces, though the prospect of a cool dip was remote. The four of us walked with little conversation.

The shrapnel wound on my shoulder was not improving and I was constantly changing the position of the pack on my back. When we stopped for a rest, Robert rigged up a pole.

'Why don't you tie your pack in two separate parcels and sling the pole over your shoulder? That should stop the pack chafing the wound on your back.'

It worked.

'The coolies who used this method of transporting goods knew a thing or two!' I said.

It took a while to get the balance right, but the rhythm of movement made the task a lot easier. We camped that night in the open air with no shelter. Sleeping in the valley floor was an eerie experience. It seemed that everything around us was dead; there was not even a rustle of leaves in the breeze.

Another day.

'When do you think the mountains bordering India and Burma will come into view?'

We encountered a few more bullock carts. Evidently these people had set out from places south of Mogaung and had picked up the trail at Kamaing. The bullocks were on their last legs and made very slow progress. Robert could not bear to see the animals suffering, and approached the families huddled in the carts.

'Please, release the animals from their yokes. Honestly, you will make better progress walking like us,' he said. They just gazed past him.

We were on the outskirts of another large village, the township of Maingkwan. Night was falling and lights appeared, dotted about the place.

'I hope the lights are those of the villagers, rather than the vanguard of refugees,' my mother said.

We were desperately short of food.

'I hope we will be able to buy some supplies from the locals, since the refugees themselves will have little to spare,' she said.

Fortunately we found the village intact despite the flow of refugees through it. Again we sought and found the local church and camped in the grounds for the night. Next day we found the pastor who, in the spirit of his religion, helped us top up our food stocks and rinse out our clothes. We washed at the village well.

'I feel much better now I've scrubbed off the dust and grime,' I said.

'So do I,' said Robert. 'Let's put our fresh spare clothes on top of our packs to dry out.'

We set off once again for the mountains.

We had passed through the driest section of the vast valley and as we drew nearer to the hills, which now began to emerge in the distance, we crossed many partially dry creeks.

'No doubt they'll become raging rivers when the monsoon arrives,' Robert said.

The numbers of people who had succumbed to exhaustion and sickness grew alarmingly. Every creek bed was a chosen spot for those who had given up their will to continue. Bodies lay close to the stagnant pools. Some were dead and others beyond help. Despite the hopelessness of the sick cases Mother always stopped to comfort the dying. It was beginning to worry the three of us.

'*Ama*, you're holding us up. We must keep moving. Just leave them be.'

She would have none of it.

'Just imagine if one of those people were you. Wouldn't you welcome the kindness of a stranger?'

How could we argue with her? We did, however, stop her from straying off the path in answer to a moan or cry from a dying person.

'*Ama*, you must not waste our precious water supply on those we know will inevitably die,' Robert urged that night. 'We are in a terrible plight ourselves. If we use up our water, we will die too. We must conserve what little we have.'

She was saddened. Mother was never known to raise her voice and shout any of us down, even when we were wrong. She simply reverted to her native tongue. In difficult situations she always felt better speaking in Burmese. I recall her once telling our father that she felt more comfortable using her language.

'It lends itself better than English to sermonising, rather than chastising or scolding,' she had said.

As we drew nearer to the mountain ranges, the countryside changed. The ground cover was transformed from stubble and stone to clumps of tall grass. We knew the grass as 'tiger grass' because it was generally believed that wherever it abounded, there would be tigers. While we were approaching a clump of grass we heard planes. The sound caught us by surprise because we had been spared an attack for a few days. Four planes flew over as we raced for cover. Robert shouldered his rifle and prepared to take a pot shot at the planes. However, they kept their altitude over the trail and then turned south and headed away. I don't suppose what was left of the refugee line presented much of a target.

Still the people died and the stench lay heavily around. It was a strange phenomenon, the sight of the dead lying in groups. It seemed that all along the trail people surrendered to death at given spots. One often reads of elephants choosing a single area as a final resting place, and here a similar scene seemed to be played out. Would it be that some humans were loath to leave their dead loved ones and in so doing gave up their own will to carry on?

Chapter 6

THE LAST OUTPOST

We reached the large village of Shimbuyang at midday. It had once been a thriving trading outpost at the end of the valley. The surrounding fields appeared to have been tilled for cash crops. Although not shown on any map, it has been said that a lot of tracks led out of this remote post to China and India and were used by smugglers of jade and opium. The village was on the banks of a fairly large river that no doubt originated in the foothills of the Himalayas. It was clean and cold and, during this dry weather, still flowed well.

It was devilishly hot and the air was still, so still that the smell of death lay like a shroud over the whole area. The first thing that greeted us was a corpse in the middle of the track. I shall never forget the sight of this body, even though I had already seen hundreds. It was covered in what appeared to be a white sheet. As we stepped carefully around it, our movement appeared to disturb the shroud. Then we saw a cloud of white butterflies rise up with a whirring, humming sound, exposing the bloated, shiny corpse of an Indian refugee. The body looked as if it had been smeared in oil and laid out in the midday sun. The butterflies must have been drawing on the juices secreted from the skin. When we had moved away, I looked back in amazement to see the cloud of white settling back on the corpse, a fitting veil for the deceased. It was a sight we were to encounter often after that.

There appeared to be no life in the village. It was an eerie experience inspecting each hut, looking for one without any bodies in it. Robert suggested we split up to look for a clean hut for the night.

'Don't mention this to *Ama*, but if by chance we find anybody near to death in any of the huts, let's all agree not to tell her. I don't think we can afford to lose any more time or rations to anybody we can't help.'

The three of us nodded to one another and set off.

We converged on the far western side, nearest the river. There were three groups of Indians in some huts and they waved us on to an empty hut next to theirs.

They approached us courteously. 'Please, we beg of you, do you have any food you could share with us?'

My mother answered, 'We have hardly any left, but please join us and share what we have. We will get our fire going and make some hot tea.'

There was little we could do to help the poor wretches. The four of us set about clearing the hut for the night's rest and preparing a meagre meal. With the fire lit and tea brewed we were joined by some of the Indians, women as well as men. They were friendly and not the least bit threatening.

'How long have you been resting at Shimbuyang?'

'About a week, Memsahib. We had been hoping to acquire some rations but our party has been plagued by illness.'

'Is there anything we can do to help?' asked my mother, who was far from well herself. 'I have a few opium straps which may help those suffering from dysentery.'

These gentle people were very appreciative. They accepted her offer of this traditional form of medication — strips of cotton cloth soaked in opium — with enormous gratitude. They had set out together from Rangoon, almost 1000 miles away, when the first air raids hit the city and had been on the road for almost six months.

Our rations had all but run out. We sat around the fire outside the hut and discussed the future.

'There is no way we can continue with what is left of our food. Perhaps we should stay here for a little while to regain our strength and look for some food,' Robert said.

The Indian man, obviously their leader, replied, 'We are in a similar situation, but we feel we must move on. Thanks to your mother, our sick ones are feeling better already. We will take the opportunity to set out in the morning.'

We went to rest pondering our future.

'It is sad that our new-found friends will be leaving us so soon,' I ventured.

'Yes,' said Mother. 'I think we should do as Robert suggests — stay for a few days and forage for food.'

The three of us nodded. We were aware of the formidable journey ahead and the sight of the wall of mountains added to our despondency.

Robert, never a robust person, appeared gaunt and thin. He seemed to be carrying the whole weight of worry for the family. Ethel appeared reasonably well physically, Mother less so, but the fact that they had been speaking very little indicated that they were deeply concerned for our survival.

On the following morning when we gathered to wave our friends off, we shared cups of hot black tea as a parting ritual. Suddenly there came the drone of an aircraft engine.

'Watch out! It might be the Japanese!'

Everyone scattered.

We lay flat beneath the hut and I looked toward the mountain, from where the sound was coming. There was some early morning low cloud in the sky. Suddenly a large plane swooped down on the village.

'Look, the plane is friendly!' I shouted.

Our Indian friends had identified it at the same time. We all rushed out into the open and waved frantically as it banked on its return run. It was flying so low that we could pick out the crew standing at the open hatch. They waved in return and the pilot prepared for another run further away from where we stood.

Suddenly a trail of bags came pouring out of the aircraft and bounced and burst open scattering the contents all over the place. They were bags of food!

After the fourth or fifth run the people on board gave us a wave and began the steep climb to get over the mountain range. Overjoyed and pumped up with excitement, we rushed over to collect the supplies. The men worked all day to collect the bags and store them in an empty hut near the river bank. Our Indian friends, who had worked on the wharves in Rangoon, were adept at stacking the goods in a way that made distribution easy.

There was now an abundance of food.

'Look! Tins of jam, hundreds of cigarettes, rice and tea!'

'Yes, and dried potatoes and carton upon carton of army ration packs!'

'Tins of bully beef! There's enough here for hundreds of people!'

'Thanks be to the Lord, who has provided for us in our hour of need.'

This, of course, was my mother, with her unshakeable faith.

Our Indian friends soon abandoned plans of shipping out immediately.

'Now we have food, we will stay for a few days at least.'

Mother said, 'We too will stay a while, and if any stragglers arrive during the next few days we will share our good fortune with them. But remember, everyone, it is very important not to overindulge in the food to begin with. Our stomachs will not be able to digest a large meal. We must take it slowly, little by little.'

The Indians paid attention to her warning, because she had gained their respect.

For the first time in weeks, we enjoyed a decent meal, though we did proceed cautiously. Some of the packs contained ground condiments, presumably prepared for Indian troops. The smell of spices filled the air and I tasted my first meal of rice and bully beef curry. Making a curry with tinned meat was unheard of in those days but it tasted wonderful, albeit salty.

On this occasion, I introduced myself to the cigarettes that were bountiful. A dramatic change came over everyone. Our stomachs were full and the days ahead were provided for, with ample stocks of food. It gave us a feeling of security.

We talked much more and planned our movements. We knew the region was renowned for malaria and Yellow Water fever, not to mention the Naga headhunters. Then there was our fear of the monsoon. We knew from living in the hilly Shan States of Burma that every mountain range presented the traveller with a valley and watercourse that invariably became a raging torrent to be crossed during the monsoon. But this had to be balanced against my mother's greatest fear — the advancing Japanese army.

'If only we knew how far behind us they are, or whether they plan to push over the mountains.'

'Ama, surely our priority at this point is to rest for a little while and regain our strength, now that we have food,' Ethel said.

She was right. We had covered more than 100 miles, an enormous distance for a family that had barely ventured a few miles on foot on good days. Here we were at the last outpost of civilisation. Ahead lay a formidable range of mountains that had many years previously defeated a well-equipped and seasoned group of surveyors. Being here made a pleasant break from the constant walking, the fear at every step of an attack from Japanese planes, the smell of decaying flesh and the sight of countless bodies lying in the sun. Yes — the first 100 or so miles had been fraught with danger. Shimbuyang was a haven in comparison.

The pleasant stay gave me time to reflect and think about the friends and other good people we had left behind. I wondered how our relatives were and wished they were with us. I thought of the mangy pet dogs and relived the fun times I had spent with Robert, who it seemed had taken a huge leap into adulthood in a short space of time. Since much of our time was spent sitting in the shade of the thatched hut resting, it gave me ample time to think of the walks we used to take to the villages around Maymyo.

The villagers had loved us two fair-skinned boys visiting their homes. They delighted in having us stay for a meal. The older people loved chatting. Robert and I were fluent in Burmese, which was our mother-tongue. Initially, when we told the elders that our mother was Burmese, they tended to doubt our word. A number of the villagers often travelled to Maymyo to sell their produce at the markets and when we said our mother's name was Daw Ni, some immediately said they knew her. But it was still difficult to convince them that we were her sons. On our return visits, though, we were made even more welcome and taken to the monastery to meet the monks. Life in a Burmese village revolved around the monastery, where children were instructed in the teachings of Buddha and learnt to read and write.

I dragged my thoughts back to Shimbuyang.

'It must have been a thriving place in peacetime,' Robert said. 'It's been ever so well planned.'

He was right. But for a few groups of dwellings scattered in the surrounding area, the main village where we now stayed was a cluster of well-constructed huts. The roofs were thatched, but the main structures were of sawn timber. Some resembled shops, with an open front.

I pictured market days, when village people from miles around, even the hill people, would have come down to trade goods. This region of Burma was noted for its wealth of gemstones. I even thought that one day, when all this was over and we returned home, I would like to spend time in this far outpost.

The break gave us time to wash our clothes, air our blankets and rest our shoes. The long hot and dusty track had worn the soles of mine until they were wafer thin.

'I'm going to go barefoot while we're here,' I said.

When the time did come for me to put my shoes on again, they had shrunk noticeably and were as stiff as boards. I felt sad. These shoes had been my pride and joy. They had been purchased from a very British trading house in Rangoon and had been manufactured in England. I can still remember the brand name: they were a pair of Saxones. I discarded them.

Shimbuyang rested neatly on the banks of a clean river, tucked away at the end of a valley shielded on the west by the blue-green mountains that formed the border between India and Burma. To the east lay the flat valley floor that stretched away for 100 miles to Mogaung from where thousands of refugees, including us, had begun their flight to safety. It had been a stretch of relatively easy walking, but now it was littered with the bodies of thousands of those same ill-prepared refugees. The penetrating smell of human decay wafting around the perimeter of the village was slowly losing its power, or we were becoming accustomed to it. Perhaps nature was doing its work. The bloated bodies were shrinking visibly as the sunburnt skin, once stretched tightly, lay limply on the limbs of the dead. There was evidence of wild animals having feasted on some remains. Jackals abounded in the region.

I would have loved to have seen out the war there now that we had food. Our Indian friends also settled into a routine of rest and recreation. One day a group of the men approached my mother respectfully.

'Would Memsahib have any objections if we torched some of the huts that contain the remains of the deceased?'

'Thank you for consulting me and of course I have no objection. It would be a good way of cleansing the area. Besides, many of these poor souls are your own people. I appreciate that this is the most fitting thing to do under the circumstances.'

The Indian group was grateful for her understanding. They gathered one evening when the wind had died down. They performed a ritual before setting the 150 or so huts alight. The huts were like tinderboxes and the evening sky lit up. Occasional whiffs of burning flesh came our way. Building after building exploded as we watched the once thriving village go up in flames.

My mind conjured up a picture of what must have once been a beautiful place — the smell of sesame and peanut oil, onions, garlic and dried fish, the evening meal for the villagers who had lived here.

I wondered if they had enjoyed their evenings as we had in Maymyo. I imagined the children delighting in the fun times that seemed part of all village life in Burma. I envisaged them accompanying their elders to the *pwes* [concerts] held in open fields, the stage surrounded by foodstalls. I thought of the times when we had joined our servants and their families for a night at the concerts. And what a night it always was. The performers on stage would entertain us all night. They enacted comic routines and delighted the crowd by taking the micky out of one another. Jokes abounded and some were certainly not fit for the ears of the younger generation. During the night, mats were laid out, snacks devoured and those of us who were tired or bored generally fell asleep until awakened in the small hours by the elders. Surely the children who once lived here in Shimbuyang had enjoyed concerts as we had.

As the fires died down and the mosquitoes took over the night we settled back into our huts.

My mother said, 'I have been observing the gradual increase of insect life. This must mean that the monsoon is not far away.'

'Yes,' said Robert, 'and no stragglers have come through in the past few days. I am very worried that our next visitors might be the advancing Japanese troops.'

My mother could not disguise her fear.

The Indians were in better spirits that night. They had performed their duty of caring for their departed brothers and sisters. There was a serenity about them. When we talked the next day they even appeared a tinge optimistic about the remainder of the trek. It seemed quite extraordinary that such a change should come over a once dispirited group who had been almost ready to give up.

However, their change of mood did not flow through to my mother. She had not recovered physically as well as we children had. She made a huge effort to mask her anxieties about the trail ahead, but I suspected that her body and spirit were displaying signs of despair that her mind would not admit to. It was the little things she said, the advice she gave us during our evening get-togethers on how we should conduct ourselves when we arrived in a new country. The thrust of the conversation did not appear to include her.

One evening Ethel, who had not said a great deal since our departure from Maymyo, spoke up.

'The situation here in Shimbuyang is surely as good as we could hope for at this point in our journey,' she said quietly. 'This little village and the surroundings are relatively pleasant. The contaminated huts have been cleansed and we have ample food. Surely we are now out of reach of the Japanese forces. Perhaps we should hold a meeting with our Indian friends and discuss plans to see out the war here.'

'What you say certainly makes sense,' Mother replied. 'Your proposal seems a sensible one, but it is not easy to arrive at a sensible solution. There are so many uncertainties. How far away is the enemy? How long will the war last? What if sickness strikes? If we stay here, how will your father and Donald ever find us? How could we protect ourselves from robbers?'

She concluded gently, 'There is nothing I would like more than to call it a day and stay in our own country, but I believe it is my duty to deliver you children safely to India.'

That was the end of the discussion. We would never have gone against our mother's authority. It was not the Burmese way. We, like all Burmese children, had been given a childhood of great freedom and fun, some would say indulgence, up until our father's decision to send us to boarding school. But we were never in any doubt as to the authority of our parents. It was a matter of respect. Besides, as far as I was concerned, my mother was the centre of my universe. I would never have been parted from her willingly. Wherever she went, I would always want to go.

Ethel did not say anything further, but her shoulders drooped a little more. How different she had become from the happy, bouncing young person who had always joked and played pranks at home in Maymyo. It seemed a lifetime since I had seen my big sister laugh with joy. She had always found fun in anything, and she had a big heart, full of kindness and concern for other people. Ever since my father had driven away her young suitor she had lost her sparkle but now she seemed to be retreating even further, into a shadowy world of her own.

Every day we could hear the sound of planes in the distance. It was not until I reached India that I learnt that the constant and daily drone of aircraft engines emanated not, as we feared, from the Japanese air force but from planes ferrying cargo from India to the southern cities of China.

Chapter 7

TO THE PATKOI RANGE

One day our Indian friends decided to move on.

'We have been watching the clouds build up over the mountains in the west and we believe the monsoon will break in about 14 days,' their leader said. 'One of the more local people in our party has calculated that if we cover seven to ten miles a day, we may make it before the worst of the rains arrive.'

I still had my doubts about a few of the women and three children. They had not recovered from the long trek as well as they should have, and were thin and drawn. They appeared feverish and sat constantly in the shadows whenever we got together in the evenings.

'Please wait a few more days to give them a chance to gather more strength,' my mother urged, but to no avail. Their plan was set.

The following morning they waved to us and set off on the mountain leg of the trek.

Sadly we watched them cross the river in single file, each with a bamboo staff, a trademark of Eastern peasants on a trek. We too cut staffs to assist us in the climb we knew we must begin very soon.

At noon, the sun high in the sky, we ate our lunch in the shade of a hut.

'It's hours since they left. I wonder how they're faring,' said Robert, peering to the west. 'Look! There they are!'

Sure enough, some tiny figures were winding their way up the side of the first range. We watched and wondered at the slowness of their progress, knowing inevitably we would be following the same steps.

A picture of range after range flashed across my mind and I began to wonder if our party would ever make it to India. That night we settled down in low spirits. There was an eerie silence and, as I lay on the bamboo slats trying to forget about the trip ahead, all I could hear was the sound of wildlife around the watering hole. The chatter of monkeys filled the air and later on the scavenging jackals wandered around the deserted village fighting as they foraged for food. In normal circumstances I would have been frightened of animals in the night, but now, when everything else seemed to be closing around me, I had no such fear.

The log fire at one end, which served as the kitchen, sent a glow throughout the hut. It was comforting to know that when I awoke I could expect a warm cup of tea laced with sweetened condensed milk. I was growing attached to this place. Every time I looked up at the mountain my spirit dropped a notch. My legs were still tired and the shoulder wound had not healed. At times it dried up but then it would break out again. We had no medication for it and my mother tried some herbal remedies that drew the pus out but did not completely heal it.

Another problem was body lice. Despite frequent swims in the clean river the little mites persisted in hanging on. We scoured around for a sharp instrument to shave ourselves but there was nothing that could do the job.

'They're driving me mad,' Robert said. 'It's time for drastic measures. Let's put some sticks in the fire to heat up and then wind our hair around them. Then we can pull the burnt bits off.'

Mother was alarmed. 'You be careful you don't burn your heads!'

She needn't have worried. We did not dare get too close to our scalps.

'Look at you boys,' she teased afterwards with a rare chuckle. 'You look like a pair of golliwogs.' Even Ethel managed a smile.

We lingered in Shimbuyang for a few more days after our friends' departure. As the youngest and closest to our mother, I watched her covertly. She was tired and her eyes showed she was not well.

Since our friends the Indians had departed, there seemed nothing left for her. The constant chatter and the sight of her children enjoying their company had held her together and kept her smiling. Now she was beginning to lose her spirit. Physically, she appeared relatively normal under the circumstances. She had lost weight, as we all had, but she had not contracted any of the tropical diseases that had taken the lives of so many in the early stages of the trek. To see her spirit draining away alarmed me and tore at my heart. I soon realised that Robert and Ethel were also desperately worried about her, but there was nothing we could do to make her better or to persuade her to stay. She was determined to see us safely into India.

There wasn't much to talk about as we contemplated climbing the mountains that loomed ahead. It seemed our family had made a pact not to mention the past.

I was not game to broach the subject for fear of being scolded. An 11-year-old chatterbox, I now found myself dreaming of days gone by. Though Robert and I were willing to take a dip in the cool clean river and even try our hand at fishing, anything more physical had no appeal. There was no running about chasing a ball or playing games the village children had taught us back home. We sat and dozed. There seemed to be nothing alive during the daylight hours, save the four of us. The black wall of mountains consumed all our thoughts. I yearned for action, but waited for somebody else to make the decision to move on.

I was torn apart thinking of better times. My thoughts centred on my mother. I was so proud of her and of the contribution she had made in bringing the Europeans, Indians and the Burmese closer together in our home town. She had accomplished this by inviting people home for prayer meetings, tennis afternoons, evenings around the piano and children's parties. She was acutely aware of the deeply embedded colonial prejudices, but she always managed to break down barriers by treating everybody equally. She set the example.

'You should never feel ill at ease in another person's company, no matter what their background or their culture,' she used to tell us. 'Subordination is self-inflicted and one only has oneself to blame for feeling inferior.'

I thought of the winter nights when my brother and I would sit up with guns waiting for the wild animals that sneaked into our garden and killed our pets. The cold nights were followed by the loveliest time of the year, spring, when our garden took on a beautiful shade of pink from the Japanese cherry trees in full bloom. I wondered again how our relatives were faring.

'I wish they could be here to give us some support,' I said to myself. I did not dare say it out loud.

I also thought of the servants in whose care my mother had left our home on the day we boarded the truck to be evacuated. Mingled with my thoughts was the prospect of climbing the mountain range that loomed in the west.

Robert was the first to snap out of it.

'If we are going to go, we must leave tomorrow. We still have a long way to go, perhaps another 150 miles. I've tried to calculate the distance by taking into consideration the undulations, and twists and turns of the mountain ranges as well as what our Indian friends told us. We must get going if we're going to beat the monsoon. At least we have recovered some of our strength.'

If he was right, we faced a long journey. It was depressing. We made some preparations and plotted a strategy but Mother made no contribution. Robert added to our woes by reminding us that there would be many flooded rivers to cross because of the monsoon rains combined with the thawing of snow on the Himalayas.

The drone of planes continued to the north.

'How I wish one might land in those uncropped paddy fields on the outskirts of the village and ferry us to safety,' I said. It was a forlorn hope. All it did was push me further into a trough of gloom.

School history and geography classes kept flashing across my mind, stories of early explorers and the terrain they had encountered. British and colonial history was taught early in Burmese schools and I had always found it fascinating. Robert, too, had often talked about the early history of the colonies. He was a mine of information. I remembered the Spanish adventurers in South America, their long and dangerous walks into the tropical jungles. Dr Livingstone came to mind, as did the early settlers in Australia — people like Lassiter and Hume. I wondered how they had coped, what they had thought about and what they had hoped to achieve. I compared my experience to theirs and wondered if I would one day look back on mine as an adventure.

I remembered the first day out of Mogaung when my mind had been filled with excitement. I had imagined the trek as just a few weeks' stroll on the road. Not in my wildest dreams had I thought of the hardship that lay ahead and the devastating effect it would have on the person I loved above all others, my mother.

We all fell in with Robert's plan to leave and spent one more night in Shimbuyang, which had become almost like our home. The nightmare prospect of the climb and the other obstacles shattered the last vestige of the spirit of adventure with which I had begun the trek.

Reluctantly we gathered our belongings.

'We should get everything ready so that the only thing we have to do tomorrow morning is roll up our blankets,' Robert said.

We had four blankets which we used as ground sheets.

'Some of the more desirable rations would add too much to the weight of the load, when we're trying to climb,' Mother said.

'We'll have to leave most of it and take what will last as long as possible.'

She selected the food and chose wisely.

'I'm taking my rifle,' Robert insisted.

Mother, who detested all firearms, tried to persuade him to leave it behind.

'*Ta* [son], the opportunity to shoot at the enemy is not very likely now. Surely that is the only reason for keeping it.'

'Well, I think we still need protection. Anyway, it might come in handy to shoot for food,' he said, and strung it over his shoulder, rather like the Japanese foot soldiers in their marches into battle. It was an extra burden, but Robert never deviated once his mind was made up.

'We must aim to cover 10 to 15 miles a day,' he added.

We set off early, just before the sun rose from the plains in the east. The mountain range was still covered in the early morning tropical mist. The occasional break in the mist gave us a view of the dark wooded mountain ahead. We crossed the river that had been our favourite watering place in Shimbuyang. The clear water was waist deep and the flow gentle.

'Look at the water marks,' Robert said. 'This crossing becomes at least 50 times deeper during the monsoon.'

We followed the path along a slight incline that quickly gave way to a steeper climb. The smell of decaying vegetation and other tropical plants hit me. When the sun was overhead we decided to rest and were treated to a grand view of the village of Shimbuyang below us. Away in the distance stretched the plains of the Hukawng Valley behind us.

'Look, there's an aircraft circling the village!'

'It's not a cargo plane, it must be a Japanese reconnaissance plane checking out the area,' Robert said. 'Perhaps it's just as well we moved off.'

A short distance away, we came upon a smoking fireplace. It was one of the first we had spotted from our camp in the village a couple of days before.

Robert fell in beside me.

'I've just seen an Indian woman lying in the bushes. I'm sure it's one of the women from Shimbuyang who was so unwell. They must have left her to die. I think she's hardly alive, but we'd better not tell *Ama*.'

I agreed. We had to keep our mother moving. It had been quite some time since any of us had viewed a dead body or a person near to death. The thought of seeing more had not entered my head during the restful days at the village.

We pushed on and managed to keep Mother's attention focused on the climb. She was struggling to keep going.

The difference between walking on flat ground and the trail we now faced awakened me to the rigours that lay ahead.

Just as the sun began to fall behind the trees, we came upon another camping site.

'It looks as if we're making the same ground as our friends did,' Robert said.

'Maybe we'll be able to use their fireplaces,' I suggested.

It did not cross my mind that beside every fire there would almost always be a body or two of those who had been unable to carry on.

Mother kept falling back.

'*Ama*, come on,' urged Ethel quietly, holding Mother's arm. 'Just put one foot in front of another. Every step helps.'

We reached the top of the first range and when we rested for a moment I could hear the sound of running water in the valley below. We decided to press on and camp the night near the water, which seemed but a short distance away. We were wrong. Sounds carry a long way when locked in the steep walls of mountains. Some hours later we came upon the river and spotted a campsite of lean-to shelters. The familiar smell of human decay hit us. There in one of the shelters was the body of another of our Indian friends from Shimbuyang. I had seen thousands of dead bodies before, but it was far worse when they were people we had known, however fleetingly.

We rested some distance away and had a meal of canned bully beef and boiled rice.

'I'm going to look for a deep part of the river and fire a shot or two into the water,' Robert said. 'I should be able to stun some fish. It will make a change from bully beef.'

Soon we heard a crack from the rifle and in a matter of moments he returned with a few fish in his billy can. It would have been convenient to rest for the night at this point, but there was a smell of decaying bodies. We did not actually see them this time. They must have lain further upstream.

The mountain track, unlike the broad tracks of the plains, was perilous owing to the narrowness of the clearway.

'We'd better keep moving,' Robert said. 'If we're caught on a hillside when darkness falls, we'll have to stop and try to sleep leaning up against the bank of the high side. It won't be very comfortable. Besides, if anyone comes upon us at night they could quite possibly walk all over us.'

We moved on up the next climb and found a level spot, settling down to sleep in the open. There was a blackness about the night. I could still hear the running stream down in the valley, but the night was strangely silent. Tropical nights can be noisy when animals, insects and night birds come to life. Tonight was different.

'Something's wrong,' I whispered to Robert. 'Everything's so silent. What could it be?'

'I don't know, but perhaps we should keep the fire stoked for a few hours.'

'Good idea. I'll do it, you get some sleep.'

I kept it up for a while, but then exhaustion overcame me and I fell asleep. Suddenly all hell broke loose.

I awoke to see the fire extinguished. The rain roared down, sheets of water beating against the leaves of the trees around us. I had never experienced such a downpour. Water gushed down the track.

'There's nothing we can do but huddle under our blankets and wait for daylight,' Robert said. 'There's no way we can claw our way up the mountainside when we can't see even a few feet ahead.'

If there was one redeeming feature, it was that the rain was not cold.

Chapter 8

MONSOON

A dull greyness signalled the day. Our food and clothing were awash, adding weight to the already heavy packs. Worse still, the track now resembled a muddy stream.

The monsoon had begun, and everyone in the tropics knew that travelling during the rainy season was foolhardy. Centuries ago, even the Wise One had advised against it. Buddhism has deemed the rainy season a time for rest and meditation. If we had been at home we would not have travelled anywhere for at least three months.

For us, there was no rest. The rain poured down relentlessly and all we could do was keep moving. Robert had, early in the trek, acquired an army issue oilskin raincoat. It was light and came in handy as a wrapper for our rice and matches.

My mind flashed back to Maymyo when we had looked forward to the day when the black skies would open and release the monsoonal rain. Every year the rains brought Thingyan, a Buddhist water festival in all Buddhist countries when everybody, irrespective of status, was doused in water whenever they ventured out. The Burmese referred to it as a time for cooling off and cleansing. After the heat it had always been a pleasant relief to get soaking wet and frolic in the flooded drains that ran along the streets.

Now, I could not have wished the rains further away. It was unimaginable that they could be so destructive. Trees were falling around us as the gushing water swept away tons of soil. The narrow track turned into a rushing stream. The sound of rain falling on the canopy of trees was deafening and we had to shout to be heard, although there was not much to say, except to warn those behind of slippages.

Not long into the day's walk we arrived at one such slip and were confronted with the problem of getting around it. It was impossible to climb the sheer face of the mountain on one side and the alternative would mean sliding hundreds of feet down the bank and scaling back up the other side of the path.

'We'd better see out the night here,' Robert said.

We spent it in an upright position, leaning against the wall of the mountain in the fear that the small area we occupied might be washed away and us along with it. For the first time, I began to feel the cold. The sound of trees crashing into the ravine below kept me awake all night.

At early light, the rain eased momentarily and we could see what damage had been done during the hours of darkness. Some trees had fallen from the ground above and their branches had jammed in the space created by the slip. Robert tested the flimsy bridge created by nature.

'It's all right, but I'll come back for *Ama*.'

We crossed over gingerly and proceeded up the track. The rains started to pelt down again. At each step we sank up to our knees in mud. We reached the summit and began the dangerous journey down toward the roaring stream below.

If climbing a mountain on a boggy and slippery path was difficult, the way down was utterly treacherous. A false step could send us crashing far below or, worse, could see us smashed against the trees during a fall. The stream in the valley was rocky, and though the waters were rushing along we managed to negotiate a crossing. We camped at a relatively flat spot on the far bank. Another night passed without anything warm to eat. We ate some of our precious sweetened condensed milk and a tin of bully beef.

Not only had the rains dampened our bodies and our packs, but also our spirits.

'This is terrible,' I said to Robert. 'I suppose we just have to set our minds on getting over the mountains into India.'

He turned on me.

'Do you have any idea just how wide the Patkoi Range is? We could be in this jungle for weeks!'

I wished I had not broached the subject. It gave him the opportunity to expound at length on the other dangers and obstacles ahead.

'The rivers in these parts rise tens of feet in a flash and we could easily be caught half-way across the water. We could be delayed for weeks while the river levels drop and don't forget the wild animals and snakes.'

'All right then, would you rather go back to the Japanese army?'

'Well, it might be better than meeting the Naga headhunters.'

Mother said, 'The things of nature we cannot control, the wild animals we can with patience and our fellow humans are never as bad as historians make them out to be.'

I thought of my father who, perhaps unkindly, I blamed for our predicament. It saddened me to see my mother and sister struggle to keep moving.

I wondered why, as a wealthy person, he had not made the effort to have us evacuated long before the Japanese overran the country. I was growing bitter and made up my mind not to talk of the trek when I met him again. I further soured my brother when I suggested he had his count of rivers wrong.

'From what we've already crossed, I think there could be another hundred or so to come.'

He snapped back, 'What we have crossed so far are only *chaungs* [creeks]. Wait till we come across some *myits* [rivers].'

The rain pelted down and the huge trees with their broad leaves afforded little protection. In fact, the leaves ducted the water in larger volumes. Instant waterfalls formed and poured down from the high ground. The track became a watercourse and, without rocks or stones, turned into a bog. We came to yet another water crossing. The current was swift but we made it across then camped, exhausted. We found some blackened pieces of wood from a previous campsite and set about starting a fire. It was not easy, but we managed. We boiled some rice and added tips of an edible plant that grew wild.

'We've got to keep moving,' Robert kept saying. 'With luck we might come across a deserted Naga village for shelter.'

We rested on a fairly level section of the trail. It gave us an opportunity to scrape away the leeches that clung to our bodies. I noticed my skin wrinkling from the continuous drenching. My sore shoulder too began to cause trouble. The wet, heavy drill shirt kept chafing the wound, so I threw it away. As we got up we came upon an Indian man propped against a tree. He seemed to be asleep, but on closer inspection we realised he was dead. The heavy rain had washed him clean and there was no sign of decay. He looked peaceful.

The rain eased a bit and visibility improved. Along an adjacent ridge there appeared an area that had been cleared for cultivation. Robert's spirits lifted.

'Somewhere near here there must be a Naga village. Look, it's obvious the land has been cleared to plant rice or opium poppies.'

We got closer and saw that it was indeed a poor crop of rice mingled with some poppy plants.

'I hope we meet some villagers,' I said.

'You're joking, they'd probably scalp us!'

But it would have been a welcome break to talk to other people and perhaps take our minds off the trek. The next night we were again blessed, finding a fireplace with a few dying embers. Robert nursed a fire and though there was more smoke than flame we huddled around it.

My mother reached into the bushes and tore off some leaves, which she heated.

'Move over here, Colin, and let me hold them to your shoulder wound.'

We had a little boiled rice and black tea and spent a lot of time scraping leeches off our bodies by the dim light of the flames.

The horrible creatures seemed to find every crevice. Their favourite spots were between the thighs and in armpits and we had to strip bare to get at them. I even had a large one on my head. Strangely, they kept well away from the putrid wound on my shoulder.

Around midday we crossed tracks with a Naga tribesman. Far from attacking us, he appeared shy and when my mother beckoned him over he approached gingerly. Mother, who could speak numerous dialects, communicated with him after a fashion. She tried to ask him the distance to the next village. He pointed to the ground, moving his whole hand seven or eight times. We did not know if he was talking about days, mountains or even rivers but he seemed to point in the right direction.

Robert and I examined his crossbow and even fired a couple of clay pellets from his ammunition. He was keen to handle Robert's rifle, and when Robert fired one of his precious bullets into the air, the fellow got quite excited and beamed, displaying a set of blackened teeth. He headed off and we made camp for the night.

Mother then tried to explain what she had learnt from him.

'He said his village was ahead, but that nobody lived there. I think he was saying that the refugees who reached there before the rains broke used guns and drove the villagers away. He and his tribe moved to another ridge, away from the trail.'

The news buoyed us all a bit. Meeting that lone headhunter encouraged us to keep going.

'Just meeting another living person makes me realise the wilderness is not as empty as I thought,' I said.

The jungle was alive and somewhere out there in the hills, there were people living happily in what to me felt like the worst place on earth.

'That poor hunter hasn't been too successful,' Mother said. 'He was carrying nothing but his crossbow. I hope he catches something so that his family can have some food.'

It was typical of Mother to think of others when we ourselves were close to starvation.

'Well, he looks well fed,' I said.

'Yes, he looks well, but we should remember that he has to live in this region, whereas we are only passing through. We should be grateful he did not rob us of our meagre rations.'

We set off in the grey light, our spirits lighter. I had never imagined walking in slush and mud would be so demanding.

To think that in my earlier days there had been nothing I had liked better than the challenge of a flooded creek! The other danger was the debris that came down with the floodwaters, large trees and branches swept down by the swift currents.

The track was heading down into the next valley and once again we all negotiated the downhill on our backsides. It was painful having the back pack thumping against my wound. We crossed the river at the bottom, but it was too early to make camp. We chewed on some wet rice left in an oilskin bag and continued the climb up the next range, camping some way up. Darkness had beaten us and we just stopped on the side of the track and huddled together to keep warm. There was nothing else we could do.

The rain eased momentarily when we reached the top the next day.

'We should keep going to make the next crossing anyway,' Robert suggested.

When we reached the bank we two boys ferried Mother across first with our few blankets, planning to return for Ethel. The rain began to pour down again in sheets, and soon the water level rose just enough to make it too dangerous to return for Ethel. Any attempt to fetch her would have been suicidal. Mother was beside herself. She could not bear to be separated from her only daughter.

'I am so afraid for her over there, alone in the jungle without any protection. It could be days before we get her.'

I took it badly too. I thought of my sister alone in the dark separated from us. I wondered what she might be thinking. The only girl in the family, Ethel had been groomed since her early years to be our substitute mother. She was a bright and cheery person, loved by everybody who visited our home. She loved playing songs for visitors on the piano. She was physically strong and played several sports. When guests were invited to an afternoon of tennis at home, Ethel not only arranged the matches but the refreshments too. I recalled with glee the time she had spiked the barley water with gin. Poor Armanath, our house boy, who also doubled as ball-boy, had copped the blame. She was an organiser, and even the nuns at her school often called on her to help run functions.

Ethel had been very keen on the young cadet officer, Noel, who had driven her to Maymyo when our schools closed. His family were acquaintances and he often called at our place. He was a decent type of fellow, good-looking too, and his prospects in the army were bright. His father held a junior position in the Shell Burmah Oil Company and like us they were Anglos. Neither of these points went down well with my father.

After Father called off the romance, there had been a noticeable change in Ethel. She kept more to herself, and from the day we climbed aboard the army truck and left our home she had had very little to say or contribute. She more or less tagged along.

Now Robert shouted across to her.

'Move away from the water, so we can hear one another!'

We attempted, without much success, to communicate throughout the night over the roar of the torrent.

The gods were kind and the water level dropped in the morning. The skies were still threatening when we hurried across to help our sister rejoin the group. My mother cried with relief. She held Ethel close.

Since we had been up all night we decided to rest and, while we sat around, two people arrived on the opposite bank. I recognised the man as a member of a family from Maymyo. The boys were good friends of ours and attended the same school. The couple attempted to cross over. The man was helping the woman, who appeared sick. I knew it would be difficult for them and called out.

'Do you need any help?'

There was no reply. In a flash the woman lost her grip and was swept away in the fast current, screaming. Robert and I stood up, but any chance of running along the bank was out of the question, for we were too weak. The man crossed over and without any hint of recognition took off up the hill and disappeared into the jungle.

The sight of that poor woman struggling in the brown waters made a deep impact upon me. I had seen many dead and dying people but it was the first time I had seen someone washed to their death. As the man disappeared from sight our little party was too shocked to continue. Light rain was falling. I turned to my mother.

'Why didn't he recognise us? Why did he keep walking as if nothing had happened?'

'Who knows, son.'

The whole scene played on my mind. Their family were good friends of ours in Maymyo. The four boys were frequent visitors to our home. Their mother was a delightful woman of Shan stock, who, like my mother, was well known in the town for her generous spirit. It was unimaginable that he had not even stopped to say a few words.

Some time later in Calcutta I recognised the same man among the crowd. I sang out his name and hoped we could have a chat about our experiences. He heard me call and turned around to see me. Then he just kept walking on, as he had on that fateful day somewhere in the jungle in Burma.

Robert, the realist, said, 'We've seen many hundreds die already, and there was little we could do to help or save them. Besides, we're in a war and people die in war.'

'It is a tragedy when the innocent have to be the casualties,' my mother said.

The drama affected our mood profoundly. Silently we packed up and headed up the next climb. It was a heavy and difficult stage of the trek. The climb was steep and slippery. The mud was almost up to our knees and the smell of rotting matter, though distinct from the smell of rotten human flesh, was overpowering. The mud was fly-blown!

We had experienced the rain for only a couple of days and I had begun to realise how damaging water can be. Gone were the days on the plains, when we covered 20 or 30 miles a day. I could not bear to work out how much ground we were covering at this point, perhaps two to four miles a day.

Once again dead bodies appeared. It was horrendous trying to get past them. The track at best was only a few feet wide and we had to tread warily for fear of slipping and falling to the valley below. I recognised some more of our friends from Shimbuyang. We could not fail to look at their bodies, since every step had to be chosen carefully, whereas down in the plains, where many thousands had perished, we could skirt a corpse and not have to look at the dead person.

The rain continued relentlessly and the day got darker.

'We've had enough for today,' said Robert, who was leading.

We gathered with our backs to the side of the track. During the night I constantly worried that another group would come along and trample us. Each time I slid into the mud half asleep, I would wake up. I was wet, cold and exhausted, and more and more leeches clung to our bodies.

The other problem was the swarms of mosquitoes that took over the nights. The only way we could prevent our bodies being bitten away was to cover ourselves in mud. But then that too got washed off by the continuous downpour. We set off again after a sleepless night. Since it was impossible to light a fire, we had to keep going without even a sip of warm tea.

The path rounded the hill and we came across a couple of lean-tos made from branches and covered by leaves. There was a corpse, but fortunately it was quite far away from the shelter, so we decided to rest. The ground was drenched but underneath the large mound of ashes we discovered some hot coals. Robert and I set about reviving the embers and before long we had a substantial fire going.

'We need to collect some water to make tea and cook what's left of the rice, even if it has turned sour.'

'There's no way I'm going to scale down the mountainside to the creek.'

'What about collecting the drips off the broad leaves of those trees?'

'It'll take ages, but it's the only way.'

There was no way to dry our clothes, but the fire provided enough comfort to let us grab some sleep. I had thrown some heavy logs on, hoping they would provide sufficient warmth.

Despite rain throughout the night the fire stayed alight. We decided to stay another day. I explored the vicinity and was surprised to come across a carcass of a bullock. Some people before us had obviously killed it and carved it up for meat. Goodness knows how long it had been lying there, but its bones and some flesh were washed white.

'Let's try to get some meat off the bones. We can cook it in the ashes,' Robert said.

We had no sharp instruments and all we could do was tear at the remaining flesh with our bare hands like carnivorous beasts. We managed to get some lumps off which we cooked in the coals.

'You boys make sure it is well and truly cooked, even burnt, before you try to eat it,' my mother said. 'I'm worried it will make you ill.'

We made certain the lumps of meat and sinews were well and truly blackened before we set about chewing into the morsels. Our small meal was washed down with tins of hot black tea. Next day both Robert and I were violently sick. What little we had devoured the night before went straight through our systems. The belly pains were gut-wrenching, but we were determined to push on, always thinking and hoping that the next mountain would be the last.

'I wish I'd never found the carcass,' I moaned. 'I knew it was riddled with maggots but I thought it would be all right if it was washed before cooking.'

Mother, a firm believer in natural medicine, produced her remaining strips of cotton cloth dipped in opium.

'Take these, they will ease your stomach pains.'

We had to suck the blackish strips of cotton and swallow the saliva that was mixed with the drug. It worked wonders and before long the stomach cramps eased, though the diarrhoea persisted.

For the first time I saw that Robert was beginning to look sick.

'Why don't you get rid of the rifle? It's completely useless now.'

'No.'

My shoulder wound flared up again and the only time I could get it treated was when we stopped at the end of each day, and only if there was a fire for Mother to heat some wild leaf to apply to it. The look on everybody's faces said it all. I wondered how long we could keep it up. It did not occur to me to lie down in the ooze and slush and give up, yet I could not shut out the thought of what had gone through the minds of those poor people who had fallen by the wayside and perished. Were they sick, were they just tired or did the will to carry on burn out? We just kept dragging ourselves along. We had run out of matches and every campsite greeted us with a corpse or two and no semblance of a fire to stoke up.

The leeches were giving me a hard time. Every morning, before we set out, we would help one another scrape the bloody suckers off. It was horrible to see the bloated creepers burst open in a splash of red blood. Goodness knows, we had little to spare! Then I had another setback. I awoke one wet morning in a cold sweat. My body ached and the intense cold had my teeth chattering. I could not get up off the muddy ground.

'Colin, try to get up! Please try.'

'Please, let me rest.'

I experienced a strange feeling — a comfortable feeling — of drifting away. After some time the shivering ceased and I felt well enough to continue the trek. It was my first bout of malaria.

Chapter 9

THE NAGA VILLAGE

*M*iraculously, the rain stopped and for the first time in days the sun peeped through broken cloud. It is impossible to describe how our spirits lifted. The track remained a bog, but it was a relief to have a dry body. The unusual break in the weather continued for another day with a light shower or two falling at night. It was during this lucky break that we reached a crest and sighted distant smoke rising from the roofs of a cluster of huts.

'Thank goodness. We can stay there for a few days.'

The very sight of smoke, which meant a fire, was enough to give us strength and hope.

We arrived at the Naga village in the middle of the afternoon. The thatched huts were set in a row of about 25 and the village was occupied by a small group of refugees. We scoured around for an empty hut and settled down exhausted but relieved. There were about 25 people besides us and before we carefully climbed into our hut, built on stilts and about eight feet off the ground, we begged for some food. But these poor people were in the same boat.

'We have not eaten for days. We had hoped that any new arrivals would have food to share.'

Nonetheless, they were overjoyed to see us. They appeared weary and thin, yet the children's gaunt faces lit up at the sight of strangers. They were a pathetic lot, as they sat around silently. What a change from the normal gatherings of Indian families in better circumstances, occasions for noisy chatter! We drank some black tea with them. They had been holed up in this village for days, living in fear of the Japanese soldiers rumoured to be heading their way. We listened to tales of their flight from Rangoon.

One older man constantly wept as he talked about his family, who had perished early in the trek. His wife and five young children had contracted cholera, we gathered, and had died.

'My deepest regret is that I had no way of burning or burying the bodies of my loved ones. The pariah dogs will be chewing their bones,' he wailed. Poor fellow, I thought. Even if he did get through to India, he still had hundreds of miles to cover before he would arrive at his village in South India.

Each hut had a single tree trunk in which steps had been hewn out as the means of entry. The village was situated a long way from water. It seemed the Nagas believed the evil spirits moved along fast-running streams. Unlike other villages in Burma, this one occupied a knoll.

It was dark inside our hut and no provision had been made for light to enter. We set about slowly getting it cleaned up. The fireplace at the end was a mountain of ash and unburnt timber. No doubt the previous occupants, surely refugees like ourselves, had just upped and moved on.

In the process of cleaning, Robert, who had been doing most of the work, pointed to the ceiling.

'Look at that row of things hanging from the rafters. They look like coconuts.'

On closer inspection we discovered that the coconuts were human heads, blackened by the smoke. The hair of each head was visible, still hanging like threads.

'Leave them alone,' Mother said.

It wasn't hard to do. There were more pressing needs than worrying about sharing a room with these relics.

It was a relief to feel dry. Without even considering the availability of food, we decided to stay for some time.

'I'm sure we will find some edible plants to supplement our rations,' Mother said.

Actually, there was nothing to supplement, save a bag of wet tea leaves.

'I'm going to try hunting for animals or birds with my rifle,' Robert said. Even as we spoke around the warm fire we could hear monkeys in the nearby trees. The next morning our South Indian friends gave us some water and for the first time in weeks we enjoyed a warm drink of black tea in relative comfort.

Robert and I took our bamboo water containers and headed off down the hillside to the stream. While we were fighting our way down the still slippery slope, we heard a tribe of monkeys gambolling in the trees below.

'I'm going to try to shoot one and take it back to camp to share with our Indian friends,' Robert said. 'They have no means of hunting.'

We went towards the noise and came across the monkeys in trees ahead. They were unconcerned by our presence and carried on munching away at some leaves. One of the larger beasts sat quite close by and appeared to be guarding the troupe. It just stared down at Robert and me, a perfect shot for a rifleman. I waited as Robert raised his sights on the monkey. He stood there for what seemed ages and then slowly lowered the rifle.

'I can't bring myself to pull the trigger,' he muttered, ashamed.

Instead, he fired a bullet into the calmer portion of the stream. Some small fish floated to the surface and we swam around, scooping them up and emptying them into our water containers.

Robert led the way back. I followed, and for the first time since leaving home I took a good look at my brother. I was full of pride that he displayed such love for animals. He had forsaken a feed that was desperately needed for our survival and the decision, I could tell, was weighing heavily upon him. He had shouldered the burden of getting the family safely to India, and there was this pathetic figure of a boy, with a bamboo container of water on one shoulder, his rifle on the other and both propped up with a pair of skinny legs.

Robert was never robust but he possessed stamina. At a time when most young boys gave very little thought to religion, he learnt a good deal from our Saturday visits to the monastery to hear the *Sayadaw* [monk] talk of the nature of life. His love for nature and living animals was a legend in Maymyo. It was this that had stopped him shooting that easy target.

Paradoxically, Robert in those days had also been a member of the Baptist Youth Fellowship. One Sunday after morning service at the Calvary Church, he got into a fight with a European boy, the son of a diplomat. The young fellow had chided him about his race and the fact that our family visited the Buddhist monastery on Saturdays. Robert was angered.

'It would do you all good if you learnt something about the culture and the language of the country in which you're guests.'

'You're nothing but a half-caste Anglo,' the other boy spat.

Robert was furious.

'I know your father is a diplomat, but what about your mother?'

He knew very well that the boy's mother was well known in the small community as a fun-loving floozie whenever her husband was away on business.

'Our mother,' he went on, rubbing it in, 'is an educated person who can speak more languages than you could name. She's also the organist at church.'

They got into fisticuffs before some elders broke them up. To top things off, Robert told the boy, and some of the other European families who had gathered around, that one day his mother's people would be running the country.

'Then the likes of you will be sent back where you come from.'

We slowly walked back to the Naga village, the skinny boy with a heavy heart leading the way. We were greeted at the hut by Ethel, who was seated at the entrance in tears. My mother stood alongside, calming her down.

'It's all right, Ethel, everything will work out for the best.'

'What's happened?'

'A group of soldiers led by a European officer came into the camp and demanded food. We said we had nothing to spare but he went through the hut and took our last bag of tea. They forced the Indians to hand over what they had, too.'

Robert was furious and, dumping the water container, took off in the direction of the soldiers.

'Come back! Don't go after them!'

But he kept going, crying out, 'I'll kill the thieves!'

We had been at the stream for a long time and the men who had taken our tea had long gone. Some time later, much to Mother's relief, Robert returned. There was a look of hatred about him. It was a devastating blow to us.

'It's not just that they took the last vestige of our rations, but the way they did it,' Ethel said.

We all just sat in silence, too stunned even to find our friends and talk it over. Mother, in her usual way, almost excused the thieves.

'Remember, their need is as great as ours.'

Despite the hopelessness of the situation, she kept comforting us, saying, 'The Lord will provide!'

It rained all night, and we drew some solace from the fact that we were sheltered, even if we were hungry; the tiny fish were too bony to eat. Our Indian friends had been kind and had supplied us with dry wood for our fire. They had taken to cutting some of the timber from the huts that had housed the dead bodies. The timber was dry and that night, with rain pelting down outside, we had a roaring fire within. The bright flames threw light on the heads hanging from the rafters. We talked about the customs of the headhunter.

'Let's have a closer look at the grisly objects,' suggested Robert.

'Absolutely not,' said Mother. 'Remember, we are guests in the village and it would be improper to disturb anything. Just leave things as they are.'

On the following morning she instructed Robert and me to collect some plants which she described in detail. We foraged and returned with handfuls of greenery. The soup was hardly palatable, but it did warm our stomachs. Then I was stricken with a second severe attack of malaria. When the fever came on, I crawled as close as I could to the fire to keep warm. Nothing, it seemed, could stop the shivers. The shaking would last for a few moments and then I would break out in a sweat. Then I felt better and could carry on in a normal manner.

Light rain was falling and we were sitting on the ground underneath the stilted hut when the sound of an aeroplane reached us. Our Indian friends had heard it too and we scuttled out and looked for the plane. It could well have been an enemy aircraft, but it did not matter. It appeared from the west and flew in low, skimming the knoll. It flew past and banked before returning. On its return sweep a crew member stood visibly at the open hatch with a loud speaker.

'Keep clear! Keep clear! We're dropping food! Keep clear!'

On its next run the plane came dangerously low and we could see a couple of the crew, whose heads appeared above the stacked parcels in the hatch, pushing the load out. The first run missed the huts, thankfully. Everybody rushed to retrieve the bags and the plane turned around for its second drop.

'Watch out! The bags might hit us!' I yelled to Robert and we darted under one of the huts.

The bags came flying down like bombs and as they hit the ground they hurtled along dangerously before coming to rest. The plane discharged four loads of food bags before it headed back to the western sky. The village was a mess. Bags had fallen through the flimsy thatched roofs and one or two huts had had their stilts broken away from the impact of the heavier bags.

Cheered by the gift of food, Robert and I went to gather some rations. Many of the bags had split open on hitting the ground and their contents had spewed all over the place. Further down the track we saw a group of Indians gathered around with hands waving.

'I wonder what they're waving at.'

'Better go and see. It doesn't look good.'

We went over and found a terrible sight. One of the men had been struck by a falling bag and it had almost severed his head. The poor fellow was dead.

'There's nothing we can do,' Robert said quietly. 'We'd better just gather up what food we can and leave the rest for now.'

There was an abundance of food. I examined one of the bags that remained intact and was surprised.

'Look! The packers have been very clever. They've wedged some small tins of jam in the rice. And oh, look, chocolate!'

There were all manner of supplies. Dried apricots, jam, cigarettes, dehydrated potatoes, tea and even some packets of US army rations, but strangely no salt. We carried what we could into our hut and told Mother and Ethel the sad news about the death of the Indian.

Around the fire that night, we ate a little and drank white tea with loads of sugar. The tins of sweetened condensed milk were most welcome. I even puffed a couple of cigarettes with Mother, who had been starved of her favourite Burmese cheroot during the trek. All else was forgotten while we talked.

'We have been provided for as I had believed we would. We must give thanks to the Lord,' Mother said, and we joined together in prayer.

On the following day, despite the rain, Robert and I gathered more bags and carried them to our hut. The rain had not as yet got through the bags of rice that had been parcelled in oilskin. During the day one of the Indian men visited us and brought some *chapatis* [Indian bread] and shared a tin of tea. With the supply of food it was tempting to settle in this village for a long spell. One day, the sun actually broke through and opened up the surrounding hills and valleys. It was a delightful place and I thought the original inhabitants had chosen a good spot.

When our Indian friend left, Mother said, 'The decision to choose the Indian route was the right one. Aren't they kind people?'

That night I was once again struck with malaria. I began to shiver and shake and my teeth clattered like dried coconut shells beaten with a stick. For a brief moment I did not know where I was and all I could do was curl up on the floor alongside the fire and sip warm water being fed to me by my mother and sister, who were quite distressed at my condition. Within the hour, the fever had gone and my temperature returned to normal. I drifted into a deep sleep.

Again the day began with light rain. The high peaks of the mountains still to be crossed were visible above the clouds. The weather was warm and, as usual, Robert and I went collecting wood. Returning from the surrounding forests, we saw our Indian friends on a similar mission, except that their method of gathering timber was to strip the empty village huts.

'We should follow their lead,' Robert said. 'It makes more sense than exhausting ourselves wandering the hillsides.'

A more demanding chore was replenishing our water supply. It was a long and arduous walk down the valley, followed by a slippery, steep climb back up. We spent the afternoons sitting beneath the stilted huts, gazing out towards the distant hills. Nobody said much and the message to our bodies was to get fit again for the next stage of the walk. Of course, there was always the hope that the next mountain crossing would be the last and we would be greeted by friends.

The abundance of fuel led us to light another fire outside the hut. Robert and I set up a place underneath the hut, oblivious to the danger that a fire beneath a wooden structure posed. However, it was a brilliant idea, and gave us the opportunity to get out of the dingy hut and away from the ever-observing skulls hanging from the rooftop.

Returning with our water supply one day we were surprised to see my mother and sister talking to a group of four children. They ranged from about six years old to perhaps 14. It was obvious that they were in a bad way. The middle two looked thin and sick and the youngest seemed to have no notion of what was going on and wept constantly. It was a sad sight. They were Anglo-Burmans like ourselves who had taken a different route and along the way had lost both their parents. We fed them and listened to their story, though the eldest boy was reluctant to say much.

'It is my responsibility to bring my family safely into India,' he kept repeating.

'Please, spend the night with us. We have plenty of food and shelter.'

'No,' he said. 'We must go to India.'

In the meantime he was shouting at the other children.

'Stop wailing! Can't you just be quiet?'

He was desperate.

Turning to my mother, he said politely, 'Would we please be permitted to have some food to take with us?'

Seeing that he was determined to leave, she said kindly, 'Of course you may have anything you wish.'

She packed up some little bundles of rations for them to carry, and gathering the young ones together he took off into the night.

We wept as we saw them walk away, the younger children barely keeping up. Prompted by the sheer determination displayed by the young lad, we sat about that night and planned to move on ourselves. We had completely lost track of time. It seemed that we had been on the road for weeks, yet on occasions it seemed like only yesterday that we had first experienced the bombing of our home town. We were also aware that although the rains had been heavy to date, a lot more wet was still to come. This thought plunged me into depression. My shoulder wound felt as if it was on the mend and I knew that the continuous wet would undo the good the rest in a dry hut had done. I could also see that Mother was almost at the limit of her endurance even though she was still fixed on reaching India. Despite her words of encouragement, she could not hide her physical weakness. Even her eyes told me that she could not muster much strength to keep going.

In this village our wills to survive were stretched to the limit. Even I felt that if we were not rescued shortly we would perish. It was at this time that were were surprised by a visit from a group of Naga tribesmen. We communicated as best we could and they, observing our condition, invited us to stay and even join them. No doubt they felt a kinship with my mother. The meeting fuelled our desire to abandon the walk and stay put. But there was still the fear of being captured by the Japanese, of whom we had no news.

Chapter 10

LOOKING BACK

The chance meeting with the Naga tribespeople brought home to me that I was truly a native of Burma.

Mother had never let us forget that we children were a product of a Scottish father and a Burmese mother.

'It is important for you to know where both your parents come from and what their family backgrounds are.'

She tried her best to make us aware of the two cultures. At home we were taught Scottish and Burmese history and were encouraged to pride ourselves on being children of a great Scottish clan. It was her desire, it seemed, to leave us to decide our birthright for ourselves. Similarly, she taught us two religions.

'When you are adults, you may choose whichever path you desire.'

At this point it was no contest. I felt I was a Burmese child and I spoke like one. I had been reared in the happiest of homes. Even in those early days it was clear to me that my mother was a special person. She was a compassionate and caring woman with a deep sense of social justice, respected and loved by Burmese and Europeans alike.

She often talked of the prejudices that prevailed, but always respected the rules by which the colonialists played. However, she believed we were all equal in the eyes of the Lord and I think that sustained her at times when those rules and regulations made life difficult.

There was an Anglo–Indian element in the town for whom she had a special place in her heart.

'They are people in limbo, wanted neither by the British who fathered them nor the Indian women who mothered them.'

She always referred to them as her friends and urged us, her children, never to feel unwanted.

Because of Robert's love of animals our home was also home to stray dogs. Every year when the winter nights closed in and the wild animals of the jungles came out to hunt, our pack of dogs were in the front line to have their numbers diminished. Each summer Robert replaced those killed by the panthers and tigers.

People often spoke of my mother as the woman with the most servants. But it was not snobbery that saw her with so many. It was the nature of the woman: she could not bear to see anybody go hungry and took on anybody who came looking for a handout. Some of them never worked for us, but were billeted in the servants' quarters and provided with food. It was fun having people of different races living together. It certainly provided plenty of playmates! So, when the Nagas' offer was made known to me, I immediately had visions of becoming part of the family of a people, of a country I loved, again.

Malaria continued to take its toll. The high temperatures had me hallucinating and weird pictures crossed my mind. My mother was always beside me in the hut.

'Here, Colin, sip this hot tea. It will bring down your temperature.'

It was always a relief when my body stopped shivering. A calmness followed. At these times, all the happy incidents in my short life came flooding back.

The images of my father and brother Donald projected clearly. I had hardly given them any thought during the trek, yet now, in the relative security of the Naga hut, I felt comfortable enough to recall my younger days: the family get-togethers and adult discussions; my mother's and father's concerns for the family; and my father's unease at the family's Burmanisation. It was a topic that had surfaced frequently, sometimes seriously, especially when he drew my mother's relatives into the debate.

During one visit from Mother's cousin, Dr Ba Maw, a heated argument erupted. As Minister of Education it was his desire to have the schools adopt Burmese as the first language and English as an optional subject. My mother, who usually kept out of it when the two men argued, became involved. She took sides with my father and I remember Uncle Ba Maw saying, 'One day we will have you British out of our country.'

It hit a raw nerve with my father, and when Uncle Ba Maw followed it up with, 'Archie, without Daw Ni you are nothing in this cultured country and the regard in which you are held is due entirely to the union with my cousin,' my father almost exploded. It would have come as a shock to him. The British were a superior lot and in many mixed marriages the Burmese side of the family came off a very poor second. Things were different with us because of my mother's background but even she could not withstand my father when he decided to send us to boarding school in Rangoon.

In defence of my father I must say that in many ways he was a generous person. I remember one family holiday when he commissioned one of the oil company's river boats to take us and some Burmese friends on a trip up the Chindwin River. It was a memorable holiday, cruising up the river from Mandalay with friends, enjoying the sights of river life. The paddle steamer called in to villages along the way and picked up cargo to ferry up-river. At night the steamer tied up at townships where we went ashore to visit friends, to be treated to a feast of Burmese food. Even Father seemed to enjoy himself.

The trip took the form of a geography lesson, with Robert rattling off the names of the towns, with a bit of history thrown in. I learnt that the huge rafts of teak logs that floated slowly past had been harvested way up in Northern Burma and were floated down a river whose headwaters were in the Himalayan snow country. There were people on these large floating rafts and we waved to them as we passed.

'Those families have probably spent two or three years living on the floating logs,' Robert said.

He pointed to a flight of geese.

'They're migrating to Mongolia.'

He even knew the fish the crew caught every day.

'*Mahseer* are the largest freshwater fish and they're only found in the cold waters flowing from the snowfields up in the Himalayas.'

The place abounded in wild fowl, and the opportunity to bag a few game-birds was too good for our father to let go by. He had packed his two shotguns and handing one to Donald they both climbed into a sampan and rowed out to get near to the feeding flock. There were a lot of passengers on the lower deck, and they all clambered over to one side of the steamer to watch the game shooting. The steamer leaned over with the extra weight, but there was no apparent danger of a capsize. As the shooters got closer the birds began to stir. Donald and Dad took aim and let all barrels go. The sky was blackened and the wild geese honked and squawked as they took flight. They fired again and bagged a few more birds. When they returned to the steamer they were greeted with cheering from the passengers.

Our mother never took kindly to my father's use of the gun and I know he was aware of her feelings. Nevertheless, it did not stop him from game-hunting. When he came aboard he gave the birds to some of the passengers who immediately set about plucking the feathers and preparing a meal of wild duck and geese.

The steamer-master set the boat for the final leg of our journey and before long we arrived at a village perched high on the western bank. We disembarked and with our luggage following, carried by coolies, we headed for a thatched bungalow overlooking the river. The plan was to spend some days at the village. Our mother had friends amongst the natives and the pastor of the church was a good friend of the family.

Roughing it in these thatched huts was fun. All the sounds of the village and the animals filtered through the thin walls and I never felt lonely or separated from the other inhabitants. The steamer continued upstream to Katha, a fairly large outpost in North Burma. The village was a delightful spot. To the east stretched the mighty river and all around us the hills were covered in teak forests which were being worked busily by teams of elephants.

Children in Burma are accorded a lot of love and are tolerated by almost every adult. Working the huge teak logs with elephants can be a tricky operation, but the workers always made us children feel welcome on site to watch. Our safety was their prime concern and at the end of the day when the ritual of the elephant bath was performed we would hitch a ride on one of these beasts down to the river.

They were allowed to wallow and play about before their 'mahout' set about them with heavy brushes to scrub the mud and grime of the day's work off their hides. The elephants were then led into the jungle on the outskirts of the village where, with chains tied to one foreleg, they were fed and permitted to graze to the length of the chain. Donald and our father took the opportunity to go game-shooting. The area was renowned for some of the bigger beasts — tiger, panther and wild elephant. Deer and pigs also abounded. The hunters seldom returned empty-handed; there was always a wild fowl or duck in their bags.

Sunday was a big day. This region of Burma was inhabited by the Kachin who, along with the Karen in south-east Burma, had been the two tribes converted to Christianity in the 1800s. Villagers, dressed in their finery and with their children in tow, traipsed off to the church hall for the morning service. We joined them and, on invitation, afterwards visited a local home for a meal followed by an afternoon of socialising.

Father was never comfortable at these gatherings. It was understandable; the two cultures are poles apart and there must have been occasions when he wished there were other Europeans around him. Even his children spoke the language of the village. Relations between Mother and Father, I observed, were beginning to get strained. The holiday away from his European workmates was fun for a while, but we children all knew that he was ready to return to his home in Syriam and work.

Being aware of the tension between our parents did not detract from the fun we were having. The weather was beautiful and the early mornings with the mist rising slowly along the river provided the signal for us to rise and enjoy a big breakfast of sticky rice and specially prepared chickpeas, a delicacy in the Kachin diet. The days flew by and then it was time to return home. The steamer arrived one mid-morning and the master of the boat signalled his arrival with a blast of the steam horn.

Practically the whole village came to see us off. We all sang a few hymns on the riverbank and then we climbed aboard. With us came all the many gifts friends in the village had given us. The generosity of the Burmese people has always been a part of their culture. They give to create merits in their journey through life, and the receiver of the gift is always thanked for creating the circumstance and thus the opportunity to build up their score of merits.

The journey south was slower in spite of the favourable current. There seemed to be more cargo to be picked up at the villages and the stops were longer. But they did give the family more time with friends and relatives. We also saw more of the hinterland.

We finally made it to Mandalay and there on the bank was Armanath Singh, our favourite house boy. A giant amongst the small Burmese, the first thing he did as the steamer pulled in was to salute us in military fashion. Armanath was a real showman and I must confess I missed him hanging around like a shadow. Our father liked him too, and on one occasion threatened to take him back to Syriam, but Mother would not hear of it.

'Absolutely not. Armanath stays here with us.'

He always addressed Father as the *Burra Sahib* [big master] and he seemed to grow a couple of inches in stature whenever Father visited Maymyo. I think it had something to do with the Pathan culture. The natives from that part of India are of Aryan descent, where the society is male-dominated and Armanath seemed to prefer taking instructions from Father, or rather he seemed more comfortable in the company of my father. Not that he ever showed the slightest disrespect to Mother, but the relationship with her was more that of mother and son, whereas with my father it was master and servant. It was always the bowing of the head and salaaming with Father, but Mother would never expect that from any of her servants.

With all the luggage and the gifts, we headed off to Maymyo in two cars. The air was pleasant and cool when we arrived home just before sunset. The servants were waiting, but not their children. They never seemed to front up when Father visited the home. I never did find out the reason.

After a few days of social whirl and afternoons on the tennis court my father said his farewells and returned to work. He always broke down when he left our home and for a few days our mother was never quite herself. He was proud of his children and during our visits to Rangoon he would show us off to his associates in the oil company.

Back at school, the first few days became a travelogue of all the pupils' holiday experiences. Each student was asked to address the class and tell his story. The most informative and exciting one from each class was printed in the school magazine. Some of the students had travelled to India, others to the Malayan States and Singapore. Since some were sons of the rulers of various ethnic states, their stories and experiences were interesting. These rulers, especially the Shan warlords, were very wealthy and maintained a feudal system in their territory. Some of them had numerous wives and the children of the first, second or third wives all attended school together.

———

Those days were gone, and here was I, in the deserted Naga village, reflecting on the kindness of the tribesmen whom the history books described as murderous headhunters. Yet only a short time ago they had been urging us to abandon our plans to keep heading for India and to join them. Strange people. Here we were, occupying their ancestral homes and land from which they had been driven by the vanguard of fleeing troops, and they were offering us hospitality! That night I felt more comfortable in the smoke-filled, thatched hut despite being spied upon by the darkened heads hanging like puppets from the dark ceiling. Robert had again intimated that he would like to examine one of the smoked heads.

'Maybe we should climb up and take a closer look.'

Mother overheard his remark and immediately said, 'You mustn't even think of such an act. Instead, think of them as our guardian spirits.'

I don't remember how much longer we stayed. Our supply of food was still good and though it continued to rain we were well sheltered. The malaria too improved, and my bouts of fever grew less frequent. The wound on my shoulder appeared to be on the mend. However, there was an occasional flare-up, especially if, during the night, my shoulder made contact with the split bamboo floor. It seemed the wound would never heal properly, and often in child-like fantasy I imagined that the bomb shrapnel had been impregnated with a poison by the Japanese makers.

Chapter 11

MOVING ON

Despite the relative comfort of our camp there was an air of anxiety about the family, the expectation that something would happen to make us decide on a plan.

'If only we had news of how the war is going.'

'I'd still gladly make the return trip home if it were safe.'

'There's no way of knowing where the Japs are.'

'We can't be far from the border now, by my calculations. Surely a final effort for another few days will get us there.'

'We have had some rest and food. It will surely be possible for you children to reach India safely.'

One night, following a couple of days of lighter rain, we made the decision to move on. The next morning, with just a few blankets and a fairly good supply of food, we set off. No sooner had we reached the floor of the valley, several hours from the village, than the heavens opened and the path became a watercourse. It did not occur to us to retreat now. The thought uppermost in my mind at any rate was to keep going, to get to India. We had to be close to the end of the trail now. The possibility of perishing on this leg of the trek was constantly with me and this fear kept me going. The alternative was to lie down and give up, as many thousands had done earlier in the trek.

We crossed a stream and began to climb the next range. Despite the heavy rain the ground underfoot was still relatively firm, an indication that it had been quite a long time since anyone had used the path. The path was hidden by thick forest growth, but I could see enough to indicate that we were facing the steepest section so far.

Late in the afternoon we had had enough.

'There must be a relatively flat spot somewhere near here to spend the night,' Robert said.

I was exhausted. The climb through mud and water, with constant stops to help my mother as she struggled to find a footing on the greasy surface of the track, had sapped all my energy. The summit still seemed far off. We encountered a few corpses and stepping around them on this narrow track made progress much more treacherous, with the risk of tripping and hurtling down into the ravine.

'Colin, you lead the way. I'll bring up the rear and push *Ama* up the steepest parts.'

I noticed another body ahead and signalled back to Robert that we might have to go a little further on to set up camp.

As I stepped over the tiny form in the mud, I recognised the youngest child who, only a short time ago, had passed through the village with her older brother and other children. I looked at the tiny puffed-up face and wondered if any of the others were in the vicinity. My sister, who had hardly displayed any emotion throughout the trek and had kept silent most of the time, wept when she looked down at the little girl's body.

We found a square of flat ground and sat down. There was no hope of lighting a fire in the deluge, so we decided to chew some dry rice and wash it down with water dripping off the steep wall of the mountainside.

Our oilcloth-covered bag of dry rice was now wet, which meant that in a day or so it would turn sour and begin to ferment. Another blow! I had very little sleep that night. We huddled together to share body warmth. My mind returned frequently to the little girl lying a few yards down the track, her face sticking up out of the mud and ooze.

Perhaps it was because I was physically drained that her face haunted me so. I had been on the road for many weeks and witnessed hundreds upon hundreds of dead and dying people, but the sight of this child grieved me deeply. In the early morning the rain stopped and miraculously Robert got a fire going. We cooked some rice and drank some black tea. Robert had returned to her body and covered her face with some driftwood. We had barely gathered up our things when the heavens opened up again.

We wandered on, the track heading down into another valley. The rain kept bucketing down and the trail, now just a muddy watercourse, was proving more and more difficult to handle. We slid, scrambled, tumbled and rode down the path. The dry rice I had eaten was giving me wrenching stomach pains but it was impossible to stop to relieve myself. The pack on my back and the thick mud that I gathered on my body with the constant slipping and sliding in the ooze, scrubbed my shoulder wound. The whole scene seemed never-ending. There were moments when we could hear the roar of the rushing waters at the bottom of the valley, yet it seemed to take an eternity to reach it. I knew that once we hit the bottom we would find a resting place, even if it were just a rocky outcrop.

Battered, bruised and cut, we finally reached the bottom. The river was in full flood and we looked for a calmer pool to wash ourselves — no easy task. A great amount of debris was being washed down. Even large trees uprooted in the higher reaches of the river drifted by. We had come to a full stop.

'We'll just have to wait for the water level to drop.'

There was not much room for the four of us to spread out, so we just sat there and waited. The night came upon us and there seemed to be no easing of the downpour. Huddled together with a sodden blanket over our heads, we waited. Falling asleep could have proved hazardous, because of the likelihood of falling down the slippery bank into the raging waters. At any rate, sleep does not come easily when one's bowel movements occur every few minutes. Mosquitoes and other insects feasted on our bodies.

We had discovered it was better to rest for the night coated in thick mud because the insects could not penetrate drying mud caked on our bodies. But here, washed clean of the mud gathered on the slide down, we were easy prey for the creepy crawlies of the tropical jungle. There is no place in these mountain ranges that is not infested with one or another insect plague. Buffalo flies swarmed all over us in the daytime and the mosquitoes took over night duty.

The day came and went and there were signs of a let-up in the rain. Some time later Robert left the group to check on the level and flow of the water. He was gone for some time and we became concerned for his safety. There was no way we could communicate with him: the roar of the waters rushing down the narrow gorge and the sounds bouncing off the cliff walls were deafening. Eventually, he crawled back along the bank.

'There are some fallen trees and debris jammed in the waterway a bit further on. We might be able to cross there if the rains don't get any heavier.'

Anything was better than just sitting on the rocky outcrop and gradually starving and enduring the torture of being eaten alive by insects.

With great difficulty we got across and staggered up the opposite bank. Initially, the slippery climb presented difficulties. All our energies had been sapped during the hazardous crossing. By the time we had negotiated the steep climb it was getting dark and I walked ahead to find a spot where we could rest in the gloom of the evening.

'There might be shelter over there,' I said, glimpsing something ahead.

There was. It was a roughly constructed lean-to. I also detected the distinct smell of decaying human flesh.

All along the trek, whenever we stumbled across some dead bodies, we found a shelter. This one was no exception and nearby were the remains of a fireplace. Someone had set alight a huge log and I was sure, despite the rains, that some embers could be revived. It had been days since we had last sat beside a warm fire and here was a chance to dry out the few rags we carried. I put my hands into the large pile of ash.

'They're still warm!'

Robert was an expert at lighting and reviving fires in adverse conditions. He slowly gathered a few dead but still wet leaves and gently laid them on the warm ash, waiting a moment. He then began to blow gently upon the base of the ash. It was a painstaking task, especially since he had hardly any energy left, but at last some smoke rose. Before long the leaves on the ash caught alight and he added small twigs until a reasonable fire was burning. My spirits rose and I mustered enough strength to stand up again.

'I'll look for some wood to keep it stoked.'

The rains persisted, but thankfully there were no strong winds. I wandered off and returned with some dead branches to see my brother constructing a tepee of green leaves over the fire. The crude structure served its purpose and gave the fireplace some shelter from the heavy rain.

The only light we had by this time was the glow of the fire. It was too dark to forage for more fuel, so I took it upon myself to ration the wood and use just enough to keep the fire alive. We huddled close to the embers and at least one side of our bodies reaped some benefit. The insects, too, kept away. In the darkness I tried to scrape off some of the leeches that had been sucking on my body for days. For the first time in a long while I fell asleep.

In the morning, with the rain still pelting down, Robert and I set out to find more fuel.

'You go that way, Colin, and I'll go over here.'

My mother and sister had found an empty tin and heated some water gathered from puddles. We had learned that a drink of warm water, even without additives, gave us a boost. My shoulder was giving me hell. The wound was spreading right up to the shoulder bone and I began to fear I might lose my right arm, which was already quite useless. We had to keep moving. Something told me we were approaching the border. The track did not appear as steep as on the earlier mountains.

My mind went back to my school days. We had had a keen geography teacher who was also an artist. He had delighted in drawing various countries on the blackboard. He would then instruct the class to note the features that he had shaded in. He then proceeded to erase his drawing and tell the class to replicate his work by memory, to the extent of naming the main rivers and the mountain ranges. It was the recollection of his lessons that led me to believe that our party had negotiated the highest mountains of the region, the Patkoi Range, and was now heading down on to the plains of Assam.

Robert was of the same mind.

'There are still some highlands to be climbed, but I think we're getting near the end of the trail.'

We moved on, and the constant resting whenever the fever took hold of me made progress slow. Time and distance meant nothing to me, but I guess that the ground we covered, as we dragged ourselves along, did not exceed three or four miles. Like Robert, I was skin and bone. My hip bones jutted out from my frame and I can vividly recall looking down at my legs whenever I was forced to scrape the leeches off and thinking how thin I was. My mother and sister too were thin but were always bulkier than we boys were.

The track became less stony, but more difficult to negotiate. We sank further into the ooze with every step. My wound got worse and I became easy prey to the flies. Very soon maggots appeared in the wound. I was alarmed by the infestation and had visions of being eaten away by the crawling creatures. I remembered viewing human bodies earlier in the trek being devoured by maggots. However, my mother reassured me.

'Don't worry, Colin. It's nature's way of cleaning a putrid wound.'

I could hear the roaring sound of the raging stream below and once again our spirits plummeted. All I could think of was how many river crossings there still were between the two countries.

In normal circumstances I would have been delighted to come across a river or stream. There is something that draws young adventurous boys to moving water. But in my present condition the sound of running water dampened my spirit. I dreaded every moment of every water crossing. The trail we had chosen to save our lives cuts through the wettest region on earth. The

Hukawng Valley is a unique area; it makes its own climate and nothing about it is right.

As the rain continued to fall the leeches seemed to multiply. People may exaggerate when they tell stories of leeches sucking humans to death, but I have no doubt that the many thousands of the dead along the trek had these blood-sucking creatures, along with other sicknesses, contribute to their deaths. Corpses appeared in increasing numbers. Hundreds lay sprawled in the oozing mud. At the foot of every ascent there were bodies of people who had just lain down and given up rather than take on the next climb.

A year later, when American and Chinese troops began to retrace the refugee trail, the horrible tragedy of the refugee hordes was revealed.

The famous Burma surgeon, Gordon Seagrave, was one of those who retraced the trail with General Stilwell. He wrote in his powerful book *Burma Surgeon Returns*:

Still standing along the road were some extremely crude shacks, each with its 10–20 skeletons of those who couldn't get up when a new day came. In one shallow stream, we were horrified to find that the Chinese had placed a long row of skulls to be used as stepping stones. Sex and age and even race could be noted, not by such elusive clues as surgeons use, but by the rotting clothes.

Thinking of his own family, he went on.

When I saw a skeleton clothed in a delicate English dress, I was thankful for Tiny's departure a year before. Looking at the skeletons of the little boys in khaki shorts I realised they might have been John or Sterling. There were men, women and children of every race and age, their hair white, grey, brown and black still lying beside the whitened skulls; there were English, Anglo–Burmese and Indians — civilian and military...

And yet in spite of the hundreds and hundreds of skeletons we saw, we didn't see half of those who had died on the refugee trail, for English and Indian and Chinese burial and cremating squads had been at work.

A few months later only a few scattered skulls were left to mark the trail of the refugees. Now we were the first of the refugees to return.

Another unfordable river, I thought. Robert's precious possession, his rifle, finally became too burdensome and without so much as a word he cast it into the fierce running waters. I watched him as he stood there. He had carried that heavy rifle as if it were an heirloom through some of the most difficult and arduous sections of the trail. He had treasured it as the only protection we had.

My heart went out to him. I loved him, and I had a feeling that, in throwing away his rifle, he had abandoned hope.

The rains eased and heavy fog rolled in. We made the crossing, continued up a steep rise and came across a cluster of huts. It was the first real indication that we were approaching the end of the trail. They were built with roughly sawn timber and resembled a staging post.

Again we were confronted with the dead lying in and around the site. It seemed the earlier dead had been moved a short distance from the campsite, piled high and set alight. The fire had not done the job and charred bodies were visible in piles in other directions. It was a gloomy sight. I felt revolted. I don't know why: I had seen so many of my kind dead and rotting along the trail. Perhaps it was the sight of the bodies stacked in a pile like timber. I could accept that people must die in difficult situations — in battle or during an air raid, for instance, but it was unnerving and deeply distressing to see corpses stacked up. It all seemed so pointless.

There was a ghostly feeling about the place. We searched the huts for scraps of food but found nothing save a few empty tins of bully beef and condensed milk. We spent the night in a structure that resembled a kitchen. The fireplace was covered with cold damp ash and empty tins. At daylight our little party moved on. None of us had the strength or the desire to walk the few yards down the trail to the river to gather some water. Visibility was not good, but there was nothing to see anyway, just the track ahead. We barely spoke to one another; speaking used up energy. Despite my condition I carried the faint flicker of hope that we would all survive. Surely somebody would find us soon. As we rounded each bend, I began to have visions of running into a party of rescuers.

The track became less muddy and the climb not so steep. Nevertheless, movement was still difficult and wearisome. We had not eaten for days and yet the little water we could gather in our palms from the indents on the track seemed all we needed. I had gone beyond being hungry. All I yearned for was to be picked up and carried along. I was not blind to the fact that I was now just a bony figure of a person. The others, too, looked very pale and scrawny, especially Robert.

Our clothes were in tatters. Mother and Ethel both wore the *longyi* [sarong], which was normally wrapped around a woman's body from the waist down. However, because it was their only remaining garment, they had each drawn it up to cover their chests for modesty. Robert and I were left with only the shirts on our backs, long khaki army garments we had found on the bombed-out train on the way to Myitkyina. Our shorts had long since been ripped to shreds with the constant slipping and sliding on the muddy track. I seldom wore my shirt anyway, because of the chafing of my shoulder wound.

I could see a hopelessness about Robert. It seemed he had given up on being the guardian of our group, the leader whose duty was to see his family through to India. Night followed day with little progress. We were still climbing the slope that led on and on. Without a word, we settled down one evening at another crude lean-to. Miraculously, the fireplace alongside contained warm ashes. Despite his exhaustion, Robert's expertise came to our rescue, and before long we sat huddled beside warm flames.

Our sense of time had deserted us, but it was probably a few days before we decided to move on. In the meantime, we had all contracted a severe dose of dysentery and were all passing blood from our bowels. None of us had the strength to move very far from our resting place to go to the toilet and as a result even the campsite was turning into a latrine.

We knew we had to make an effort to move. We were driven by the desperate hope that help might be just around the next bend, over the next crossing. We felt sure we were near India now. The question was, how far was the border? How much more did we have to endure?

Chapter 12

WHITE BUTTERFLIES

One morning Ethel, Robert and I arose to move on. But Mother, who was leaning against a tree, gestured that she could not muster the strength to get up and keep walking. She kept begging for a drink of warm water.

She whispered, 'The pain in my stomach...'

I searched around the campsite hoping to find a utensil for heating some water. Buried under some ashes in another fireplace I found a squashed piece of metal, a flattened cigarette tin. I managed to prise it open, scooped up a little water from the muddy ground and placed it in the hot ashes.

We all sipped the warm fluid, which miraculously did ease the stomach pains.

'We have to get going,' Robert insisted.

'*Ta* [son], I cannot get up.'

In frustration Robert pulled at her hands, but he was too weak to raise her. She said in a faint voice, 'My children, you must leave me. Go along and seek some help and come back to get me.'

I asked, 'But, *Ama*, what if we do not return? What will you do?'

'Maybe, God permitting, I will go back to my own country and my people. When the war is over you will be able to come back and find me.'

She slipped off her rings and reached for Ethel's hand.

'Take these, to exchange for food or anything else in India.'

Ethel said nothing. She was beyond words and beyond tears. She just took the gemstones — sapphires, rubies and emeralds — and gazed at Mother, her face stricken.

I was shattered. My mother was my great love and I could not bear the thought of leaving her in the jungle. I could not accept that this could happen. After all, we had survived the long journey from our home in Maymyo 800 miles away, the bombings, the long trek along the plains with the threat of attacks from the air, the climb over the mountain ranges and the crossings of dangerous rivers. I could not believe that any of us would not survive. And now it seemed that one of us had reached the end of the road.

My whole life had revolved around my mother. I had a special bond with her and had frequently been reminded that I was the most Burmese of all the children.

I remembered my father, on one of his visits to Maymyo, asking my mother, 'Why does Colin persist in speaking only in Burmese?'

I think it was the Burmese in me that created that special bond with my Burmese mother.

The whole of my young life came flooding back. The reality that I could lose my mother overwhelmed me. Suddenly all I could think about was the fun I had experienced as a child growing up in the care of a person who had showered me with love and affection. There had been hardly a moment in my younger days, until I was forced into boarding school by my father, when I was not near my mother. She was always there like a guardian angel. I could not accept that all those good times were soon to end.

Mother kept drifting in and out of consciousness, awakening to tell us to move on. She repeatedly whispered, 'Your father is waiting for you, he is expecting you.'

Robert and Ethel were utterly broken.

Full of grief, Ethel took my arm.

'Colin, nothing more can be done for *Ama*,' she whispered gently, but I would not budge.

The two of them had somehow accepted the situation, and they began to move off together. They were too weak even to cry. I watched them dragging themselves up a slight incline into the mist that had descended. I tried again to get my mother up, but it seemed that her spirit to continue had gone. She looked at me and I sat down and hugged her, and that special smell of a mother, the scent that bonds a mother and her child, flooded back.

It was the scent of her body I had experienced so often during the days in Maymyo, the days when we all gathered around her on the verandah of our home at night to listen to the sounds of insects and animals as they foraged around in the bushes that surrounded our home.

Despite having witnessed the death of thousands along the way, I did not ever foresee this situation. Day after day along the trek, even during the most difficult times, I had never contemplated our death. Certainly there were times when, utterly exhausted, I felt like lying down and drifting into a long sleep, but death, never! But now I had reached the point in the trek when I would willingly have stayed with my mother and died with her.

I looked up the track. Ethel and Robert had disappeared from view. My mother touched me.

'Ta [son], it is your duty to leave me and join your brother and sister.'

'No, no, Ama, I can't. I can't leave you.'

'Son, if you love me, you will go and seek help. Go ... I will wait until you return ... if anything is altered, I will try to go back to a village ... you may find me when the war ends.'

'What will happen if I can't find you, who will look after me?'

She whispered, with words that have remained embedded in my mind, 'The world is full of good people ... I know you will find them and be well cared for, for the rest of your life. Son, you must walk on ... don't look back.'

I promised myself that I would one day return to seek her out, and sit at the spot where I had parted from a mother who had displayed such love and devotion to me.

I hugged her for the last time and walked away. I never looked back.

I lived with that memory for years, never prepared to accept that my mother had indeed passed away on that hillside in the jungles of Burma. I willed in my heart that, miraculously, she may have been rescued by some Naga tribe and carried back to a friendly village to see her days out.

Year after year, decade after decade, I sought the means to return to Burma and the northern regions to seek my mother. At every step an obstacle was placed in my path. I sought the assistance of the government of Burma, but because of the internal security problems that prevailed in that country after independence, I was refused an entry permit time and time again. When the country was finally opened, and seven-day visas were granted to selected persons, I, with the help of the Reverend Roger Bush, sought assistance from the top man in Burma, General Ne Win.

To my surprise, I was granted a 21-day visa and support from the military authorities to travel in the country. However, the area I wished to go to was out of bounds. Nevertheless, with my eldest son and his wife, I finally returned to the country. It was 1982, 40 years since the trek. We travelled to my birthplace and after some enquiries contacted a long-time family friend who had connections with tribal chiefs in the Hukawng Valley.

He was able to tell me, 'Your mother indeed did die during the trek.'

I was sad, but profoundly relieved. The uncertainty was finally over.

Many years later, while catching up with friends from Burma in Western Australia, I met a Captain Minus, now retired, from the Burma Army. He had known my family during peacetime and had often visited our home. By strange coincidence, he had later married one of my mother's relatives. In the lounge room of his Perth home he, rather reluctantly, told me of his trek out along the same route after losing his platoon. He had broken through Japanese lines and followed the refugee trail a few days behind our group.

Bit by bit, his story unfolded.

'I stopped by the tree under which your mother sat, and talked with her. She was very near death and I was sad that I could not be of any assistance.'

He had offered her some water and, in a state of delirium, she had replied, 'Thank you, but my servants have just left to get me some water from the well.'

––––––––

Time meant nothing to me. I had completely shut off and do not recall the next stage of the trek. When I found my brother and sister sitting, resting, some way down the track, they were tremendously pleased and relieved to see me.

Robert said, 'I was convinced that we wouldn't see you again.'

I said, 'We've got to keep walking. We must get help for *Ama*.'

The desire to save my mother was the only thing that was keeping me going. Ethel and Robert said nothing.

Catching up to them brought me back to reality. I was glad to see them. In fact, I felt acutely conscious of my surroundings. I remember continually urging them to keep moving, but Robert was finding it very hard, as he was convulsed with dysentery and was bleeding badly.

We crossed a wide, rocky stream. It was knee-deep, and many bloated bodies were wedged between the rocks, partly floating in pools. I knew that most of the dead were natives of India, but seeing all these bodies half out of the water, bleached almost ghostly white, seemed strange. A feeling of unease came over me and I was driven to get away as far as possible from this horrible scene. The rain had eased and some shacks came into view up ahead. The rough lean-tos were scattered on both sides of the trail and every one was occupied by a group of corpses. We found one that had collapsed, but part of the platform remained. It was better than lying in the mud.

There was no sign of life and even searching for some warm embers was out of the question. We just huddled together a few inches off the ground on this shaky platform and slowly attended to the ritual of scraping off leeches. My shoulder wound opened up again but I felt no discomfort from it. All three of us continued to suffer from dysentery and the wrenching stomach pains and constant bowel movements kept us awake most of the night, but it was Robert who suffered the most.

As we huddled together under the last blanket, we were joined by a man. In the dim light I could see that he was tall, dressed in ragged khaki clothes and had a revolver strapped to his waist. I naturally thought we were at the point of being rescued, but then he asked if we would let him share the shelter with us. He introduced himself in English. We had become so used to speaking only Burmese amongst ourselves on the trek that this came almost as a surprise.

He told us that his name was Mr Rossiter and he was a district commissioner in Burma. He had been posted in the far north and when the Japanese overran it he had escaped. He had travelled for days behind Japanese lines and had eventually picked up the refugee trail. He, too, had not eaten for days and, like me, had been stricken with malaria. He talked of his family — in England, I thought — and asked which route we had taken.

We must have drifted off to sleep. I thought I heard other voices, but it may have been just the hallucinations of malaria. At first light, I moved off the platform to relieve myself, taking care not to disturb our companion's sleep. Robert had awakened too. He stared at the man for a moment and then leant over to touch him.

'He's dead.'

I was surprised. He had walked right up to us the night before. I wouldn't have thought he was weak enough to die. Perhaps he was more ill than I had realised. We rolled his body just off the platform and I noticed that his belt and revolver were missing. I didn't look closely at his face.

I mentioned the missing revolver to Robert but he just replied, 'Perhaps he lost the belt when he went into the bushes at night to relieve himself.'

Perhaps he did. Or perhaps it was even somebody else. We were so close to death ourselves that we had been drifting in and out of consciousness.

We set about covering the body in leaves to hide it from our view and to give the man some dignity and privacy in death. We were in no condition to drag his body any distance.

Then Ethel looked up. She whispered, '*Ama's* rings! They're gone!'

We just looked at her. The jewellery was gone, our only resource should we make it to India. We were too weak to react. Normally, Robert would have become angry. He would have wondered whether we had somehow been robbed in the darkness and he would have gone looking for the culprit. Perhaps somebody had taken the dead man's revolver and our jewellery during the night. Or perhaps it was just a coincidence. Perhaps the rings had dropped from Ethel's thin fingers. She had had to wear them on her hands; she had nothing in which she could carry them. Robert was too ill to say, let alone do, anything about it. I don't think he had any anger left in him.

Mother, like all Burmese women, possessed a fair amount of jewellery. In Burma, a person's wealth is measured by their ownership of precious gemstones. Even our servants seemed to have some jewels tucked away. Mother preferred to wear simple items — her heavy, broad gold wedding band and a few pearls. But she had brought her most valuable rings with her when we set out on the trek, to use as a form of currency. She also had some gold coins, which she must have used earlier in the trek to pay our way.

I remember our father bought her the best Ceylonese sapphires, cornflower blue stones set with diamonds like sparkling flowers, when he went back to Britain on furlough every three years, stopping off in Colombo on the way. She also had rubies, the prized Burmese 'pigeon's blood' stones that changed colour, from deep pink to blood red, depending on the light. But he refused to have anything to do with local sapphires from the Burmese–Thai border region, saying they were inferior quality and badly cut. He gave her emeralds from South India and opals from Australia, which he bought in Colombo also. I remember that she did not really like the opals, although the Indians loved them and would barter valuable emeralds for the semi-precious stones.

Now they were all gone, and it did not seem important. Nothing mattered anymore. We just sat around, too weak to move on, drifting in and out of consciousness.

The next morning I awoke, overcome by a strange coldness. The three of us had been resting huddled together. Robert was close beside me and the coldness I experienced was his body. He had died during the night.

I had not anticipated this. I knew Robert was terribly ill — more ill than I was — but we had all still been hanging on. Now I just wanted it all to end. I wanted to join my brother. He looked so much at peace curled up, dead, beside me. Ethel too was deeply grieved. There were no more tears for either of us to shed. I just wondered what it was all about. I had stepped over and around many dead bodies along the trek. Now my own were suffering the same fate as those poor people left along the way.

I had not known that Robert would die. I had never thought his life would just slip away in the night. Perhaps his big heart gave up the battle. I will never know.

Yet something in me willed me to fight for survival.

I had learnt that it was customary to say a prayer whenever one saw a coffin on the way to a burial. In a country like Burma, where death was a common occurrence, one seemed to pray daily. The prayer was just a few words Mother had taught us: 'Lord, give those left behind the strength to carry on.' The words came upon me, but they conflicted with the teachings of the *Pongyi* [monk] which were, 'You yourself can only overcome the problems of the day.'

I was confused, and managed to whisper to Ethel, 'Why is God putting us through this?'

I received no reply. She could not speak.

I covered my brother's body with the last blanket. Ethel and I, though very weak, managed to gather a few leaves and sticks to lay over the blanket, to shield our brother from people's view. I loved him. We had grown up together as the closest of friends, although we were very different. He was the brains and I the brawn. We argued for one another and we fought for one another. He was loved by all for his earnestness. The servants, the stallholders at the markets and the teachers at school all spoke highly of him. There were times when I tired of all the nice things people said about Robert: it was difficult to live in his shadow. But he always encouraged me and never, ever put his young brother down.

His love for animals was demonstrated in Maymyo when our neighbour, who was a Commissioner of Forests, shot and brought home a man-eating tiger one day. While we all gathered round to view the magnificent beast, Robert asked the Commissioner, U Nu, 'Why did you shoot it?'

'It was a man-eater and very dangerous.'

'Surely the reason it killed people must have been either that it was hungry, or was guarding its territory,' Robert said.

The principal of the school in Maymyo once described him as a child prodigy. He was invited to sit for an open examination with students much older than himself, to select the nation's top scholar. He streaked the field and achieved a near perfect score in all subjects. He even topped the Burmese paper. He was a talented musician and an above-average sportsman, although there were many things he preferred to do other than prove himself on the playing field or in the pool. Above all, he was a gentle person blessed with the gift the Buddhists call '*Karuna*' — a compassionate spirit that revelled in the success and joy of others.

The rain had not eased for some time. Ethel and I, without a word, struggled off the rough slats that had kept us off the ground and moved away up the slope. On the other side we hit a quagmire on a flat section of track. We were some yards apart, both only inching along, and could not have been far from where Robert's body lay. Ethel sank down as if to rest a moment. I moved on a short distance further, then I too let my body down into the ooze.

I felt completely at peace. There was not a thought of food or water in my head. I just gently created a pocket in the mud that was comfortable and warm. For the first time in many weeks I had found a resting place for my aching bones. The mud provided a cushion which would normally have been provided by flesh, but I had hardly any left.

As I lay there so near to death I observed, or perhaps I dreamed, a cloud of white butterflies floating down towards me. It was a comforting vision and I was not afraid.

I cannot remember how long I had lain in this comfortable position when I was aroused by a noisy group of people. At first I could only hear their shouting. My eyes had closed when I had dozed off and some mud had covered them. I must have wiped them open to see what appeared to be a huge European man looking down at me. He tried to stir me with his foot. It was extremely painful. I uttered something.

'Who else is with you, laddie?'

'My sister is somewhere nearby,' I managed to croak.

'Get up!'

I did not want to get up or be helped. I felt at peace and for the first time in many days I felt warm. A strange feeling of being with people I loved came over me.

'Please let me rest,' I pleaded.

He roared at me about people giving up the will to live and not fighting to keep going.

Being pulled out of the mud was excruciating. I remember my rescuers very kindly trying to wipe the oozing stuff off my body with a blanket. It was agony. My shoulder wound and body sores screamed in pain.

Then they laid me on a grey blanket, which they then hitched to a pole slung between two Indian natives.

That is how they transported me to a camp at Ledo, I learnt later. It was a devil of a ride. My shoulder wound was painful and as the bearers negotiated the uneven ground my body sometimes scraped along the dirt and mud. I recall very little of the trip. I must have drifted in and out of consciousness from pain and starvation. I do remember that it was still daylight when we reached the camp. Evidently I had almost reached civilisation unaided.

I did not know it, but it was nearing the end of August 1942, three and a half months since we had set out on the trek from Mogaung. The camp had been set up by the tea-planters of Assam, of whom my rescuer was one. Their Indian labourers had carried me to the campsite.

When I was finally laid down outside a hut, I observed a lot of activity. Fires were alight everywhere and men were moving about pouring themselves mugs of liquid from drums atop the fires. I was offered a drink. It was a strong brew of tea, laced with salt. Somebody opened a tin of apricots and I made an attempt to eat the fruit. I was violently ill and when I came to, I found myself in a long hut occupied by sick and wounded soldiers. They had transported me to a place called Tinsukia, a jungle hospital away from the front line.

There I was head-shaved, bathed and sprayed with DDT powder to eliminate the body lice. My shoulder wound was also attended to in a fashion. I was then moved to another section of the field hospital where for the first time I saw some women dressed in nurses' uniforms. They were Anglo–Indian nurses working with the troops on the Burma front.

I remember being told by somebody early on that my sister, too, had been rescued, but had passed away. I was not able to react. I was too near to death myself at that point to feel my own emotions, let alone respond to what I was being told. Perhaps it was my mind's way of preserving what little was left of my body.

Later, the Scottish tea-planter who had saved my life told me that Ethel had been carried to the camp alive, but had survived for just one day after being rescued.

'Your sister died in the camp before we could get her to the military hospital. She drifted away peacefully.'

He was very kind in the way he explained it. I was deeply upset, and he saw that I could not talk about it. I could not bring myself to ask him whether she had been buried. I just lay there silently. He quietly left me, and I was grateful for his understanding. For her to have come so close to survival and then to miss out on living was beyond my comprehension.

I had not been as close to Ethel as I had been to Robert in recent years, because she was older and was rapidly becoming a young lady. But when I was small she had always been there for me like a second mother, cuddling and comforting me if something went wrong, laughing and telling me stories, carting me about the place and spoiling me rotten. She had always been deeply protective of me. Now she too was gone, and I was truly alone.

II

MOTHER INDIA

Chapter 13

HOSPITAL

For days I drifted in and out of consciousness. Then one morning I began to notice what was going on around me. The wound on my shoulder was troubling me and the smell was unbearable. The nurses said there had not been much they could do about it while I remained so ill.

'Now that you are a little better, it's time to begin treating it.'

The daily ritual of dressing the wound was the most painful experience I had ever encountered. Whenever the time came I would break out in a cold sweat and cry aloud. It was torture and the two nurses hated every moment of it as much as I did.

There were times when they would weep with me. The wound had opened up into a gaping hole into which the nurse would prod a gauze bandage.

'It is the only way to drain the pus and clean the infected area.'

I was fed a battery of tablets to treat my malaria and to stop my bowel movements. The liquid food of concentrated chicken essence went straight through me.

As the days went by my vision, which had been cloudy at best, became clearer and I was more inclined to speak with the nurses and some of the other patients in the bush hospital. A lot of the other Indian patients were casualties of battle. Some were laid low with malaria. It was a pitiful sight to see these half-naked people who displayed such courage, despite having lost limbs and carrying bullet wounds to their heads and faces. Some of them gave their time to sit alongside my bed and talk. I still believe the nurses had instructed those fine fellows to visit the boy at the end of the makeshift ward.

My voice began to improve in strength, although I had not been aware that I had been speaking in a whisper until somebody pointed it out to me. Whenever I talked to a nurse or a visitor, there was a strange drumming sound in my head, as if I was bellowing.

As my health improved the events of the past weeks kept flooding back. One of the nurses who was particularly kind to me would sit beside the bed.

'Think only about getting better,' she said.

Whenever she came to visit or administer some medicine, she would take her leave by saying, 'God is looking after you and has a mission for you.'

I think she was a Catholic girl because every time she went she crossed her heart.

The nights were hard to take. Many of the wounded soldiers had difficulty sleeping and one or another was constantly crying out in pain. The packs of jackals and the hyenas too began prowling at sunset and created a lot of noise as they scavenged for food in the compound.

The rope bed was painful. I was so thin that only skin covered my bones — there was no flesh to act as a cushion.

Some time during the week the doctor said, 'It is time we had this young man weighed.'

The problem was how to do it. The scales were the old-fashioned type used to weigh carcasses, hung from the rafters in the roof. The nurses had to devise a means to get me hanging off the hook. It was a painful exercise and I protested aloud. Eventually the staff had me slung by a sheet and hooked on to the scales. I weighed 50 pounds.

'He has heavy bones,' one nurse commented.

'Whatever would he have weighed if he had a light frame?' the second nurse replied.

I recalled having weighed myself at the commencement of the trek at the railway station in Mogaung, during an idle moment while the family was deciding which route to choose. I had weighed in then at around 124 pounds.

I asked my favourite nurse to get me a mirror because it had been months since I had taken a peek at myself. She went away to find one but soon came back.

'I'm sorry, but there don't seem to be any mirrors available,' she said.

Much later, during a brighter moment, she confessed that she had lied.

'The doctor instructed me not to let you see yourself — it was part of the process of lifting your spirits.'

Either I was developing a sense of awareness, or my eyesight was now improving daily. I began to watch things and people along the long ward. I was desperately sad, but also had moments when I thought of the poor souls around me. I was not alone. I was sharing these times with very sick and dying soldiers. They too were far from their homes and loved ones. Surely they must have felt as abandoned as I did.

A skinny Indian soldier befriended me and was a constant visitor. He was swathed in bandages from head to feet, but still managed to hobble around the ward. We spoke in Hindustani and he told me about his life in a village in Central India, talking lovingly of his wife and children. He had joined the army when the Japanese invaded Burma, not so long ago. After a short training session he had been posted to a regiment in Burma just before the defeat of the Allies there and had been wounded in a mortar attack. He was a humble fellow.

'My only regret is that I never ever had the opportunity to fire a bullet at the enemy,' he said.

I think he would have liked the chance to kill one of them because he could have returned to his village and boasted of his deed.

'You might get an opportunity to go back into action when you recover from your wounds,' I said, but I did not fancy his chances. He surely would be invalided out.

Not once during the long sessions he spent alongside my bed did he mention or ask after my family. He, like the other patients, had probably been instructed not to ask me anything about the trek. It was the way things were handled in those days. Nowadays children are encouraged to talk about their traumas in an effort to help them, but things were different then. It was considered best to leave painful memories alone.

Some time later, the nurses propped me up on the *charpoy* [bed] which gave me a better view of my surroundings. During the day, when the long side flaps that acted as windows were opened, I could view the surrounding countryside and the mountains beyond. Initially, the blue hills in the distance did nothing but bring on a deep sense of sadness. All I could think about was the trail beyond and the horror of the trek: the days my family and I had spent pulling ourselves out of the mud at every step, the torrential rain and the flooded crossings. The nights, too, haunted my thoughts as I lay looking at the distant hills thinking of the darkness and the hours spent scraping off the blood-sucking leeches.

So obsessed was I with this view of the hills that in my dream world I used them as a gauge of my progress to better health. On good days I pictured myself returning to those mountains and once again tackling the obstacles. On other days my mind would conjure up the gloomy scenes of the trek. Whenever my favourite nurse sat beside me on a better day, I would talk about one day tackling the ranges again. She never questioned me about the past, but encouraged me to speak positively about the long walk.

'I would love to accompany you,' she said.

Time went by and still I was kept on a fluid diet. Every time the other patients were fed, the smell of curry made me wish I could sit down and join them. To see those poor soldiers tucking into the rice and chapatis made me long to be well.

'Couldn't I just have a small bowl of rice and curry? I'm fed up with clear soup.'

'I'm sorry, Colin, but we cannot risk setting your recovery back with a bout of diarrhoea.'

All I could do was look on and hope that one day soon the staff would bring me the meal I longed for.

My medication was changing. Quinine tablets were discontinued and I was dosed with a new wonder drug for the treatment of malaria. Atabrin and Metabrin tablets were pumped into me and I was forced to drink what seemed like gallons of water. They also introduced a new treatment for the wound on my shoulder, which was a relief. The daily draining of pus via the gauze cloth was replaced by a medicated pad that drew out the pus. The constant chafing of the rope-bed caused bedsores to break out. The humidity was not helping the process of healing.

Despite these minor irritations, I was on the mend. I began to ask a lot of questions of my whereabouts.

'Has anyone told my father that I survived? What is happening with the war? When will it end?'

My carers took my new-found curiosity as a good sign.

'The fact that you are asking all these questions means you are definitely getting better!'

I detected a change in them. They appeared more cheerful when they attended to me. Even my Indian friends in the ward appeared happy with my progress. As they walked past my bed I remember their display of white teeth as they smiled.

Then one day the doctor had news for me.

'The authorities have been informed that your father is an employee of the Shell Burmah Oil Company. You are soon going to be transferred to the oil company's modern hospital at Digboi, an oilfield to the south.'

'But I don't want to move!'

'You will receive better medical treatment there. But we won't allow you to be moved until you have been tested on a diet of something other than soup.'

His other concern was the imminent threat of bombing, or even of being caught up by the advancing Japanese army. This alerted me to the fact that the Japanese were still on the offensive and were heading into India.

My diet was altered and I was fed boiled rice three times a day in a very watery gruel. It was very palatable, I thought, even if the cook was heavy-handed with the salt. The nurses watched me closely in the days that followed: I was to be taken off the partial solids if my bowels reacted in any way. They did not. I was gaining a bit of weight. Sweetened condensed milk was added to the rice for the evening meal. It was delightful, and tinned milk in my tea made drinking it a pleasure instead of the chore it had become.

The sound of planes increased.

'What's going on? Will anyone tell me?'

'Now, Colin, you know that in wartime nobody talks very much.'

The air-raid alarm sounded on numerous occasions but as I lay in bed awaiting the thud of bombs nearby, nothing eventuated.

By now I really had a feeling that I would make it. My whole body seemed to be responding to the kindness of my carers. Again I asked for a mirror, but again my request was turned down.

'But you are looking fine,' I was assured by the nurse who had always shed a tear whenever I had had my wound treated in the early days of my hospitalisation.

'Your hair is beginning to grow nicely and your teeth are beginning to return to a white colour after all that scrubbing.'

I knew I was thin and the fact that I could not yet hold up my arms signalled that all my muscles had wasted. The only part of my body I could view as I lay on my back was my lower torso. It reminded me of the walking skeletons on the trek. Nonetheless I knew I would get better as the days went by, and a tinge of desire to live on became evident. Every day seemed to bring with it positive news of my recovery. The Indian doctors, always smiling, would give me a good report.

'You are making excellent progress. Soon you will fly the coop!'

One day they said the hospital would be evacuating its patients.

'Why?'

'The Japanese are advancing on India and it will be safer to move further inland and away from the range of their bombers.'

In the early hours of one morning a nurse came alongside my bed.

'Colin, are you feeling well enough to travel?'

It did not occur to me that I would be carried. All I could say was, 'How can I move? I cannot even stand on my feet.'

But a stretcher was brought and two nurses lifted me on to it and carried me out to a waiting ambulance, which was to take me to the oil company hospital at Digboi.

The trip took about four hours. It was slow and bumpy, and when we arrived I was hungry and thirsty.

'I think I will pass out if I do not have some water,' I said to my carer. He was kind enough to fetch me a drink while I waited to be admitted and handed me a clay cup of rose water, a favourite with Indian children.

I was lifted out of the ambulance and laid on the grass near the entrance to the hospital. I lay there looking up at the large series of buildings, all painted in white, as most public buildings in the East are. I was left for what seemed an eternity and became frightened of being abandoned. I longed to be back in the military hospital at Tinsukia. As I lay there I thought of the many friends I had left behind. The memory of being carried through the large ward and the waves of the other patients was fresh. The roughly constructed military hospital had become my haven.

A European couple came by, both dressed in tropical white. They looked down at me. I managed a smile.

'Is the hospital admitting natives nowadays?' the woman asked the man with a surprised look on her face. I must have looked like a poor village boy.

Eventually I was carried into the building and up some stairs to a room. The place was spotless. Even the floors glistened, as if they were scrubbed every day. The bed was a welcome change from the military rope cots and the sheets were bleached white, but as I was lifted on to the clean bed I caught a glimpse of myself in the mirror. I was horrified and my spirit hit a low. I did not believe I would pull through after seeing the skeleton in the reflection. I could even appreciate the remark that woman had made out on the lawn because I looked so brown and sick. I now understood why the doctor had refused to allow those good nurses to furnish me with a mirror.

Doctors and nurses came and went and I spent the next few days crying and completely depressed. Many people walked past my room, visiting friends and relatives in other rooms, but the only visitors for me were the professionals who cared for me.

Then one day, while the nursing staff were getting me up for my first steps in a long time, a giant of a man entered the room. He watched while the two nurses coaxed me to take a step. He beamed at me and cried out, 'Come on, laddie, you're not going to give up again!'

I recalled his Scottish voice instantly and recognised him as the man who had rescued me on the track. It all came flooding back. His words were similar to those he had used when he picked me out of the mud when I had begged him to let me lie in peace and he had shouted, 'You're not going to give up the will to live!'

Now he came up to me and, plucking me from the two nurses, forced me to stand up and make the effort to move.

It was soon afterwards that he came to tell me what had happened to Ethel. I was overwhelmed with grief.

I soon got my thoughts into focus and for the first time in months became aware of the days of the week and the months. It was October now; almost five months since I had set out with my mother, Ethel and Robert on that early morning, the sixth of May, from the deserted railway station at Mogaung. I had witnessed the death of many thousands and the thought of those tragedies brought me no joy as I lay in the comparative comfort of a clean hospital. People I had never met began to visit me. I suspected that the burly Scottish tea-planter who was responsible for my survival was also responsible for the visits of these people.

Despite my poor physical condition, I was forced to undertake mandatory air-raid drills. They entailed climbing out of bed when the alarm sounded and lying on the floor beneath the mattress. It was a huge undertaking for me. Lying on the hard floor for even five minutes was not easy because I was still skin and bone and the lack of any body padding made contact by my bones with the floor hellishly painful. During my stay at Digboi we experienced many false alarms. Japanese planes approached, but their main targets were the airfields some miles away.

As the weeks went by, I grew stronger and with the aid of the staff was able to take a few steps and wander down the corridor and out to the balcony. It was good to be able to sit in the open verandah and view the countryside. The township was down to the left and to the right I could see the oil derricks at work. Digboi was not a vast oilfield and the number of derricks seemed quite insignificant compared to the fields in central Burma, at Yenangyaung.

One day the doctor said, 'The time has come to upgrade your diet.'

'That's good. May I have some rice and curry please?'

He laughed. 'I'm afraid not. We have to keep you on very bland food for some time yet, young man.'

The meals were indeed completely tasteless but no doubt they were nourishing and they were certainly performing the job of getting me fatter. It was still a slow process but I could feel myself getting stronger as the days sped by.

Very soon I was able to wander along the corridors of the hospital, chatting with the staff. Everybody seemed happy going about their duties. I still kept things close to my chest. Some of my European visitors would ask about the trek, but I was not keen to talk about the immediate past. I had pulled the curtain down, creating a refuge.

My hostility towards those who had forced me into this situation grew. The question, 'Why my family?' kept haunting me. I began to blame almost anybody in authority for my condition.

My bodily functions repaired well and gradually I gained the energy to undertake longer walks in the gardens. My hair grew longer and I could now view myself in the mirror and comb the locks. Even my teeth seemed to have lost that dark stain and though they were not entirely white, I was now much more confident of smiling at people. The deep brown tan I had developed during those months in the jungle was fading. There appeared to be more activity about the place. Native staff were kept busy clearing up and the buildings were given a new coat of paint. I also saw festoons of lights being strung across trees. It dawned on me that all this hustle and bustle was taking place in preparation for Christmas.

Chapter 14
CALCUTTA

*C*hristmas Day was not a joyous one. I was still depressed, and could not push myself to join the staff and celebrate the day. Besides, I was still on a restricted diet and the goodies were denied me.

Unbeknownst to me, my future was being mapped out by oil company executives, government agencies and the missionaries whose lot it was to care for refugees. One day the doctor gave me a thorough medical examination and pronounced me fit to travel.

'Arrangements have been made for you to go to Calcutta, to stay with some people who belong to your father's church. They will care for you until the end of the war.'

I was kitted out with basic clothing, provided with a suitcase and driven to the railway station. There I was introduced to a European woman, the wife of an oil company official. She was returning to Calcutta after a short visit to Digboi. We were to share a carriage for the four-day trip. The woman was pleasant but distracted as she checked out other passengers. Thankfully, this saved me from telling her too much about myself. I was keen to take in the sights as the train moved through this strange land. She settled down to read a book and drink liquor which she had brought aboard in an ice box.

It was a spacious two-berth carriage and, just before nightfall at one of the stops, she said a railway attendant would come aboard and convert the carriage into a sleeping unit. The trains were not equipped with refreshment cars and all meals were taken at the refreshment rooms at designated stations along the way.

We had been travelling for the better part of the day and I was enjoying the ride. The countryside was lush and there seemed to be pockets of water everywhere. The rivers we crossed were swollen by the recent monsoonal rains and the thawing of the snow on the higher slopes of the Himalayas which fed the many rivers and streams in the eastern part of India.

We travelled through mile after mile of cultivated fields dotted with villages. Children waved and cheered as we sped past. I was beginning to feel good. The smiles on people's faces at the stations cheered me up immensely. Dinner in the refreshment rooms was a grand occasion. Despite the war raging not far away, European travellers were always treated to a feast.

During the first dinner, which I ate quickly, I excused myself from the table which I shared with two British army officers, and wandered along the railway platform to mingle with the throng of natives. There seemed to be so many people rushing about with possessions on their heads seeking a seat on an already full train. The food hawkers walked back and forth, loudly proclaiming their wares. I was completely absorbed in this mass movement of humans. Some appeared anxious and others were laughing merrily and talking loudly as they farewelled their friends and relatives.

I spent the night listening to the wheels on the track. As the train pulled into a station early the next morning a man arrived in our carriage carrying a tray.

'Breakfast!'

The server stayed in the carriage until the next stop where he alighted with the trays. Not long after, the train stopped at a large town. As we drew slowly towards the platform it seemed as if the whole community had trotted down to the station to welcome us. My mind went back to the months gone by, when the very sight of even a small group of people moving about signalled life. Now the mass of people boosted my spirits. Living was beginning to be worthwhile.

Further down the track the train came to a stop. I looked out the window and beyond the mass of people I saw the river. It was probably a tributary of the Bramaputra. It was very wide and still muddy from the rains.

Railway staff came along.

'Everyone must disembark here.'

'Why?'

'The bridge was washed away a few weeks ago and passengers will be ferried across the water to join another train on the other side.'

The European woman travelling with me put on a turn and became abusive to the staff.

'This is terribly inconvenient. Isn't it dreadful how inefficient the Indian railways are compared to ours in England!'

I walked away and let the porters take care of my scant belongings. We crossed on a barge and were directed to our carriage. I rather enjoyed the break in routine. During the crossing, my companion joined a group of travellers. They were all of the same ilk, a miserable bunch of colonial types who gave me the impression that they were here in this vast and beautiful country under sufferance.

Back in the train the English woman had not got over the incident.

I asked, 'Did you have prior arrangements in Calcutta that have been broken now?'

'Not exactly, but it means I will miss out on another day of fun in the city.'

I could not think of anything to say except 'Enjoy the journey'.

That night during dinner in the refreshment room she consumed a deal of liquor. She was in a happy mood and appeared to have hit it off with one of the officers and took me aside.

'Colin, I wonder whether you would be agreeable to switching carriages with this officer.'

I moved into another two-berth carriage with another army officer. Evidently, they were on leave from the front line. My new companion was full of war talk and, with a tongue loosened by the alcohol, he tried to impress me with tales of his exploits in the jungle. I resisted telling him that what he had endured was a Sunday outing in comparison to what I had been through.

I tired of his ramblings and tried to get some sleep. I had hardly dozed off when I smelt liquor near my face. He put his hands around my neck and, pulling me up, tried to sweet talk me into moving over. I was terrified. I knew what he was up to and, despite my physical disadvantage, managed to push him away. It was late at night. The train pulled into a station. I rushed for the door and stepped out onto the platform. The place was surging with people; it seems that every rail station in India, no matter the time of day or night, is a hive of activity.

I walked along and spotted two military policemen, both Indian. I spoke in Hindi and told them of my problem. They led me to the station-master, a slightly built Anglo–Indian, and relayed my story. Together we returned to my carriage and the station-master began to question my European companion. He was well and truly under the influence of alcohol and became aggressive.

The two military policemen then dragged him from the carriage and led him to the station-master's office.

While I waited in the carriage one of the policemen approached.

'Sir, you have no need to worry any further. We will take care of the matter. We are holding the man in custody and he will be shipped out on another train.'

He went on to tell me about the problems they had experienced with drunken white men. Relations between Britain and India were turning sour and Indian Congress leaders who had been agitating for home rule had been imprisoned. I had the impression that this military policeman, too, was keen to see the British out.

The train moved on and I had just fallen asleep when I was awakened to a banging on the door, and confronted by a bearer with my morning breakfast. I had expected a visit from the lady with whom I had begun the journey, but I did not see her until the train pulled into a station for lunch. She inquired after my travelling companion and I told her the whole story. She turned white and looked agitated.

'I'm dreadfully sorry for having left you with him,' she said, and hurried me back to our carriage. She could not have been more pleasant.

'May I ask whether you intend to report the matter to the authorities at Calcutta?'

'No. As far as I am concerned the episode will be forgotten. Actually, I did not even give the officers my name.'

She was quite overcome with relief. Happy that I would keep my mouth shut, she returned to her lover, saying she would rejoin me later. I was alone again and enjoyed the peace — a kind of joy in solitude.

We arrived at Soaldah station in Calcutta. My escort was met by friends, said her goodbyes and hurried away. I stood around for a while with my belongings and viewed the scene in awe. I could hardly appreciate the vastness of the building and was overwhelmed by the sheer number of people milling around. It was chaotic — soldiers in transit, people rushing about shouting at one another, women in colourful saris and naked children begging with hands outstretched. I had very little money and the prospect of spending the night on the platform with beggars was rapidly becoming a real possibility. Yet I did not feel threatened; in fact, I felt at home, among friends. I was reminded of my mother's words back in the jungle, 'You will always be cared for.'

There was nobody to meet me. I waited for a while, then decided I had better fend for myself. I found an office marked 'Registration of Refugees'. The

Indian official and I went through a mountain of papers before we set about filling in any forms. I was restless and still physically weak but he wanted to write down every detail of my background. Nobody else seemed in a hurry to be processed and no hostility was apparent among the crowds waiting for instructions.

I was taken to a refugee camp somewhere in the suburbs and billeted in an old building. The place was primitive and the outdoor toilets consisted of a hole in the ground. One day, when using the toilet, I heard the cry of a child in another cubicle. He had fallen into the pit and was standing up to his knees in human excrement. I hauled him out and we went to the communal tap and scrubbed ourselves clean. Not long afterwards, I was called to the front office and introduced to a very apologetic European couple.

'We are so sorry we did not meet you at the station. We were wrongly informed about the train from Assam. Are you all right?'

Mr and Mrs Smee were an elderly couple who belonged to the same church group as my father. Through their web of connections they had heard that a child of the flock had survived the trek out of Burma.

'It is our Christian duty to take care of you, Colin, until peace is restored and you can join your father. We have been informed that he is presently in Abadan, in Persia.'

I accepted this news without asking them anything further. I had not really imagined that he would still be in Calcutta after all this time.

They were a kind and gentle couple who had retired to Calcutta after years of missionary work in the field on the sub-continent. They had no children and were very formal in their ways.

We drove through the industrial suburbs, through teeming crowds, and entered a leafy suburb close to the heart of the great city. They did not miss any opportunity of slipping a bit of Christian teaching into our conversation. In the hot car they had a captive audience. I took it in my stride; if there was one thing I had learned from our family visits to the Buddhist monastery in Burma, it was that we should practise tolerance of everybody's religious views.

They warned me of the traps and pitfalls of the devil's path.

'Seek guidance from above daily, Colin. Remember we are living among hordes of disbelievers.'

I had heard it all before.

We arrived at the house. It was set back from the street, a large colonial building which, though in need of refurbishment, was nonetheless impressive. The garden, too, needed attention. It must have been a grand home during the heyday of the British Raj. I was shown my room and given the schedule of daily activities. My mind flashed back to boarding school in Rangoon. I accepted the house rules but kept alive the hope that the war would end soon and I would be on my way back to Burma in search of my mother.

I fell into the routine with the elderly couple: meals on cue, quiet moments during the heat of the day, Bible reading at nights and off to bed with prayers of thanks for the good day passed. Sundays were days of rest and quietness. The church was not far from their home.

Soon it was six months since I had lain, a bony body, in the military hospital at Tinsukia, in Assam. I put on weight. I was well looked after, but the nagging feeling that I was a 'cared' child of Christian missionaries disturbed me. Was I an object of their good works? A banker in their quest for merits in the afterlife? I was even afraid that they were preparing me for a life in the missionary field.

That the Smees cared for me I have no doubt, but I was not in any condition to feel uplifted by their doomsday preaching. They were blissfully unaware that I had been brought up in a household where freedom of movement and association was encouraged.

One day Mr Smee said, 'We will be travelling out of town for the day, Colin. You must stay here. Don't venture outside, in case you become lost in the big city.'

I chuckled to myself. Had I not crossed many miles of unmapped terrain without someone to direct me? Within minutes of their leaving I ventured out of the house in the direction of the street at the end of the garden.

'I am going out for a little while,' I told the servant, who had followed me. The look on his face signalled disapproval, but he did not dare deter me.

I swung open the wide metal gates and stopped to view the movement of humanity, vehicles and animals of one of the world's most populous cities. I was overawed at the crushing movement of people. There were masses of all ages heading purposefully in every direction. I realised how remote the Smees' house was from this city of millions. I could have been on another planet. I felt alive breathing in the smell of cooking, human bodies and car and truck exhausts. Tram cars rattled past, skinny black men hauled carts laden with goods. The air was filled with chatter as the people shouted to gain an audience among the throng. It was a revelation and as I stood on the dirty pavement of fractured concrete, I felt, for the first time since the trek, truly alive.

I was tempted to board a tram car that had stopped to pick up passengers, but realised I had no money for such an adventure. The heat of the day was intense. It was pre-monsoon time once again, and very little breeze stirred the air. Unlike many Asian cities that have a distinctive smell of herbal cooking, Calcutta gave off an odour of decaying garbage. The deep gutters, a signature of monsoonal cities, overflowed with all manner of refuse accumulated since the previous monsoon. I was not put off by the smell and squalor. This was Calcutta, and the freedom I experienced that day was enough to make me fall in love with the dingiest of all cities.

I returned reluctantly to the quiet of the Smee compound and paused in the shade of the large trees that lined the driveway.

At dinner I decided I had better admit to my adventure before the Smees found out.

'Today, while you were out, I went for a walk in the street,' I said casually.

My elderly caretakers looked at one another in disapproval.

'It was fascinating! I would love to spend more time in the city,' I ploughed on.

'Colin, you are not yet ready to face the heathen frontier. You must be more circumspect. If you ever feel the urge to venture out again, you must be accompanied by a chaperone.'

'I understand,' I said, but I did not feel the least bit repentant.

Try as they might, these two well-meaning people were not equipped to care for somebody of my age. We were poles apart and I became desperately unhappy. I went off my food and neglected taking the prescribed medication. Malaria hit me again and the Smees took me to the Calcutta Infirmary where a kind Indian doctor examined me.

He was a jolly fellow and exclaimed, 'My God! You're like a scarecrow! We shall have to fatten you up.'

He added that I was all out of proportion.

'At your height, you should be tipping the scales at ten stone and not five and a bit. But never you fear. I will have you as fat as a *babu* [fat Indian merchant] before you leave us.'

The activity in the hospital and the smiling faces of staff and visitors gave me a lift. I enjoyed talking to the cleaners, the other patients and their relatives and friends in Hindustani. It was like old times when I was most at home playing and fighting with the children of our servants. The Smees visited frequently and I was conscious of their concern. Because my diet at the hospital had been substantially changed from their European fare, my weight climbed at a tremendous pace. Perhaps the doctor was true to his word and may yet have me tipping the scales at the level of a fat, contented Indian merchant.

I was content with my lot there and spent a lot of time observing the masses moving about in the street below. They moved briskly, oblivious to the cruel heat. Back in the wards the ceiling fans were never switched off. Between the cycles of high fever I returned to normal and took myself to the verandah to watch the spectacle, yearning to be part of the scene. I began to feel the world was leaving me behind. I reflected on the past and planned my future. But making plans without an inkling of what lay ahead was terribly demoralising. The thought of returning to Burma constantly crossed my mind, but how and where to start were questions that tormented me.

On the other hand, I was enjoying my stay in hospital. Indian hospitals are vast institutions. I could almost trick myself into believing I was in a village full of people, such was the atmosphere. When I left hospital after a week or so, it was with a tinge of sadness.

'I'm going to miss all the characters,' I told the doctor when he gave me my last examination.

He laughed.

'The whole world is waiting for you and you are certainly in a much better shape now than when you came in.'

But the hospital had been a refuge. I would miss the people, not to mention the smell of antiseptics mixed with the cookhouse aromas of spices and the inescapable pall of *bedi* [Indian cigarette] smoke.

The Smees drove me home on a Sunday and broke the journey with a visit to the local church. The fiery sermon was preached by a red-headed elder whose theme was the wages of sin. He repeatedly exhorted the congregation to repent.

'Seek God's forgiveness before you are all called before the throne on high!'

Even at my young age I could not believe that any intelligent people would willingly sit and listen to someone telling them they were sinners.

Chapter 15

GETTING AWAY

*B*ack at the Smees' home I became restless. They recognised this and decided, without consulting me, that they must do something about it. One night they called me.

'Colin, I must admit that your few months with us have been somewhat different from what we had envisaged,' Mr Smee said. 'We have come to accept that it is not a simple task for two people in their twilight years to understand the feelings of a young lad.'

Mrs Smee nodded.

'I have been in touch with a fellow Christian in the South of India who has a young family,' Mr Smee went on. 'The time has come for you to be brought up with children of your own age. You will attend the same school as the two youngest Beer children. The arrangements are made. You will be leaving us in two days' time. We will always keep you in our prayers.'

I displayed qualified enthusiasm. I was torn. I yearned to get away, and wanted to be with other youngsters, although I would have baulked at the idea of boarding school. The thought of joining a family was appealing, but I could not be certain that the move to another strange household was the right one. How I wished I was physically fit. I could have walked away and headed back into Burma. With bags packed, a few words of advice and a good dose of spiritual bidding, I was on my way to the great South land. The train journey to

Bangalore would take several days, this being war-time, and I was to stop off at Madras along the way. Mr Smee drove me to Howrah Station on the Western bank of the Hoogly River. It was late afternoon and all pedestrian traffic seemed to be headed to this wide muddy stretch of water.

The rivers I had crossed during the trek out of Burma had been relatively clear, but the Hoogly looked like an outpouring of melting milk chocolate. My knowledge of geography told me that the river was a tributary of the mighty Ganges. This stretch of water must have moved along many hundreds of miles through the most populous regions in India. Along the way it had probably served as a huge sewer; that would account for its appearance. At the station forecourt we were set upon by a horde of scrambling porters all eager to carry my worldly possessions tucked away in a fibre suitcase.

Howrah was no different from any other stations in India, serving not only as people movers, but also as centres for hawkers, pimps, thieves and families. They ate, slept and defecated in the concrete structures amid the odour of rubbish, cooking and the ever-pungent coke-fired engines. The walk to my compartment was an obstacle course and the din from hissing, steaming engines and the clanging of goods was deafening. I entered my compartment, a four-berth carriage, and smiled at my fellow travellers. They were Indians who appeared to be well-educated government employees. I soon settled in and long before the train set off we were chatting like long-lost friends.

Of all Britain's achievements as colonial masters, the most notable must surely be the construction of a remarkably fine rail system. It is cheap and has the capacity to move many millions of Indians around the sub-continent. Our first-class sleeper was decked out in the finest leather and woodwork. Since the tracks were wide, at 5 feet 6 inches, the compartments were very roomy.

I was eagerly awaiting the train's departure, and looked forward to seeing the countryside before darkness settled in. My three travelling companions focused on me. I told them briefly about my trek out of Burma, without much detail, and perhaps this window into my tragic past swung their kindly attention to me. At every stop, and there were many, they offered me all manner of Indian snacks and drinks. As is usual on the Indian railway, the morning began with *chota hazari* [light breakfast] delivered to the compartment.

I was excited. I had learnt about the Coromandel Coast in my geography lessons in Burma, and now I was to experience the journey. I was in a good frame of mind to absorb every detail of the two- to three-day trip south. The journey begins in Bengali country, shuffles through Telugu country and terminates in Tamil country. It is a long ride through three distinct ethnic boundaries, with a view of three very different cultures. Even the smells at the various stops were different; so was the food on sale at the stations along the way and the costumes of the people too. I enjoyed every moment of being part of a changing scene. I noted the little things that made the people of this country so different and interesting. To add to the enjoyment, my three companions were also of different backgrounds.

The politics of the day came into our conversation.

'It is very true that we have done well under British rule,' said one of the men, and the others agreed.

'However,' he went on, 'there is some doubt about what will happen when India finally gets its independence.'

'The war years have been tough,' said another. 'Food has become scarce and the unusually heavy influx of people escaping from the eastern states has confused the administration.'

One of the passengers was a Muslim and although the atmosphere in the cities was tense between the Hindus and Muslims, my companions seemed quite able to accept one another. They talked about the chances of partition and wondered how it would affect the country. The subject turned to the imminent famine in Bengal.

'The wealthy traders are to blame for what could become a major catastrophe.'

'Yes, it is a terrible situation which could backfire badly.'

Their predictions came true some months later. The Bengal famine took the lives of a million or more people. The news of the war was a priority, naturally, and hence not much was written about the disaster.

It was a fairy-tale journey. The gentlemen spoiled me. During the day, when there was so much to see, they took a nap and let me soak in the sights. With mountains on our right, we tracked south. Occasionally we caught a glimpse of the Bay of Bengal on the left. Villages dotted both sides of the track and mile after mile of cropped fields appeared. I never tired of looking at the green fields which, I knew, had been worked by hand.

I have always thought of Indians as open-minded people who didn't hide anything from strangers, unlike some other Orientals. Shyness never came into their behaviour and every happening in India was a sideshow. The whole country was a stage and the people the actors.

I recalled a fleeting walk down a street in Calcutta. The pavements had taken on the look of a stage; barbers, dentists, hawkers, car cleaners and letter writers were everywhere. A haircut under a black umbrella beside the street would draw many onlookers, but the two that drew the biggest audience were the dentists and the ear-cleaners. The poor person seated for an extraction inevitably had a big crowd watching every move. People pushed and shoved to get the best view of the patient's open mouth. When the tooth was eventually pulled a loud shout of '*Shabash! Shabash!*' [well done] went out. The removal of ear wax was not something I took an interest in, but I knew that once a blob of wax had been removed the patient was rewarded with a few drops of warm, sweet-smelling oil to soothe the ear.

Perhaps the Indians had nothing to hide because so few had anything at all. A glance out the window on any Indian train at dawn would prove my point. There, on a path leading from the adjacent villages, the natives lined up for their toilet session. Bare bottoms could be seen, always with their backs to the railway line, but this was India, where more than half the masses walked around half-naked anyway.

I decided to take my evening meal with my companions. We all bought something different from the hawkers, the tasty food washed down with tea served in earthen cups which were thrown away after use. I loved watching *char wallahs* [tea vendors] dispensing tea. The art was to pour the drink, laced with heaps of sugar and whitened with condensed milk, from a great height. The vendor held the clay cup in one hand, the jug in the other and poured the hot liquid from one to the other. The buyer ended up with a cup of delicious, sweet frothy liquid.

After a few loud burps from my companions, the evening chatter began. We talked of old India, its customs, traditions and politics. I learnt a great deal about India's rich history. They told me about the formation of the Congress Party and Gandhi's fight with the British over the iniquitous salt tax. I learnt that Gandhi, before the war, had travelled the countryside breaking the caste system and encouraging cottage industries. In a short space of time they gave me a free lesson in Indian history, geography, social studies, politics and religion.

The train crossed the Godavary River around midday. It was dry and a low bridge spanned the sand for about two miles.

'When the monsoons come, water washes from one end of the bridge to the other,' they said.

As we rode south, the station names began to sound different. There was an absence of animals or chickens. The hawkers' food baskets took on the smell of fish and a lot more fruit was for sale.

'Look at all the food being sold! We're never out of sight of food on the train, yet this is a poor country!'

My companions chuckled.

'We are coming into Tamil country. They call this the Garden State. You will see many more trees here, and the people's skins are darker.'

'Ah! Then we are getting close to my destination.'

The towns grew larger, factories appeared and more and more people clambered aboard our over-crowded train. People piled on to the roofs and some hung dangerously on the running-boards. A glance from the window brought up a sea of smiling faces right along the carriages, all facing the rear because of the soot from the engine.

The train pulled slowly into Madras station. The speed appeared intentional, as the hangers-on took it as a signal to jump off. Some stumbled as they hit the rough ground, but always with a laugh. Others ran alongside and waited for a friend to throw their belongings from within the carriage. As the train crept through the outer shanty towns that housed the city's workers, I noticed a group of men dressed in finery, their faces masked with make-up and their bare chests accentuated to resemble women's breasts.

'What's this all about?'

'Those men belong to a caste that perform duties at various functions. They are hired by the wealthy as mourners for funerals, to cry and wail for the departed soul.'

'We don't have them in our part of the country,' the Muslim put in. 'They're "gender men",' he added.

I had thoroughly enjoyed the train journey. It was drawing to an end and I hadn't even thought about my destination or how I would be received.

The train stopped at a platform already packed with people. The doors flew open and hundreds more spewed out to join the throng. The place was a shambles. If I had expected to see a recognisable face it would have been nigh impossible.

Madras is a hot city; even the sea breeze is hot. Back home in Burma we thought of Madras as the curry capital of India. South Indian cooking is the hottest and spiciest in all India. People say the fiery diet opens the pores of the skin to release sweat and the breeze blows over the skin to cool it.

A gentleman in a light cotton suit greeted me and introduced himself.

'I am the head of the Church Mission,' he explained. Another gospeller, I said to myself. Full of missionary zeal. How else would he choose to live in such a state of unholy heat? I spent the night at his residence in the shadows of the first Christian Missionary to India, Saint Thomas. Not far away was the shrine erected by Catholic followers. The Catholic church has a large and dedicated following in this part of India.

The missionary was an interesting fellow. His great love, apart from the Gospel, was Indian trains. We discussed rail gauges and engines.

'I was fortunate enough to have travelled the length and breadth of India by train during my years on the sub-continent,' he said, and proceeded to give me a most interesting brief history of the construction of the track that had transported me to Madras. His interest in the subject extended to the station buildings.

'The architecture is Victorian, with minor variations.'

'Sir, I was fascinated with one station, two hours out of Calcutta.'

'Ah, Barrackpore. It is not only a major link station but also a centre of the military and air force.'

'Why does it have just one platform, with a track on either side?'

'I have no idea why it was built like that, but it can accommodate four trains in one line. It extends along about a mile.'

'It must be a nightmare for travellers on the other three trains!'

A few days away from my caretakers in Calcutta, I had already absorbed a great deal of knowledge about a country I was falling in love with. My young mind had been filled with Indian history, geography, political science, culture and now the mechanics of rail transport. I wondered if any other 12-year-old had been so blessed. Perhaps my mother had foreseen my future. I felt a growing confidence in my ability to mingle with my elders. My attitude towards the world was taking a positive turn.

The trip to Madras had been enjoyable, thanks to my Indian companions. I was now alone on another train, on the last leg of my journey, with the prospect of a new life staring me in the face. As the express rumbled along and the four hours elapsed, I kept my ears trained to the station announcements identifying the town. There were no names posted on the stations. This was a war-time precaution in case of enemy attack.

'The next stop will be Bangalore East,' came the announcement. I prepared to get off quickly.

'Bangalore East is a small station and the train will only stop for a few seconds,' the station-master at Madras had warned me.

On the rather deserted platform stood my new caretaker, a portly gentleman who, by his manner, I immediately recognised as of a military background. Despite his age he did not shuffle. One knew right away that he had spent many an hour on the parade ground. He shook my hand.

'Welcome to Bangalore, Colin. I am Dr Beer. I hope you will be very happy with us.'

He escorted me to a horse-drawn carriage and we rode around the corner for a short distance and arrived at his home.

'Bangalore is a cantonment city,' he explained on the way. 'In peacetime the British always garrisoned their troops in the cool centre of South India for respite from the heat.'

Situated a few thousand feet above sea level, the climate bordered on the temperate. It was clean and the British colonial influence was patently obvious. The streets were wide and lined with avenues of trees. Parks abounded and no occupied city of the colonial masters would be deemed conquered unless it displayed statues of military generals and governors in every park — a constant reminder of the brave empire builders!

'When I retired from the army I chose to remain in India and devote my life to missionary work,' he said. 'My wife and I have six children, three girls and three boys. The youngest, Lily, is your age and William just a little older than you. I hope you will become friends with them. They are very much looking forward to meeting you.'

As soon as we arrived at the house, I was greeted by the family members. Each one embraced me warmly.

Mrs Beer said, 'We are absolutely delighted to have an addition to our family!'

I was touched by their warmth.

The family had obviously been briefed on my background. For the first few days I spent a long time speaking with the good Doctor. He knew how to get me to open up without peering into my past. I was fascinated with the stories of his garrison duties in the north-west frontier of India. At St Paul's in Rangoon I had read of the difficulties the British had encountered in trying — and failing — to 'tame' the wild and fiercely independent Afghan tribesmen who inhabited that unforgiving mountain country.

While the younger members of the family went to school, I was given time to settle in and found myself with a free hand to wander around the countryside.

'I want you to explore and familiarise yourself with your new surroundings,' Dr Beer said.

It was a sort of marking out of new territory for me, and after what had felt like imprisonment at the Smees, the freedom felt good. I struck up an instant rapport with the servants and in no time was picking up the rudiments of

Tamil. The cook's assistant, a young man, was particularly good to me. We spent hours exploring the district and the villages.

The day arrived when I was enrolled as a pupil at a school just a block away. Clarence High was a Mission School and accepted students from all walks of life. There was a sprinkling of European children and they mingled with the Anglo–Indian and Indian pupils. It was co-educational, my first experience of a mixed-sex school.

Chapter 16

BANGALORE

$\mathcal{T}$welve months of 'freelancing' had come to an end. It was with a degree of trepidation that I entered the schoolyard.

'Please go to the principal's office to be introduced and assessed for a class.'

There, I was questioned on the level I had attained when I had last attended school. I was not very helpful. Twelve months was such a long time in a young person's life and all I could recall were my experiences since the trek. Everything else was blocked from my mind as I sat at the school principal's desk.

After morning assembly, I was escorted to a class of boys and girls my age. I was conscious that all of their eyes were fixed upon this tall skinny rake of a fellow. I took my seat at a desk with an Indian student.

'McPhedran, please stand and introduce yourself.'

I took a deep breath.

'My name is Colin McPhedran and I am Anglo–Burmese. My father is a Scotsman and my mother Burmese. I am in the care of Dr Beer, whom most of you know as a governor of the school.'

My health was improving dramatically. I loved the Indian food served up at the Beers'. Dr Beer, who was a medical doctor and was therefore able to monitor my condition with an expert eye, was delighted with my progress, but he constantly added words of caution.

'You must not, as yet, take part in any of the school sporting activities.'

I was not impressed, but dutifully accepted his advice. He was, as always, kindly.

I then reached a stage in my development that concerned the good doctor. I put on too much weight!

'I am not going to put you on a diet, because that would be inappropriate in such a close family atmosphere. Instead I have devised a series of exercises for you to do every day, with the hope that you will shed some pounds.'

It worked, and at my monthly medical examination he said, 'Well done, young man. You have a clean bill of health. Now it is time to lift the restrictions on your sporting activities.'

Straight away, I joined in all the school sports and games. I was determined to make up for lost time. Every spare moment of my young life in Burma had been spent playing cricket, football and native games taught to me by children of the various ethnic groups.

Outside school sports, I now enjoyed learning what the locals played too. I taught them Burmese games. Marbles, top-spinning and kite flying became favourites among some of the poorer families with whom the Beer children mixed.

I was not one of the glamour boys on the block, but they did invite me to play whenever any game took place. I was wanted, and I began to feel good. Certainly at times my mind went back to the trek. The question of whether my mother had survived lay heavily on my mind. At times when the family was taken into town for a shopping trip the sight of children grouping around their mothers would set me off. I would become silent and withdraw for a while into my own world. The Beers never commented on my mood, but they must have noticed. After a while I would cheer up and start joining in the conversation again.

As time went by, I began to realise that I had to put in some effort at my studies. The teachers had been lenient but gradually they began to put pressure on me. I could easily cope with the workload but had no drive, until one day the history teacher took me aside.

'You must pull your socks up, McPhedran.'

He hit a raw nerve by adding, 'What will your father think of you if you *plough* (fail) your exams?'

I turned on him.

'I couldn't care less what my father thinks of me.'

He appeared shocked and mumbled something about being ungrateful and unchristian. I managed to bite back my response.

India's only aircraft factory was located on the outskirts of Bangalore. The city was also the training centre for air crew recruited for service in the Burma Campaign. All manner of planes flew in the clear skies above us and whenever my mind went off my lessons, I would gaze out of the classroom window and watch the planes darting about the sky.

Living on the fringe of the city gave me the opportunity to mix with the villagers. I enjoyed talking to farmers on their way home from the city markets, their carts laden with unsold produce.

The goat herders too were an entertaining lot as they drove their flocks past our house to market. The native owner waved his arms as he urged the flock along. With my sprinkling of Tamil I realised they were not being kind to the wayward beasts but were abusing them along the road. Strangely, both in Hindi and in Tamil profanity carried a female connotation, and it was the poor mother of the offender who copped all the abuse.

The land around the state is very fertile, hence its name, 'The Garden State'. The villages were quite small and the community compact. Every village had a watering hole — the village well — which, especially just before sundown, attracted all manner of people. They would draw water and sit around and socialise. Others would move away a short distance and proceed to wash off the day's work grime.

Wells in South India are surface affairs, pond-like structures about 30 feet in diameter with walls of stone. Generally, there were crude steps leading down into the water. Bathing near the wells was never encouraged, but on very hot days I would be invited to take a quick plunge into the cool waters. The wells were also used extensively for irrigation. I spent many an afternoon after school watching bullocks hauling water out of the wells in skin bags which then emptied into bamboo pipes stretching out into the fields.

Back at the Beer household I talked about these excursions. Dr Beer never discouraged me.

'It is a good idea to see how the natives live. You might come to love these people, just as we have done.'

During one visit I invited a fellow student to come along and wander amongst the villages. He was a Tamil, whose family was Christian and had moved a rung or two up the social ladder.

'It isn't customary to mix socially with the village types,' he said.

'But it's fun. Come on, let's go.'

'All right, I suppose so, but not for long.'

We walked through the Indian cemetery on the way to a village. It was a peaceful and shady neck of the woods. The trees were the fruit-bearing tamarind and we climbed one to pick the ripening pods.

While we were up the tree, we heard loud voices along the trail. A woman and a man of merchant appearance were walking in our direction, talking loudly. The woman carried a tray of goods on her head. They stopped beneath our tree. She laid her tray down and they began an animated conversation. My friend, who understood every word, nudged me.

'They're going to have sex!'

'Good!' I said. 'We can have a good view.'

In a moment the woman lay down and and pulled her sari up to her waist. The man proceeded to kneel down between her legs and while still talking continued with the act. A few squeals later from the woman and it was all over. The merchant-type handed over some coins to the woman's outstretched palms, she set the tray atop her head and walked toward the village. The man walked back toward the town. While all this activity was taking place, the monkeys that abounded in this part of the country were enjoying the fruits of the tamarind. They were fun to watch — more so than the monkey business that had just concluded on the ground, alongside some unknown person's gravesite.

We climbed down and wandered off towards the village. The young people I had befriended were there to greet me but my Tamil friend was ill at ease. He never spoke to them in the vernacular. A couple of the villagers spoke a smattering of English and it was to them that he directed his conversation. History had taught me that India was battling the caste system that kept its people apart, so I accepted that my friend was following the traditions of the day.

Back at school, word got around that the boy from Burma had an unhealthy fascination with village life. I was sometimes teased about befriending the younger boys and girls who occasionally ventured out of their villages to meet me at the school gates.

During this time I got to know another Anglo–Burmese, a girl whose family had migrated to Bangalore and who was a fellow pupil. Hillary was great fun. She was very athletic, with boundless energy. She was a link to my country. We always talked in Burmese. It was fun to say what we liked about the people around us. One day I mentioned that I thought the Anglo–Indians were conceited.

'It seems as if most of the students at school who are of mixed blood are ashamed of their Indian connection.'

She turned on me. 'Everyone is talking about your friendship with those village kids.'

'What's the big deal? I like playing with them and, besides, they're happy with their lot.'

We remained friends, but I could never get her to come with me to see these good people for herself. I felt dissatisfied, but there was nothing I could do about it.

Dr Beer had a very different attitude from my classmates. He was not a wealthy man and so the family did not get away much in the holiday season. I had formed a close bond with one of the Indian servants, who one day approached me.

'Please, would you do me the honour of visiting my family during the school holiday?' he ventured politely.

'Thank you. I would love to, but I had better talk to Dr Beer about it.'

Dr Beer was enthusiastic.

'It is an excellent plan. It will give you a fine opportunity to learn more about village life and observe the customs of the people.'

We made arrangements to set off on a train journey to the servant's village in the Nilqiri Mountains, south of Bangalore.

'I'm going to travel with him in a third-class compartment,' I told Dr Beer. 'I would be embarrassed to travel in style when he can't. Besides, it will be an interesting way to go.'

I had never appreciated just what the natives had to endure when travelling in this vast land and I was excited at the prospect of being with them. As the train chugged in, it looked like a slow-moving centipede. Hanging off the sides of the carriages were hordes of people with arms outstretched in balance. Others sat quite comfortably, cross-legged on the roofs of carriages, oblivious to the risk of nodding off to sleep and sliding to their deaths.

When the train came to a standstill my friend grabbed me.

'Quick! We must get in now.'

He pushed me through an open door which was discharging other travellers. We pushed and shoved our way along the narrow central corridor, pounced on a tiny space and threw our bags down before sitting on them. The trip would take a few hours before we changed for the mountain line.

As the train pulled out, I thought again of the last train trip in Burma I had taken under very different circumstances — the trip to Myitkyina. The two had some similarities. Most of the passengers then had also been of South Indian stock, fleeing home from the invading Japanese. Even the composition of the passengers — mothers and children — and the odours of their bodies were the same as on that fateful trip. The only things different now were the looks on the faces of the passengers. They were a happy and boisterous bunch, whereas those on the Burma train had been sad and fearful as they constantly looked out for the next air raid.

We arrived at a station at the foot of the mountains. I was exhausted, my limbs were sore and my clothes smelled of tobacco. Everybody of all ages seemed addicted to the common rolled-leaf cigarette, the *bedi*.

A little puffing Billy with three open carriages in tow, somewhat like a tram car, pulled into the station. There was ample seating and it was a pleasure to be able to stretch out and enjoy the journey up the mountains. The tiny train followed mile after mile of tea plantations as it ground its way up the steep track.

'This train journey must surely rank as one of the most picturesque in the world,' I said, half to myself. My companion flashed me a big smile.

Then the grinding clatter of the central cog line that helped pull the little engine up the steep grades stopped. We had arrived at our destination and were greeted at the station by the house boy's relatives. Having been raised with the Oriental custom of living with relatives, I was not at all surprised to see so many there.

Coonoor was a delightful little township. The air was clean and crisp. The town was the centre of the tea-processing industry and also the site of one of India's most prestigious girls' schools, Hebron.

We declined an offer of a pony-cart ride to the village which was only a short distance away. I preferred to walk with the people who had made a day of greeting us.

The family home was on a small block of land that sloped down to a creek. Rows of Indian corn appeared ripe for harvesting. It was a clean mud-floor dwelling and I was invited to eat. We talked after a fashion, a bit of English and a bit of Tamil.

'Your country?'

'It is similar to your own region,' I said, waving my hands to try to convey the meaning.

The family seemed delighted. As the night closed in, they lit kerosene lanterns and everybody prepared for sleep. I was shown a large earthenware container just outside the front door and invited to scoop cold water out and wash for the night.

Our stay was to be a week. The days flew by; the weather was fine and cool, being what South Indians call the mid-season. I was taken to the markets in the morning, where the family sold its produce. By mid-morning we would stroll around to various temples and mingle with devotees of the Hindu gods and the Saddhus. Then it was back to the market for the afternoon. I was delighted to help around the stalls and ate with groups of other village stallholders. European residents frequently walked by and many a curious glance was directed at this white fellow amid the group of Indians.

The journey home to Bangalore was just as chaotic as the first trip. It seemed that Indian people loved trains, for they were constantly moving from one town to another. Every train in every direction was filled to capacity. Arriving at East Bangalore station, the house boy and I took a short-cut by scaling a barbed-wire fence that ran between the railway track and the Beers' house, instead of trudging the long way round by road. In minutes we had arrived at the door.

'Colin's back! How was the holiday?'

'It was great.'

The whole family was happy to see me return unharmed and Dr Beer, beaming, said, 'Colin, you're a good boy and no doubt you have made a lot of people happy back in Coonoor.'

I felt good, but puzzled.

'It was I who had a good time.'

'Yes, and your visit will have lifted the status of your host family.'

'But this is their country and they have a right to feel proud.'

'I know, Colin, but that is how it is.'

Chapter 17
FAMILY LIFE

The two children closest to me in the Beer family were William and his sister, Lily. Lily was my age, William two years older. They filled the space of the brother and sister I had lost on the trek.

We were constantly in one another's company. We ate together, studied in the same room at night and chatted a lot.

They often begged me to tell them about my experiences as a young boy.

'Please, Colin, tell us more about Maymyo!'

William and Lily listened intently to my stories about our socialising with families of different cultures, the camping trips in the jungles and our close connection with villagers around Maymyo.

'How ever could you have been so involved with outsiders and still have close ties with the Church and the Buddhist monastery?'

'Well, Mother always said she wanted us to see the different paths in life.'

'But when did you find time to study your school lessons?'

'Perhaps that is the reason why you are such a clever fellow and I am not!'

I was joking, but William was a clever fellow and a very hard worker. I did not feel any discomfort or envy at his achievements. I admired him. Anyway, I felt quite comfortable with the situation. I was used to being around a brainy older brother although the two were very different. Robert's had been an effortless brilliance that he seemed barely to notice but which others paused to admire.

In turn, however, I was surprised by William's and Lily's narrow outlook on life. Nonetheless they were happy. Their world revolved around their family, church and the Christian community.

They were good for me. My health improved dramatically. I was beginning to shed the feeling of a loner. This in turn improved my relationships with the other kids at school. I became more involved in school activities, especially inter-school sport.

Cricket was my first love and when the season came around, I set my mind to play well and help lift the school team against the other schools which had dominated for a long time.

Bangalore boasted some very fine private schools, exclusive and expensive. Bishop Cotton and Baldwin were two outstanding examples. Their students were drawn from wealthy families of Europeans and the ruling class in various Indian states. Both were private boarding schools, run on the lines of famous English establishments. The students were immaculately attired and even I envied the dark green blazers of the Cotton boys and the deep maroon of the Baldwins.

Clarence High, our school, was a poor cousin. We had no uniform; the students' families could not afford such luxuries. Despite this lack of identity, Clarence boasted an above-average academic record. It was in sports that our school usually fell short.

Soon the cricket season was in full swing and, for once, Clarence performed well. We reached the finals and were drawn to play Baldwin for the Bangalore Cup.

It was quite an event. Because of our school's poor facilities we had to play on Baldwin's home ground. It was a magnificent oval, and the parents of practically every Baldwin student were there. We had the support of just a few girls and boys and a smattering of parents.

We won the toss.

'We will bat.' This was our captain, a skinny little fellow with the spirit of a tiger. He was an Indian Christian named Joseph, an inspired character who was undaunted by the occasion.

We went to the crease in the morning and were bowled out before lunch for 120 runs. I thought it was a reasonable total, but not so Joseph. The sight is etched in my memory of this skinny Indian lad jumping up and down waving his arms at the team.

'A hundred and twenty! We should have scored at least a century and a half!'

He meant 150 runs. I could not help laughing at the quaint reference — it was century this, quarter-century that and half-century the other!

'McPhedran, this is not funny. We are in dire straits here.'

We took to the field after lunch and it was hot. The score had moved along to double figures when Joseph called me on to bowl.

Most Indian bowlers were spin bowlers. I was not one of them. I could not spin the ball, but I did possess some accuracy and hurled it down the wicket with all my strength. The first few flew down to the boundary past the wicket-keeper, who persisted in standing over the wicket as for a slow bowler. At the second over I bowled one of the batsmen out. Joseph cheered up considerably.

'Keep up the pace! You have frightened the devil himself out of these fellows!'

The match ended before tea break. Baldwin were all out for a little over a half-century. No catches were taken. I had bowled the whole team out myself! Joseph was ecstatic.

'We have shown them how to play cricket! McPhedran, you saved the day.'

On the following Monday at morning assembly, to my surprise and joy I was presented with the ball of the match. It was a big moment for me.

One day, out of the blue, Dr Beer called me aside. He looked quite delighted.

'We have received some very good news. Your father has arrived in India from Abadan to see you, and he will soon come here with your brother Donald, who has secured leave from the army.'

I accepted the news with no outward display of enthusiasm but my mind was a turmoil. Would my father take me away with him? Would he be able to tell me anything about my mother? I knew that was a remote possibility, but I could not help the desperate hope. The news from the front in Burma, such as it was, was all dreadful — of camps full of starving prisoners of war and Japanese atrocities against the Burmese people, especially the Anglos. I had heard nothing at all about the refugee trail after I left Calcutta.

I was filled with a mixture of hope and dread. Indeed, I believe the good Dr Beer was more excited and happy than I was at that point.

He remarked on this gently one night.

'Colin, you do not seem overjoyed with the news of your father's visit.'

'I'm all right. It's just that it has been so long.'

Actually, I was happy, but many things were going through my mind. How would I react to my father? I still carried deep resentment against him, particularly the question of why, despite the resources available, he had chosen to leave his family in Burma during the invasion.

The last time I had seen him was a couple of weeks before our school in Rangoon had closed. It had been a brief meeting and under those circumstances saying goodbye had been hardly a sad occasion, as we had fully expected to see him again soon. Now I was to meet again the man who had become a stranger in my mind.

I was more eager to meet my brother Donald. I was curious to find out what had happened to him after that sad day at the railway station in Maymyo when we had waved him goodbye. My mother had never seemed the same afterwards. I hoped I could tie up some loose ends. But I was also fearful of being interrogated about the trek. Surely, if my father did not ask me about it, my brother would. I was stricken with terror at the thought of being probed. I had hidden the events of the trail inside my mind, and I could not bear to bring them out.

One day the principal called me to his office.

'McPhedran, your teachers are becoming concerned about your schoolwork. They say there has been an adverse change to your attitude in class. I hope this will be just a temporary state of affairs, while you are waiting to see your father and brother.'

He was very kind and genuinely sought to help but I remained mute.

The day of the visit arrived and the Beer family were tremendously excited. The house had been cleaned from top to toe. The vases were full of flowers. Friends from the church gathered for the reunion and within myself I became overjoyed at meeting my own flesh and blood once again.

My father embraced me and I could see the absolute happiness on the faces of those present. As he spoke in his deep Scottish accent he asked, 'You're surely not going to speak to me in Burmese, lad?'

He had not forgotten that, of all his children, I was the only one who used to reply to him in Burmese.

'No, Father, I will talk to you in English, if that is what you prefer.'

He glanced sideways at me as if to see whether I was being insolent, but he said nothing.

The few days together flew by. We shopped for new clothes for me and even had time to have a family portrait taken of the three of us and one of me alone in my new suit.

I recall very little of the visit. I don't even remember where they stayed. But I do remember being very glad that they had come to see me.

According to my brother Donald, the first thing I asked my father was, 'What have you found out about *Ama*? And why did you leave us behind in Burma?'

These were questions to which my father apparently had no ready answers, and I don't even remember asking them. But Donald later told me that I displayed feelings of deep anger at and disappointment in my father. He said I was quite insistent that our father provide answers about our mother's whereabouts. The only thing on my mind, so far as Donald could tell, was an almost obsessive desire to return to Burma as soon as possible to find her. I certainly remember that desire, for it stayed with me for years while I made every attempt to get back into Burma from Australia. I just don't recall talking to them about it.

Thankfully, neither of them asked me about the trek. It seemed to me that my father had no desire to open up the events of the last year or so; in fact, quite the opposite.

On the last day he took me aside.

'Colin, it will be for the best if you forget the past and set about focusing on your studies. You must aim at getting a good pass in the Cambridge Certificate so that you can attend a decent university.'

He was back at his old game of directing his children on the paths he had planned.

I had got the message. Father was returning to Abadan and he was not taking me with him.

What would have been in store for us children if the war had not intervened? I was getting the distinct impression that boarding school in Rangoon might have been simply the first step in a deliberate plan to remove us altogether from our mother's Burmese influence. I even had an inkling that boarding school in England might have been on the agenda, as it was for some Anglo–Burmese children, who were sent 'home' against the wishes of their heartbroken Burmese mothers. There was no doubt about it, my father was at heart a racist. He did not really want to see the Burmese in us children, at least not in the long term.

We said our goodbyes and none of us showed any sorrow at parting. But I was deeply saddened. Once again, I felt abandoned. I wondered why a father would not want his son to join him. I decided he must have had his reasons and, of course, it was still war-time.

After he and Donald had left, I began to pick up the threads of my new life. Nothing concrete had been said about my future, except about my education, and even that had been put in general terms. No mention had been made of a return to Burma. It was all rather unsatisfactory. But I was left with a feeling that, despite everything, a remnant of my family was still alive and would be there if I needed them.

There had been some mention of Donald's service in the army but nothing about what had happened since that fateful day at the railway station when we had farewelled him. Many years later, from Canada where he lives, he sent me a description of his activities after that day.

It turned out that his visit to Bangalore was not the first time he had seen me since the trek. He had come to see me at the Smees' house in Calcutta not long after I had got out of hospital, but the visit had never registered on my mind. He wrote:

I managed to get a job with the American Supply Group that was ferrying arms to the Chinese army, engaged in war with the Japanese forces.

I drove trucks in convoy along the Burma Road to Lashio, a town near the Chinese border. The American involvement grew and when General Stilwell assumed command of the China/America forces I was used as an interpreter. As the Japanese forces pushed the Allies north, I was informed that my family had evacuated to the northern town of Myitkyina from whence they had hoped to be transported by plane to India.

In the interval, we in the American strategic force retreated into India via the Imphal route. The journey took about 10 days and the terrain was not as intimidating as I had expected. The weather was extremely hot and the track was well used. We lost some members of the group along the way. Some succumbed to tropical illnesses. I left the group in India and made my way to Calcutta where I had some friends.

I soon learned that the airfield in Myitkyina had been destroyed by Japanese bombers and the only way out of Burma was via the dreaded Hukawng Valley Pass. School geography had taught me the Hukawng Valley had never been patrolled during the British occupancy of the country. The textbooks wrote of a part of the country where the timber was impenetrable and there were numerous rivers and high mountains. The area was also home to the Naga headhunting tribe of which little was known. Yellow water fever and malaria were also prevalent.

Shortly afterwards, I made contact with my father and was enrolled in the Scottish College of Calcutta University. News filtered through of the refugee trail through the Hukawng Valley. I was without news of my family in Burma. I was certain that they had not been able to secure a flight out and I wondered if they had made the decision to chance their luck by trekking over the mountains into India.

A refugee reception centre was set up in Calcutta and I spent all my spare time visiting the centre to hear some news of the survivors. All the authorities would tell me was that a few had survived the trek and those who did were holed up in refugee camps in Assam. With news that the refugee trail had dried up, I took some comfort in the thought that perhaps the family had decided to remain in Burma to stay out the hostilities.

Some time during late August 1942, three months after the fall of Burma to the Japanese, I was given the news that one of my family had survived the trek. My youngest brother, Colin, was the sole survivor. At this point things moved quickly and I left my studies and enrolled in the army.

My brother Colin in the meantime was plucked from the refugee hospital in Assam and moved to Calcutta where he was to be cared for by some Christian friends. It was here I met my brother Colin, the youngest of our family.

I remembered Colin as a strong kid brother, always involving himself, even at the age of 11, helping those less fortunate. I called on him at the home of the Christian friends. Seeing him gave me such a shock, I was dumb and inarticulate for a minute or so. He had become withdrawn and non-communicative. He answered my enquiries in monosyllables and was not forthcoming with any information whatsoever.

I observed the depth of the sadness with which he had witnessed the death of our mother and also that of our sister and brother. I wanted to know the details of the trek, but I was not about to force him to relive the agony he had so recently endured. Colin was very close to our mother and the loss must have been traumatic. I left the house wondering if my visit had registered in his mind.

Donald was absolutely right. Even now, I do not recall his visit to me at the Smees' house in Calcutta at all.

In another, longer account of his life during those years, Donald expanded on his observations during his visit to the Smees:

Under normal conditions there is an opportunity to grieve one's loss but in time of war, that luxury or benefit is denied one. I have always wanted to know the details but I was not going to force my brother to relive the agony that he had so recently had to endure ... To this day the veil that has enveloped these horrific details has not been lifted from my perception and it was only many years later that Colin said that our mother, even in those circumstances where water was more precious than gold, gave up what she had so that a fellow traveller who was on the brink of death could slake her thirst ere she crossed the Rubicon.

What I also did not know was that Donald had taken exception to Mr Smee:

Mr Smee was quite a skinflint and the way he was being so stingy with Colin really irked me. I was in no position to make or demand that he make any changes but luckily Colin did not remain under his care for very long.

My brother also applied himself to the terrible question of why my mother had made the fateful decision to walk out of Burma:

Due to the rapid advance of the Japanese army and the sad way the British in Burma underestimated the ability of the Japanese army in jungle terrain, the airport in Myitkyina was made unusable and my mother and siblings had to make the fateful and disastrous decision to trek out of Burma along the Hukawng Valley route to northern Assam.

They were among the thousands who made that decision and one must understand that it was not a very easy decision for my mother to make. We knew from the way the people in China were treated, that the Japanese conquerors were ruthless and extremely cruel. For them the Geneva Convention did not exist, as proved by their treatment of prisoners on the Thailand to Burma railway.

Also, there was my sister to think about and had they been captured, she most certainly was a prime target for rape.

I feel sad that I was unable to share with Donald the details of the trek. He was entitled to know. It must have taken great strength on his part to refrain from interrogating me. I suppose I was simply too traumatised to unlock the door and let him in.

Chapter 18

GROWING PAINS

As time went on William Beer and I grew close. I was beginning to accept him as a brother. We discussed intimate matters more freely and the subject of 'boy meets girl' was high on the agenda.

Though he was a studious character, he was now of an age when young fellows begin to fancy themselves with the opposite sex.

He took to mentioning some of the girls who attended our church.

'What do you think of her?' he would ask, of any who took his fancy.

'What makes you think I'm an expert on the subject?'

Nonetheless, I felt privileged.

'I think that if I fancied a girl, I would make my feelings known to her.'

'Really? But what if she didn't feel the same?'

'I'd take my chance anyway,' I said with more bravado than I felt.

As one can appreciate, at that age every second or third girl takes one's fancy, but there was one he liked whom even I thought fitted the bill.

'Tell you what. I'll pass the word along to her.'

'No, please, I wouldn't know what to do.'

'Look, William, if you think she is desirable, go tell her yourself then.'

'I couldn't. I simply couldn't. Can't you help me out here?'

So, one day after the Sunday Gospel service I arranged a get-together with some others, so William could at least utter a few words to the love of his life.

We all stood about chatting, and he managed to work himself around to where she was standing with one of her girlfriends.

On the way home, I grabbed his arm.

'How did it go? She seemed to like you all right.'

He blushed.

'I say, Colin, it was good of you to arrange it.'

I enjoyed the role of decoy, and our friendship firmed appreciably.

The Beer family had recently employed a new cleaning woman. She was a young woman with a city background, well groomed and stylish. Both William and I took a fancy to the new recruit who, like a lot of South Indian women, did not wear a bodice underneath her sari. I don't doubt she had a hunch that the two young fellows were onto her.

'Tell you what we'll do. Let's entice her into the air-raid shelter.'

William, though keen, was nervous.

'What would we do then?'

'Oh, for Heaven's sake!'

However, he spoke to the maid.

'She's agreed, but we have to be careful.'

We kept a watchful eye out, but she always had the excuse that the time was not right.

One day the adults were away.

'Right, William, this is it. Pass her the word that I'll be waiting in the shelter.'

I waited and waited. I could hear voices nearby but no movement. In exasperation I emerged and saw the pair in conversation. William was looking embarrassed.

'Tell her that I'm no longer interested,' I said, and marched off.

I never again let my emotions drift towards this young woman. Since then, I have occasionally pictured this woman, who once created such a stir in William's and my lives, slavishly tending half a dozen of her own children in a tenement somewhere in South India.

William was a keen student. He could absorb schoolwork and even in those early years had set his mind on medicine. Though he never wavered from his goal, I believe my presence in the family had made him aware that there was more to life than school, prayers and church: harmless, yet pleasurable things such as picnicking with girls and boys, taking walks and swimming in waterholes.

We also had vigorous discussions. One day, during a debate about class distinction, I said harshly, 'You seem to forget that I am a half-caste and in discussions of race I have two crosses to bear, the Oriental and the European.'

William looked up.

'You're the best thing that has happened to me,' he said simply. 'And I really admire your principled stand against what you believe to be the evil treatment of the natives by the white population.'

I was overwhelmed by his praise, but all I could say was, 'Thanks'.

There was a remarkable transformation in the way William now viewed things. I even detected a hint of the rebel in him. When I convinced him that my use of a swear word or two meant nothing, he began to slip in a phrase or so, albeit sheepishly and out of earshot of his parents. He could never quite muster the appropriately casual attitude, but he worked at it. We bounced off one another and I grew more at peace.

The understanding and familiarity between us extended to Lily. We studied together and often broke off to talk.

I liked Lily as a sister and felt I could pass on some knowledge of worldly things.

She was deeply interested in the way people in love behaved.

'What do you think makes one person attracted to another?'

'I don't know really. I suppose it's something to do with biology.'

'You know, Colin, there is a boy whom I really like. I think he might like me a little bit, too.'

I gave her the same advice I had given her older brother.

'Let the fellow know your feelings and get on with it.'

Unbeknownst to me, she did. A clandestine affair developed. One night she told me all about it.

'Lily! I didn't mean you should take my advice quite so literally!'

She was devastated.

'Oh, Colin, please don't say anything to anyone,' she beseeched.

In 1950 I visited Lily and her sister in London. She had become an attractive woman. We talked of our school days and surprisingly she brought up the subject of the boy in Bangalore. I was so embarrassed that I feigned a loss of memory.

Everything was going well. I felt I fitted in with the family and they, it seemed, had accepted me completely. I was growing to love the people who had taken me in and given me a new life. I had also settled back into school after the upset of my father's visit. I was into my second year with the Beer family and the time was flying by.

Then two things happened that made it impossible for me to stay.

William and Lily had an older sister, Cora, who was about 10 years older than Lily and me. She was kind-hearted but there seemed to be something missing in her life. Despite her age, she did not appear to have a relationship with any young man. Yet she loved to touch and embrace us all. She often came into the room I shared with William and, if her brother was out, she would sit on my bed and touch me.

The touches became more frequent as she manufactured any excuse to flit into my room. The touching turned to rubbing. Her visits embarrassed me and I feared William would one day walk in. This went on for quite some time until one day she entered my bedroom knowing the family was away for the afternoon. She suggested something quite extraordinary, coming from a devoutly religious person.

'I am proposing a friendly intercourse.'

I was shocked and scared.

'What if somebody comes home?' I stammered.

That made her think for a moment.

'You're right. We had better be careful.'

She then proceeded to masturbate me. When she left, I tidied myself up, left the house and went to the cemetery nearby to try to take my mind off the embarrassing affair.

Try as I might, I knew things could never be the same again in the Beer household. Cora became aloof. I felt terribly sad and guilty.

I could not wipe the incident with Cora out of my mind. My schoolwork deteriorated. I even grew suspicious of people and it seemed the wave that had been carrying me along in pleasant circumstances had somehow lost its way. My school reports reflected my attitude. When they reached Dr Beer, he called me aside.

'Colin, this is very disappointing, especially since you had been doing so well. Is there something the matter?'

How could I tell this good man the truth? In a moment of despair, I turned to him and said, 'The only thing I am interested in doing is returning to Burma.'

Of course this was all fantasy. The war was still raging in the border region. Nonetheless the urge to get back home and look for my mother burdened me constantly, and ever since the incident with Cora my mind had been drifting back to my quest.

'I am sorry, Colin. I wish there was something we could do.'

I appreciated his concern. I had thought I had pushed the tragedy of the trek way into the darkness of my mind, but I began to have nightmares about it. Instead of concentrating on my schoolwork, I spent the days dreaming about my lost family and home.

Then something else happened.

One day at school, sitting at the desk I shared with an Anglo–Indian girl, I was staring out of the window.

India's only aircraft factory was in Bangalore and the allied forces used the base for training. I was gazing at two planes in a mock fight, a Hurricane and an American plane, the Lightning.

The Lightning was distinctive, the only fighter I knew that had a dual fuselage. As they circled, the Hurricane climbed steeply, did a flip and commenced a dive at the Lightning. It was a noisy manoeuvre and my eyes remained glued to it. I was enjoying the show, when the diving plane sliced through the Lightning and with bits and pieces flying about continued its downward flight. With a dull thud it crashed into a nearby paddock. I bounded out of my seat and raced out towards the crash.

As I ran I looked up and saw the pilot of the Lightning floating down under a parachute. When I arrived at the site of the Hurricane crash, a few Indian villagers were already there. The plane was embedded in the soft ground and only its tail section was visible. Some of the debris was very hot to touch.

There was nothing anybody could do to save the pilot. He was buried deep in the ground. Before long air force personnel arrived in trucks.

'Everyone must move off! We are going to seal off the area!'

The crowd dispersed.

I did not have the heart or spirit to return to school. Instead I walked along a back lane that led to the cemetery, clutching a fragment of the perspex canopy which I had souvenired.

I sat there with just a few monkeys romping around. I grieved for the pilot, whoever he was, and the family who would be notified of his death. In my short life, I had witnessed thousands of deaths. I had seen many planes crash from the skies, yet this incident lay heavily upon me. Late in the evening I walked back to the Beer home, not even realising I had left my school case in the classroom. I stayed silent as everybody in the family related their versions of the accident.

The next day I was called to the principal's office.

'McPhedran, you know it is unacceptable to leave class without permission. Please explain why you did so.'

I tried to form the words, but they would not come out. As the silence grew, he became angry.

'That is not good enough, young man. I will have to contact Dr Beer to discuss your conduct.'

The events of the war in Burma came flooding back. The accident had triggered a vivid recall of the tragedy of the fighting and the trek. I somehow left the principal's office and the rest of the day passed in a dream. I only remember walking home that evening thinking that surely by now he must have been in touch with Dr Beer.

Dr Beer was in his study when I arrived.

'Colin, please come and sit with me for a while. Tell me what happened.'

I sat there, mute. He put his arms around me, and at that moment I burst into tears. He comforted me, saying, 'It's not fair that one so young as you should have had to witness so much tragedy.'

I wiped my eyes and replied, 'I'll be fine,' but I was desperately sad and did not know where to turn. Everything seemed to be going wrong. I was acutely aware that I was not living up to anyone's expectations.

During the next few days I pondered my future with the Beer family. I was beginning to feel fenced in.

One day while we sat at the study table in the bedroom, William, who was finishing school that year, cleared his throat.

'You know I'm going to university soon. Personally, I'm feeling quite excited at the idea of going somewhere different. Do you feel as if you need a change from Bangalore too?'

'Maybe I do,' I said slowly.

He was right: I wanted an escape. But where to?

'The trouble is, the only thing I want is to go back to Burma. But everyone says it's still out of the question.'

'It's true. Father says the Allies are having a difficult job keeping the Japanese from advancing into India.'

The state of war was seldom discussed at family gatherings. It seemed the children had been forbidden to talk of the hostilities, lest they revived memories of my recent tragedy. The Beers were a considerate family.

One evening, at the end of nightly prayers, Dr Beer asked me to stay behind for a moment.

'Colin, I hope by now you truly know that we love you as one of our own.'

I nodded silently.

'I cannot stand by and not do something to help bring happiness into your life. You are still young and you have so much life ahead of you. We want to do the best we can to help it be a fulfilling life, despite the tragedies you have endured.'

He did not wait for me to answer.

'I have had preliminary discussions with a Christian colleague of mine. He is the principal of a boarding school in Ootacamund in the mountains of South India, near where you went for your holiday. The majority of students are children of missionaries who are working in the field, families quite like us. It is a co-educational school, and quite broad in its approach. There is also a lot of sport and the educational standard is high. Would you be interested in going there?'

His description of the school had me interested. I brightened up.

'It sounds all right,' I said cautiously.

I knew I had reached the stage in my education where I would have to make a special effort to attain reasonable results in the final couple of years — something drummed into me by my father.

So the decision was made. Plans were set in motion to move me to Breeks Memorial. I was to begin in February 1945. The months flew by. I knew I would miss the close support of the Beer family. But my time of shifting from one situation to another had taught me to develop a barrier which I did not permit anybody to breach unless I so desired.

In the Australian summer of 1998–99 I received a letter from a Dr William Beer of Bangor, in Wales. He wrote that with help from the Lord he had traced me to my address in Perth, Western Australia, where I was living at the time. His 54-year search for me, he said, had ended. He was due to fly to Christchurch, in New Zealand, in January 1999, for a medical conference. His itinerary allowed for a five-hour stop-over in Sydney.

We arranged to meet at the international terminal on 27 January at 7.30 am.

I was looking forward enormously to meeting up with the young fellow whose family had taken me in as one of their own in India in 1943. I arrived at the airport as the passengers were walking through Customs. There he was, the same dapper little fellow, wearing rimless spectacles and his hair brushed back on to his head. He stepped briskly through the barriers with an air of confidence.

We recognised each other immediately. It was an emotional and joyous meeting with a man who had shared nearly two years of his youth with me. He introduced his wife and told me that Lily was living in Canada.

I could see William was hoping that I had continued my links with the Christian church, so I quickly explained that I had chosen to follow the Buddhist path. He wasn't the least bit surprised, and he respected my choice.

'But I will never give up praying for you in the hope that one day you'll return to the fold,' he said.

'You're not the only one,' I said. 'My brother and my Burmese relatives in Perth still pray for me for the same reason!'

Over a cup of coffee his wife said, 'Now that we're all sitting here together, tell us the story of how this young refugee boy, Colin, came into your life.'

William took a deep breath and, speaking in the same old-fashioned, rather formal manner that I remembered so well from the years I spent with the Beer family, he began his tale.

'My father,' he said, 'was a missionary doctor in Bangalore, South India. Since leaving the army he had devoted his life to caring for the sick and homeless among the poor in India. Our family of six lived in a modest house in East Bangalore. I was the youngest boy and Lily, my sister, who was about Colin's age, was the youngest. At our nightly family prayers we were always reminded of the war in the border region and our concerns and prayers were directed at the thousands of refugees who were being displaced as a result of hostilities.

'During a prayer session one night, Dad quoted a passage from the Bible. It read, "My children, let us not live in word, neither in tongue, but in Deed and Truth." Father was spurred to do something in a practical way to display charity and provide a home for a refugee child. He got in touch with missionaries in Bengal and arranged to have one child sent down to his home, to be cared for by the family.

'Colin arrived. He was a thin, tall, melancholy chap in his early teens. My mother, in her wisdom, advised the children to give the newcomer space to himself. Within a short period of time, this young, despondent person was transformed into a spirited teenager, mature beyond his years. We became firm friends. A brotherly relationship developed. Nearly two years later I moved to university. Colin too moved on and was enrolled in a boarding school in Ootacamund in the Nilgiri Mountains.

'It has been nearly 55 years since we last talked with one another. I must say, I have found him, as expected, an independent sort of chap, a survivor, and, it seems, one with that same love of people he always displayed. Having known him for those years he spent with us in Bangalore, I was always confident that he would never fall by the wayside.'

We said our goodbyes at the airport. It was a memorable reunion with the kind man who, as a teenager, had helped fill the lonely void left by Robert's death. We promised to keep in touch, now that we had found one another again.

Then, in 2000, I received a phone call from his wife. William had been killed in a car accident in Wales. He had been on his way to fly to India to comfort the widow and surviving daughter of a missionary who had been brutally slaughtered, along with their two young sons, by Hindu extremists. William, it seems, was doing good deeds until the very last.

Chapter 19

A FRESH START

February in Bangalore was a glorious month. The weather was cool and the moderate rainfall from the north-east monsoon helped keep the town fresh and clean. The train trip would take about 12 hours, via Madras and on to the foothills of the Nilgiri Mountains. The whole family came to see me off, and we all said tearful goodbyes.

The train, like all Indian trains, was packed. I was travelling first class and the reservation had been made days ahead. I shared the compartment with several high-class Indians.

Before long we had struck up an acquaintance and the chatter kept us all awake until the time arrived for me to change trains. It was the middle of the night and I waited on the platform for my connection, which was overdue by two hours. I whiled away the time observing the Indian travellers moving briskly back and forth along the station. Food hawkers plied their wares and the drink sellers kept up a song, advertising hot tea and cold drinks.

Ever so slowly, the train pulled into the station. The hordes on the platform were jockeying excitedly to be first on to an already crowded set of carriages. Since my seat was pre-booked I did not hurry aboard. However, the poor devils who were alighting were forced to battle their way over the clambering commuters and their baggage. It was all done, despite the seeming chaos, with good humour. There was no violence and it amazed me to see these people accepting the hassles of travel as their lot.

When the flow of human traffic thinned out, I proceeded to my carriage, which was easy to identify, and went aboard. I shared the leather-trimmed eight-seater with one Indian gentleman. He seemed tired and no doubt had been awakened by the noise of the last stop. We exchanged smiles and did our own thinking for the trip to the bottom of the mountains, a journey of about four hours.

I dozed off in the luxurious seat, but not before pondering the situation of the third-class passengers who were herded together like cattle. My mind returned again to the 400-mile train journey with my family from Mandalay to Myitkyina. We had been in a similar situation to the poor devils now in the carriage behind, with the additional danger of being strafed twice by Japanese aircraft. I nodded off to sleep.

It was still dark when the train pulled in at the end of the line. Most of the passengers had alighted along the way and there were not many of us left to continue up the mountain. The sun began to creep up over the horizon. The station was divided, the broad gauge on one side and the narrow tracks of the funicular train on the other.

It was a glorious morning and, to the south, the mountains seemed to sprout straight out of the plain. A porter carried my bags and beckoned me to follow him to the other platform. There awaiting us was a 'toy' train, a miniature version of the early engines with their long funnels. The engine appeared out of place surrounded by the giants of steam. The carriages were open-sided and reminded me of tram cars in larger cities.

The trip up the mountain was delayed for a long time, but the old porter seemed reluctant to leave me. We wandered around the comparatively deserted station and shared snacks purchased from the hawkers. Communication did not come easily, I with a smattering of Tamil, he a bit of English and Hindustani. Aided by body language we managed to get some messages across.

People stared, perhaps wondering what was going on between the old man of India and this half-caste youngster from anywhere. In that short time a fondness developed between us and I discovered that he had travelled widely in his younger days in search of work, to keep his family fed. He had worked in pre-war Burma, as had many natives of the Coromandel Coast.

Burma had had a huge enclave of Indian workers in the early days of British rule. They came from all parts of India and were engaged in all manner of work and business. The North Indians, who comprised the higher caste Hindus, were generally merchants and moneylenders. The mountain men, recruited from the foothills of the Himalayas, became the guardians of law and order, employed in the police force and the army.

My porter friend, who was a South Indian and of lower caste, was one of many who had been employed to do the menial jobs in the development of Burma. They had been the coolies, porters and street cleaners. They had been recruited in the poor regions of South India, the British-owned shipping companies ferrying them across the Bay of Bengal to Rangoon. Many thousands of these South Indians remained in Burma, acquired small land holdings and grew food for the markets of the bigger towns.

Because of their Buddhist faith, the Burmese displayed tolerance to these low-caste Indians. The traditional caste separation of these darker-skinned folk in their own homeland was never a problem in Burma. As a consequence, many thousands of the Tamil people were integrated into the Burmese population. I had been reminded of this during my trek out from Burma through the Hukawng Valley. Of the 20,000 or so refugees, more than two-thirds had been of Tamil origin.

I was beginning to accept that throughout my stay in India I would constantly be reminded of the trek, try as I might to shake it off. However, these flashbacks led me to a realisation that I did have to get on with my life and not dwell on the past.

The other passengers began to board the miniature train. Among them were a few blonde European girls being farewelled by their parents.

A couple of European boys introduced themselves.

'I say, you must be heading for Breeks too. Why don't you sit with us?'

I was glad to, and we soon joined the group of girls.

'They're bound for Hebron High. That's our sister school in the mountains at Coonoor. It's 15 miles below Ootacamund. We always see them on the train.'

'I know Coonoor. I've been there before.'

It was the place I had visited with the Beers' house boy.

They were a happy crew, and it occurred to me that if they were a sample of what I could expect in my new school, I would be lucky. They were living the life I had lived in Burma. Living was for the day, not for the future nor for surveying the past.

The countryside was beautiful and as the air got cooler the landscape looked greener. The train made very slow progress.

'We're going to get off and walk beside the track for a while. Do you want to come with us?'

Of course I did. I was ready for anything. We hopped off and trotted along beside the train, getting back on again when our legs began to get tired.

A festive air prevailed. The tea-pickers had completed their morning harvest. The long line of women with straw baskets on their backs headed toward the buildings of the tea-processing stations.

As we climbed up above 5,000 feet the dark green tea bushes gave way to misty grey-green plantations of Eucalyptus trees.

'They were introduced from Australia and they're cropped for an oil which is sold to pharmaceutical companies,' one of the girls said helpfully. 'How do I know that? My parents are Australian.'

'Really?'

'Yes. They're missionaries from Tasmania. Do you know where that is?'

'At the bottom,' I said promptly. I had always liked geography.

Months down the track, this young girl and I became good friends. Helen was blonde and a little overweight, with blue eyes and slightly protruding teeth. She was not in line when pretty looks were handed out, but what she lacked in the beauty department she made up for in the sweetness of her nature. She was a typical missionary's daughter with a terrific attitude of inclusiveness. She also had a natural, outgoing manner that was typical, I would discover years later, of Australians. In the months to come, whenever the two schools got together for social functions, Helen would seek me out.

'Come over here, Colin, and let me introduce you to some people. Everyone, this is Colin. He's from Burma.'

We pulled into Coonoor and the train was half-emptied as the girls from Hebron High alighted. It was mid-afternoon when we reached the end of the line. The school had dispatched some horse carriages to ferry us the two miles to the boarders' quarters.

'The school itself is in the town,' said one of the boys as we swayed along. 'Look, there it is, over there. Boarders don't live there. We stay in buildings up on the hill. They're right next door to the Governor's residence and the botanical gardens.'

It was a pleasant introduction to the final years of my secondary education. The principal, a gentle man, met me at the entrance and shook my hand warmly.

'McPhedran! Welcome to our school.'

He briefly outlined what was expected of the pupils and led me to my bed in the dormitory.

It was two days before classes commenced and boarders were free. I was the only new one that year. The eyes of the domestic staff seemed to pick me out as I familiarised myself with the place.

The head of our house was a woman, a mother figure who, though strict, was a tremendous source of caring if anything went wrong. She was a large, heavy-boned woman, a spinster who had devoted her life to Christian ideals. A strict disciplinarian, she was devoted to us boys and treated the injuries we incurred on the playing fields. On one occasion I had to ask her to attend to a boil on my backside. I was extremely embarrassed, and she knew it.

'Just imagine I am your mother!' she said.

I had the feeling that Breeks Memorial was what I needed. I did expect some lessons in religion since the school was established by missionaries, but I soon realised that I could talk freely about many different aspects of living and playing.

A few days later more boarders arrived and an assembly was called after dinner that night. The principal welcomed us and, after a brief talk about his expectations, he briefly told the assembly about the new boarder.

'Please make McPhedran's stay a pleasant one,' he said to the boys.

We were awakened early the next day.

'Shower, then breakfast in the dining room.'

After breakfast we assembled in the courtyard and marched to our classes, a mile or two down the road as my new friend in the train had indicated.

My first morning at school was taken up with selecting subjects. I was piled high with textbooks and writing paper. The realisation that I was already into the final two years of my secondary schooling hit me and I was soon given an ultimatum by my father that he expected me to perform.

He never wrote to me himself. The messages were always relayed downwards to me by the school principal. I don't even know whether he wrote directly to the school either, for that matter. As I was to discover, the travel company Thomas Cook had been appointed to handle my finances. My father provided well, but he did not think it necessary to communicate with me. I still felt abandoned, but I did not wallow in it. I had grown used to the state of affairs and, for most of the time anyway, managed to push aside my resentment.

So it was passed down to me as a message from on high that my father wanted me to put the events of 1942 out of my mind and knuckle down to my education. This was the same thing he had said when he had visited me in Bangalore.

I was left under no illusion that he expected me to give him value for the money he was spending. I could understand his concern, although I did not take kindly to the prodding of someone who had so little to do with me. Nevertheless, I set my mind on proving to myself that I could perform.

All the boarders were male but the school had male and female teachers, as well as girl day-students.

'Most of them are the daughters of missionaries or businessmen who use the cool hill station as their country residence,' one of the boys informed me. 'Some are the daughters of the European tea-planters from around here,' he added.

Despite the heavy workload, the school was proud of its record on the playing fields and inter-school carnivals were taken seriously. I involved myself in every sport, with a particular enthusiasm for soccer, which I had learned as a child in Burma.

During one match, when the school was pitted against an army team, I was approached by an Indian gentleman.

'I am the president of a local sports and cultural club for Indians,' he explained. 'Would you consider becoming a junior member of the local Tagore Club? It is a social club that encourages many activities, some on the playing field and others based on the studies of the Indian philosopher Rabindranath Tagore.

'Thank you, but I will have to consult the school principal.'

I went to see him the next day. He was a very reasonable man.

'Certainly, if you wish,' he said. 'The Tagore Club is very reputable and it will give you an opportunity to meet people from outside the school. But school activities must take precedence. We will review your involvement if your schoolwork begins to lag.'

'I understand, sir. Thank you.'

So I became the first non-Indian member of the South Indian branch of the Tagore organisation. My involvement was not extensive. The games were mostly at home and took a couple of hours at weekends, and I enjoyed the association. It was a release from the strictures of school and provided an opportunity to meet and mingle with locals. Despite some barbed references to my association with the 'Chi Chi' crowd, as the locals were called by my fellow students, I continued to play for the club and cultivated many enduring friendships with my Indian team-mates and their families. I fitted in.

On one occasion, one of the senior students at school buttonholed me.

'What's this I hear about your association with the native boys?' he asked.

I took the bait straight away.

'I don't know about you, but I've never felt threatened by any person of a different race or culture.'

Our differing attitudes would fester into a sore of rivalry. We were each guilty of using our differences about the then accepted standards of European behaviour to a ridiculous degree.

Henry, as he was called, was a quarter-caste Indian but his appearance displayed no trace of his Indian ancestry. He was intensely racist, as were most of the whites and part-whites in India during the British Raj. Henry could never come to terms with the fact that I boasted of my Burmese connection. He extended his dislike for me into every facet of our school life. On one occasion he goaded me into a challenge tennis match, a scheme he hatched with his friends. He was a talented player and I knew he would walk all over me on the sand court. I sent a message back with one of my friends.

'Tell them I concede that he is the better player and I will not be taking up his challenge,' I said.

I could not resist adding, 'I have no reason to prove my superiority, because in my own heart I know I am a better person than he could ever hope to be.'

Henry became incensed.

'I'll have that half-caste drummed out of the school,' he told my unfortunate emissary. He might have succeeded but for an ally in the classroom.

Mr Subramanium was a Brahmin, a high-class Indian. He was also the science master. In spite of his strict and demanding attitude in the classroom, he was truly Indian and displayed, though not too openly, a dislike for the colonial masters of his country. He was highly regarded by the governors of the school for his dedication to his position.

Our relationship was a master–pupil one during school hours, but outside Subramanium and I developed a firm, respectful friendship.

We talked at length of our families and our discussions spilled over into the history of the East — the great rulers of India, the religions and philosophies of the Orient. He explained the caste system and elaborated upon the strange traditions of the different groups of nationals that made up the population of the sub-continent. Seldom did we talk of classroom activities, although he did once advise me to reconsider my choice of subjects for the Leaving Certificate.

'I get the impression, Colin, that you are struggling to grasp the fundamentals of the science subjects,' he said tactfully. 'Perhaps you should consider concentrating on subjects with which you have a greater affinity.'

I did try to keep abreast with the other pupils. I was never in the top bracket, but plodded along quite comfortably somewhere in the middle. With a few exceptions, I got along famously with my fellow students. They loved talking about my experiences before coming to Breeks but, to their credit, they never broached the subject of the trek out of Burma. They had been instructed by the principal to refrain from raising it.

What they did ask about, and I was delighted to tell them, was the freedom of travel that had been afforded me, and would continue to be afforded to me, in the short time I had been in India.

As time wore on, I would have more stories to tell them. I had no family in India and nowhere particular to go in the school holidays. It was a school rule that boarders could not stay in the boarding house during breaks, and so I had to go somewhere.

The first school vacation would soon be upon us and the principal buttonholed me.

'Where are you planning to go for the break, McPhedran?'

It was a fair question. The system demanded that I give notice of my plans.

I couldn't wait to get back to Calcutta. This was my chance to explore it without the restrictions the Smees had placed upon me.

'Calcutta, sir,' I said immediately.

'That's a long way. Are you familiar with Calcutta?'

'Yes, sir, I spent my first few months in India with some family friends there.'

He seemed satisfied.

I knew little of the arrangements my father had made with Thomas Cook, but they proved to be generous. All I had to do was notify them of my destination, and they arranged my itinerary, including hotels.

Chapter 20

SCHOOL DAYS

No two train journeys in this vast sub-continent are the same. Along the way, at the many stops, different scenes are played out. What never changes is the crushing presence of humans.

From Madras onwards, I shared the compartment with a soldier returning to his unit in Calcutta. He was quite a jolly Englishman and I took the opportunity to tell him as much as I could of India and its history.

Then, at one of the stops, a woman and her daughter knocked on the door of the compartment from the side of the tracks. I realised the woman was plying the trains and selling her body for a few rupees. Her hands did the speaking and in a moment my companion and she had struck a deal.

The lights were turned down and the two of them went into action. It was embarrassing to sit there and listen to the two of them indulging in a sex act. Having finished, the soldier produced a bottle of alcohol and offered it around. He pointed to the woman's daughter, who would hardly have been older that 10 years old.

'Why don't you have some fun with her?' he suggested.

I was horrified, but just said, 'No thank you, sir.'

The woman kept pointing to her daughter with the obvious suggestion that I take her little girl. Again I waved the suggestion off. The two drank some more liquor and then the soldier turned to me.

'I fancy having her for myself,' he said with a leer.

The young girl moved over onto the other side of the compartment and lay down. I walked into the toilet and shut the door while my companion committed the act with this girl whom I considered a child. When the train pulled into another station, mother and daughter got off between the tracks and headed away.

It was raining heavily when the train pulled into Calcutta's Howrah Station. I boarded a taxi and drove to the Grand Hotel, on Chowringhee, in the centre of Calcutta's business district. Nothing had changed since my stay at the Smees' house. The airstrip in the middle of the city was still being used by fighter planes. The hotel looked out on to a park, a popular recreation area.

After a brief rest I walked down the street and booked into a movie. It had been a while since I had set foot in a theatre because my Christian connections did not encourage visits to what they considered to be the domain of the devil's children.

Back at the hotel I made a point of speaking with anybody in uniform. The guests were generally British and American officers, all friendly and prepared to talk about the front line and the action in Burma, where the Allies were breaking through. The Japanese were being pushed back on all fronts. The Allies had taken Bhamo in December, and the Chinese had taken Namkham in January.

'Any day now, Rangoon will fall,' they said. 'The Japs will be on the run.'

I had been growing so quickly that all of a sudden I had put on a tremendous amount of weight and was bursting out of my clothes. The only set I had that still fitted me was the new school uniform Dr Beer had ordered for me when I began at Breeks.

I went to see Thomas Cook to arrange my return trip and diffidently mentioned my need for new clothes to the clerk. He went away and spoke to someone, then came back and told me the name of one of the big stores. I don't remember whether it was Jardine's or Whiteway's, but he said, 'Go and buy what you want. The bill will be taken care of at this end.'

Relieved, I found my way to the men's department of the enormous store and one of the assistants took me under his wing. He measured me up and said, 'You can pick up the clothes tomorrow.'

He was as true as his word. The next day I went back and collected two brand new pairs of casual trousers, three white shirts, a set of cricket creams that were my pride and joy, one pair of English leather shoes, rubber shoes for sport and some new underwear. I remember the trousers were the most important because I could barely do up my old ones. Newly kitted out, I set off to explore Calcutta.

I was determined to get out and about. I was doing what I had yearned to do on the day I had been left alone at the Smees' house during my first stay in Calcutta. I pounded the streets, rode the tram cars, visited the slum areas and ate and drank with the Indians. I even went to the gates of the Smees' residence and looked around at the scene I had last viewed that day early in 1943.

In the street were the same people, almost, with the same air of going to a destination. Even the smells were there, as were the pariah dogs, sniffing the ground for a scrap of food. I walked along the streets beside the dirty Hoogly River and roamed through the business district and further on to the wharves. There I watched the native labourers unloading foreign ships.

Each day I had lunch at a cheap curry house and in the evenings I explored the affluent suburbs of Tollygunj and Ballygunj. They were clean, with tree-lined streets, and statues, on most corners and in the parks, of long-ago British conquering heroes and distinguished governors. It was the time of day when the wealthy returned home in chauffeur-driven cars and their children came out to play tennis and ride horses in the cool of the day. It was a great city of contrasts — the rich at play, and the poor also playing, but in the gutters. Both were unmindful of the sick and dying in doorways and on the pavements.

My visit to Calcutta was far too brief for my liking, because the school vacation was only short. I vowed to return soon to the city which held me in its thrall.

————

Sunday was a free day at school, when we would sit around and discuss our encounters with girls. All the versions of our experiences were tinged with exaggeration. Most of the liaisons included the girls from our sister school at Coonoor.

One of my best friends was Peter Turley. He had developed a close friendship with Helen, the girl who had befriended me on the train up the mountain, the vivacious blonde with the happy face. The pair would often disappear into the gardens in search of a secluded spot.

'Give us a whistle when it's time for the girls to go back to Coonoor,' Turley would say.

I would, and the pair would reappear, rather sheepish and flushed. I constantly but lightheartedly teased him about her teeth.

'How do you enjoy getting a mouthful of them every time you kiss?'

He pointed to his chest and said, 'Who needs kissing when a girl is built like Mae West?'

Whenever I saw Helen after that, my eyes were drawn to her upper tunic like a magnet.

David and Shirley were another couple. Shirley was the daughter of a tea-planter and David the son of the aide-de-camp to the Nizam of Hyderabad. His family lived in one of the many palaces the Nizam owned in South India. He was a fine fellow, but rather serious and subdued. He seldom boasted of his conquests and I admired him for that. However, he and Shirley became very close and I feared that one of them would get hurt. Some months later I was told that Shirley was pregnant and had been removed from school. It was a bitter blow for David, and he became a recluse.

The time flew by. Boarders were given a remarkable amount of freedom. Unlike my earlier stint at boarding school in Rangoon, we were trusted to do the right thing. The boot-camp mentality of the Catholic priests that had dominated the lives of young pupils in St Paul's was not in evidence here. Corporal punishment was never practised. The system was permitting me to develop freely, although Christian values were slotted in during the compulsory Sunday Gospel service.

Church was not all bad. I enjoyed the rousing hymns and it was an opportunity to view the day girls in a different light. It was pleasant to see them wearing colourful dresses and cute hats, compared with the plain white blouse and blue tunic of the school uniform.

After the morning service the boarders would march back to the boarding school in military file.

'Did you see Fiona? Didn't she look good?'

'Yes, nice legs, too. I caught a good flash of them when she bent over.'

'What about Maureen? That was a different hat she was wearing.'

'Who cares about hats. It's the bits further down that matter.'

The lesson of Salvation that some visiting evangelist had spent hours preparing was quite forgotten.

What a far cry Breeks Memorial was from that horrible place with a saintly name in Rangoon. How could I ever forget my stint at St Paul's? My father's decision to send Robert and me to that Catholic institution had certainly taken the sparkle out of my mother. Seeing her carrying the burden of hurt extinguished what little love I had for him. He had enrolled us to be taught by the very Catholic brothers whom he had always called idolaters. The school stood for everything my father detested, yet he went ahead and enrolled us.

One Sunday at Breeks my roving eye latched on to a particular girl, Flora, who was in my class at school. Every Sunday she attended the service with her mother. The male boarders sat together on the right-hand side of the church and Flora and her mother occupied the seats diagonally ahead, across the aisle.

During the week Flora looked like any of the other day girls. She was part of the school scene. However, on Sunday, she wore long, plain dresses and a black straw hat. It was the simplicity of her dress that made her stand out from the rest of the girls at church.

One lunch break at school, I was getting ready for the afternoon session with a teacher who was going to test us on a subject I hated. I was so worried that I could not eat. I sought help from classmates, but they were busy chatting up the girls. Then I spotted Flora reading in the shade of the school verandah. I sauntered over and joined her on the bench. I told her of my predicament.

'I don't suppose you would be able to help me.'

'I'm sorry — I am in the same situation. I really don't understand the lesson either!'

We talked for a while and it struck me that she was not quite as perturbed as I.

'Aren't you worried about being singled out as a dummy by the teacher?'

She shrugged and pointed to the mangy dog that frequented the playing field in search of an odd crust of food.

'See that dog, Colin, it is not at all concerned about what's going to happen to it when we are called into class. It will just move on and make the best of what lies ahead.'

I looked at her and noticed her long hair had been plaited into two pigtails. It made her look younger still. The bell rang and we walked into school together. The second period arrived.

'I am most dreadfully sorry,' the teacher said at the outset. 'You must have all been wondering what the question was all about. I didn't give you the correct information!'

I caught Flora's eye and our friendship firmed from then on.

Flora was my first love. We talked and talked whenever the opportunity arose. She told me about the death of her missionary father, and she was the first person to whom I opened my heart about my family tragedy. We cried together as I recalled the trek. There were times when my thoughts flashed back to the Saturdays I had spent at the Buddhist monastery in Burma listening to the monks explain the theory of rebirth as written in the Buddhist canon. It occurred to me that perhaps Flora was the embodiment of my sister.

This partial belief made me look upon her as somebody to cherish and love, but not to speak about in the sexual way my friends spoke of their girlfriends.

There was nothing soppy about our relationship; it could be better described as a discovery that we were soul mates.

However, it did not inhibit my desires for the opposite sex. I continued to flirt with some of the girls from the sister school. Henry, my arch enemy and a real 'pants man' with the girls and, indeed, the younger female staff members of the school, was mad about the daughter of a wealthy Englishman. She was friendly and open and Henry was very possessive, even though she wasn't actually his girlfriend. Any attention paid to her by other boys was met with veiled threats of a hiding. If he couldn't have her, no-one could.

Cycling and exploring the wooded hills around Ootacamund were popular recreations on Sundays.

My little mate, Turley, said one day, 'I want to take Helen for a ride today, but she is stuck with her friend. Why don't you come along and make a foursome? She's a nice girl.'

As soon as he mentioned her name, I realised she was the very girl of whom Henry was so possessive.

'Are you out of your mind?' I asked. 'Henry will go berserk.'

Turley, undaunted, said, 'Well, Helen says she doesn't like him anyway. He can't just monopolise someone who doesn't want him. Besides, if you don't come, I'll be saddled with her, and that won't be any fun.'

'Oh well, then, I suppose so,' I said.

We rode along a path that was used by a small tribe of little-known Indians, the Togas, who lived in the high country. We crossed some green fields and found a rocky outcrop. Turley and Helen chose a space between two rocks.

'Leave us alone. There's a place on the other side where you can go.'

Great guy, I thought. Here he was with his favourite girl, wedged in a secluded spot, and I was left with a nice girl for whom I had had no desire, not even to be her escort for the afternoon.

Our embarrassment was compounded by the squeals and laughter coming from around the rock. I stole a glance at the girl's blushing face. She was actually a beauty queen, blessed with a fine complexion, growing out of the awkward period of her life but not yet ready to blossom into maturity.

It was agonising, sitting there like a couple of rawhides waiting for the first draw. How did I get into this situation and why was I not doing anything about it? There was Turley acting out a love scene, one he would delight in bragging about back at the boarding house. He would no doubt make me verify his story.

The girl was sitting with her hands around her knees.

I half turned to face her, gently pushing her backwards until she lay on the sloping ground. I drew my body up to hers and kissed her on her neck. She squealed softly but offered no resistance. The petting grew heavier and I soon found my hand under her blouse and on her breast, but I went no further. Holding her tightly, I said, 'Come on, let's get those two. We'd better get back to the boarding house.'

Back at the boarding house the boys were reliving their weekend's experiences. Some, children of wealthier parents, had returned with baskets of good things to eat. Others reminisced about delicious cakes at the coffee house down town. The more athletic described hikes in the hillsides. And there were those who could not go beyond the subject of the opposite sex. Today I was one of that group. Although I had been caught up in the foursome quite by accident, I had to admit it had been fun.

But I took exception to the way the other boys — even Turley — expected me to reveal every detail.

'Well, McPhedran, how far did you go? Did you get into her pants?'

'No, I did not, if you want to know, and I object to you fellows bringing her name into this.'

'Oh, come on, we all know who she is.'

But I wouldn't be drawn anymore. She was a decent girl who did not deserve to have her name dragged along the corridors of a boarding house full of randy young fellows.

Fortunately, Henry never did find out about our assignation. But later on I discovered, to my chagrin, that our friends from the sister school indulged in almost exactly the same sort of gossip about us as we did about them.

Some years later, in London, I attended a reunion of former pupils of Breeks Memorial. To my surprise, the same girl turned up. She had matured into a self-satisfied young woman, typical of the well-heeled, smug British upper-middle classes of the time. I was slightly disappointed, but not altogether surprised, to see that despite her early promise she had not blossomed into a truly beautiful woman.

I began to focus more on study. The word which filtered down to me from my father indicated that the consequences of failing would not be pleasant. I still played sport, but the weekends spent flirting were over.

Flora and I spent more time together and most of our energies went into revising. We grew close and I sometimes played with her waist-length hair and learnt to plait her dark locks whilst she read aloud. Often her mother was present and we talked about the work of missionaries in India.

The political situation was hotting up as the war with Japan was being won. I wondered what Flora and her mother would do when India finally achieved its independence. One day they asked me where my future lay.

I told them I would catch the first transport home to Burma and enter the Hukawng Valley in the north to seek out my mother who, I was convinced, would still be alive and living in a remote village.

One Sunday, while Flora and I were waiting for her mother to emerge from church, she said, 'You know, Colin, Mother cried for you after you told her about your mother. She has constantly prayed that you will find her alive and well. Mother says you will not rest until you find out what happened to her. She prays that you will go on and have a joyous life no matter what you find in Burma.'

I was touched. It seemed there were people around who were genuinely prepared to share the burden of somebody else's grief.

Through the years, the images of Flora and her mother have never dimmed. I often see them dressed, as they always were, in plain clothes, heads covered with straw hats, stepping out of the red brick church on the hill in Ootacamund.

Chapter 21

WAR IS OVER

1945 rolled on. The war in the Pacific was drawing rapidly to a close. The soldiers I had spoken to in Calcutta earlier in the year had been absolutely right about the situation in Burma. Rangoon had fallen shortly afterwards, on 1 May.

Since the news from the war was so encouraging, I decided I should pay another visit to my beloved Calcutta during the long break. It was so close to Burma that I would surely meet somebody from the war zone who could tell me what was happening up in the mountains.

It also meant that I could stop off at Madras to meet my brother Donald's wife, of whom I had only recently learnt. Unbeknownst to me, Donald had met her in Calcutta while he was a student at the university. She was an evacuee from Burma who, with her family, had been imprisoned in Myitkyina in a concentration camp run by the Japanese during their occupation of upper Burma.

Her family, the McRaes, had suffered dreadfully at the hands of the Japanese. After Myitkyina had been liberated in 1944, the remaining members of her family arrived at the evacuation centre in Calcutta before joining their grandparents in Madras.

Donald had fallen in love with Pamela, who was a real beauty, a former Miss Burma, and they married in Madras shortly afterwards. He left university to join the army. A few months before my visit, Pamela had given birth to their first baby, a boy named Robert, after our brother.

The visit was not a success. Donald was away in the army, and Pamela was all at sea with her young baby. She immediately seized upon me to help out with him, and so for the few nights I was there I babysat the poor little fellow while she went out. It did not suit my teenage temperament and I did not feel welcome. I was glad to get away, and put the visit out of my mind.

So I found myself back at the Grand Hotel in Calcutta, booked again for me by Thomas Cook.

With the war drawing to a close, security had loosened considerably and after the hotel guests, mostly soldiers, had consumed a few drinks in a relaxed environment, I learnt quite a lot about the Allies' advance to Rangoon in April.

Calcutta was getting over the ravages of the famine that had killed an estimated one million people. People were still dying on the streets and it was a common sight to see emaciated people scavenging through rubbish bins outside the hotel.

The Indian Congress Party was creating some problems for the British authorities. Gandhi and Nehru, the two leaders of the Party, were stepping up their agitation for self-rule in India. People gathered daily and when the beating of drums had summoned a crowd, a Party member would address the gathering.

There was always a heavy police presence and on some occasions, when the mob got out of control, the police would step in, their batons flailing at anybody nearby. The mood of the citizens was certainly changing. Some Indian youths took to abusing Europeans brazenly. I kept away from any trouble spots.

I befriended a young university student whose family were well-to-do Indians and lived in the Central Provinces. One day, loudspeakers blared out that Gandhi would be addressing a meeting in the park.

'Let's go and hear the great man speak,' my friend suggested.

I was afraid initially.

'Don't worry, the police will be in control if hostilities break out,' he said. 'Besides, there will be over a million people there to hear Gandhi, and it will be an experience of a lifetime for a young fellow like you!'

I joined the throng heading toward the meeting place. There were people on bikes, some riding in horse-drawn vehicles, others walking and even some limbless people crawling along the dusty road. I had never experienced anything like it, and probably never will again. When we arrived, the seething masses were being bombarded with speeches from the preliminary speakers, whose voices screamed out from loudspeakers.

Pushed and jostled by this frenzied mass, I felt nervous, but my companion said, 'How can you go back now against the flow of people? You may as well stay with me until the great man speaks and then we will be able to move back with the crowd.'

It seemed logical. Gandhi spoke in Hindi and as I could pick up only a few words in the distorted din, I was none the wiser afterwards. Back at the hotel, elated, I recounted my experience to some interested listeners.

'I am so glad I was present at such an historic event!'

'Just as well you didn't get crushed in the crowd, young man.'

A visit to the back streets of Calcutta soon brought me back to earth. I now understood what was disturbing the local population. I wondered whether this might be my last visit to Calcutta and I set out to see as much as I could of the large, sprawling city and to mingle with the people. I knew the Indians were becoming restless and were thoroughly sick of foreigners running their affairs.

One day I received a message from the offices of Thomas Cook. I went in to see what they wanted.

'You are invited to visit a Miss Coutts, a friend of your father's,' the clerk told me. 'She is Principal of the St Andrew's Presbyterian Orphanage near Kalimpong, a few hours by train and bus from Calcutta. I have your itinerary here.'

Kalimpong was a town near Darjeeling in the Himalayas. I arrived by bus at the gates of the orphanage, which was a few miles outside the town. Miss Coutts appeared to be in her early 40s, a similar age to my mother. She was a good-looking Scottish woman with a strong accent, quite matronly but with a certain kindness in her manner.

There must have been a couple of hundred Indian children in the orphanage, mostly from Sikkam, on the border of Tibet, and Nepal.

'Welcome, Colin, I hope you enjoy your stay. It's a great pleasure to have one of Archie's sons here for a visit. I'm so glad you could come. I'll let your father know how well you are looking.'

She was obviously on very close terms with him, but I didn't dare ask how or why. At that point it did not occur to me that they might have been more than friends, but it did strike me as curious that she knew him so well.

She had some news for me. A Burmese neighbour of our family in Maymyo had evacuated from Burma early in the war and had come to live in Kalimpong. Miss Coutts had arranged for me to visit.

The lady's name was Mrs Bellamy, and she had been married to a Tasmanian, a bookmaker who ran a book at the Rangoon Turf Club. Mr Bellamy had passed away just prior to the start of the war in the East.

Mrs Bellamy had been quite friendly with my mother, and she and her daughter had been frequent visitors to our house, Jamshed Villa. They were of royal lineage — Mrs Bellamy was one of the daughters of the last reigning king of Burma, King Thibaw. When the British had annexed the whole of Burma after the teak wars, they had exiled him to India in 1885, thus ending the rule of the monarchs in the country. After she grew up, she had returned to Burma to live.

Mrs Bellamy's Burmese name was Princess Ma Hlat ('the pretty one'). Her daughter, June-Rose, had inherited her good looks and became a very beautiful young woman.

Years later I heard that, after the war, they returned to Burma and some time during the 1970s June-Rose married General Ne Win, the Burmese dictator who had seized power in 1962. He had been bewitched by her beauty. She was his second wife and the marriage only lasted a short time.

Divorced, June-Rose went to settle in the United Kingdom where she wrote a book describing in detail her short spell as Ne Win's wife. Apparently, she detailed the General's inadequacies in the book and, before publication, he struck a deal with his ex-wife to have the draft of the book destroyed. June-Rose was more than a match for the General. She drove a hard bargain and it is said to have cost him the crown jewels, literally, to win the settlement. The last I heard of June-Rose, she was living in Switzerland.

I spent two days with them in Kalimpong and feasted on Burmese food. When it was time for me to return to the orphanage on the second afternoon, I decided to walk along the mountain track rather than catch the bus. I hoped to view the scenery and chat to the villagers whose huts were dotted along the bush track.

As the afternoon wore on, I suddenly realised that the light was fading fast. I hadn't a clue how far I had to walk and before long the night closed in. I was guided by the flickering lights in the huts along the way. The Sikkimese people who inhabit this region are Buddhist and there were numerous poles outside most of the dwellings, laced with prayer flags fluttering in the breeze.

Eventually I became rather concerned, so I stopped and asked some villagers the way. I arrived quite late and was met by a very relieved Miss Coutts.

'I was so worried that something had happened to you! You gave me quite a fright, young man.'

———————

Back at the hotel in Calcutta's renowned Choweringhee, the scene was changing. The pavements were seething with people in uniform. Mingling with them were hordes of pickpockets, hawkers and prostitutes. Every day, after a clean-up, I had dinner and strolled down the street into Park Street to sit down in one of the better-class cafes where I took in the scene over a cup of coffee and some French pastries.

The war news was encouraging.

'The Allies are giving the Japanese a pounding!'

'It can't go on much longer.'

'The war will soon be over.'

Indeed, everything pointed to the end of hostilities. There seemed to be more drunkenness in the city. Black African troops and their white counterparts swayed on the footpaths with heavily made-up Indian girls in tow. Still there was an undercurrent of resentment by many of the Indians, including the middle class and the merchants.

I returned to my hotel. The drinkers in the bar always overflowed into the rather small lobby. To reach the stairs one had to push past men and women with drinks in their hands. I walked through to the garden lounge and found a seat outside. The spectacle of men and women emptying their glasses as if their lives depended on it was overwhelming. I wanted to get away from it all and wondered what the ordinary people of Calcutta were thinking.

It doesn't take much to stir dissatisfaction among people struggling to survive, while around them they see a scene of lavishness. Certainly, the very poor and the street beggars' lots were marginally better, since a fair amount of money had found its way into their hands. But it was those of the higher caste who, I thought, displayed a mood change. It was getting uglier every day, although I had not struck any trouble. Perhaps I had been kept safe because I had followed my instincts and moved with the crowd.

The waiter came over.

'I'll have a gin and lime, please,' I said, remembering it was a favourite with Europeans in the East. I felt guilty about consuming alcohol at my age, but if ever there was an occasion for it, this was it. The khaki-clad officers were becoming rather boisterous. The Indian waiter came back.

Speaking with his hands as well as his voice, he said, 'War finished!'

I was overcome with joy. The first thing that flashed through my mind was that now I could make plans to return quickly to Burma and search for my mother. I had no thought of returning to school to complete my studies. I had to find a way home. I remembered there was a government of Burma in exile in India at Simla, a hill station some days from Calcutta by train. I even thought of boarding a ship and hoping it was heading for Rangoon.

I wandered out into the streets and asked anyone I could about a passage to Burma. I had no luck. Everything was a whirl.

On my return to the hotel there were officers everywhere. They were sprawled in the lounges, in the corners and on the floors and every one of them appeared to have a painted doll clutching him. Outside the hotel many a brawl erupted. I wanted to get out of the city, which no longer seemed like the one I so loved.

I had planned to go to the movies but they were closed, no doubt to keep the celebrating hordes out. Instead, I sat in a corner and took in the scene. A waiter approached.

'Would you like a lady for the night?' he asked.

'I beg your pardon?'

'My sister is a beautiful girl and she has had a Catholic education. Would you celebrate with her?'

I didn't know what to say, but it did not matter. In a matter of minutes he reappeared with a young woman in tow.

The waiter left us, pushing through the mob, and returned with two glasses of gin and lime. I don't recall much of our conversation. I was on a high one moment and in deep depression the next. However, we talked and I noticed that she was quite attractive and well-spoken, with a set of beautifully formed white teeth. Every time she smiled, her teeth gleamed.

Even after I took her to the room I shared with another officer and made love to her, still half-dressed, all I remembered was her beautiful teeth. There was nothing mind-boggling about it, nor did any bell ring out in my head. My memory of that moment was simply this dark-skinned young girl looking up at me with beautiful white teeth. I paid her for the privilege, as this seemed to be the norm, and never saw her again.

There was nothing more I could do. I had pursued every avenue I could about returning to Burma. I had broached the subject of returning to Burma with a few of the soldiers at the hotel. They were brutally frank.

'You're crazy. It's turmoil over there. You'd be mad to try to go back. You'd probably be killed.'

It was time to get back to school and get down to the task of passing the exams.

I left Calcutta for the last time, though not without difficulty. The turmoil had thrown train schedules into chaos. Thomas Cook had trouble getting me on to a train to Madras because I required a sleeping berth for the two-and-a-half-day trip. However, they eventually found me one and off I went back to school.

The train headed down the Coromandel Coast to Madras. It was a dreary journey this time, shared with a couple of Indian scholars from a university in South India. I missed the hustle and bustle of Calcutta but I knew I would not return.

Calcutta had brought me joy and sorrow. It was there that I had taken my first steps into adulthood at the ripe old age of 15. It was the city in which I had learned how to truly survive. I was as streetwise as the locals. It was the friendliest city in India. I loved the people but hated the poverty.

Back at school, my friend Turley was waiting to hear all about my holiday.

'Did you have a good time in Calcutta?' he asked. I told him all about it.

He was happy for me that the war had ended but he realised it was a turning point for me.

'Have you made any plans to return home to Burma?'

I told him I had tried, although I could barely admit, even to myself, that an immediate return to Burma was a pipe-dream. But one part of me accepted what the soldiers had said: that Burma was in chaos and there was no way any Anglos would be welcome. Besides, my father would never have allowed it and without his financial support I was clearly helpless at this point.

To lighten the mood, I told Turley about the girl in Calcutta.

'What was it like? What did she do?'

He had a giggle when I conceded, 'All I can remember is the smiling face of a young Indian girl with beautiful white teeth!'

'You're joking!'

I never told anyone else of that brief encounter.

As I grew into manhood people would often ask, 'What do you look for when you first meet a woman?'

And I always had to admit, 'It's the teeth that capture my attention.'

Inevitably, the reply was, 'You're having us on, McPhedran!'

Chapter 22

WHITE FLOWERS

Back at my desk, listening to the teachers was paying off. Encouraged by Flora, I really put an effort into the subjects I had elected for the Cambridge Certificate exams, which we were due to sit towards the end of 1946.

Time flew by. I had not given much thought to the next break until one of the Indian servants approached me and asked where I was going.

He had obviously noticed that at the end of each school term the other boarders were always picked up by their parents but that nobody ever came to meet me.

'Do you have a home to go to? I cannot help but see that the other boarders always seem happy to be leaving for the holidays, but that you always have a look of slight sadness,' he said.

He was spot-on. I dreaded the end of each term and especially hated the way the principal, Mr Willa, always asked, 'Where might you be going for your holidays, McPhedran?'

It was, of course, a fair question — nobody was allowed to stay at school during the holidays — but to me it always underlined the painful facts of my situation.

Thomas Cook had a network all over India and I was already quite a seasoned traveller. Yet, despite the prospect of being able to travel far and wide in India, school holidays also meant some lonely times for me, a boy staying in an adult world of hotel rooms and guesthouses.

On the bright side, I learnt a lot about Indian cooking when on occasions I would forsake the formal lounges of the hotels that had been booked for me, and descend to the kitchens to find some human warmth. There I was always treated royally and I have never forgotten the cooking lessons I received from the chefs in these establishments.

They taught me how to grind and mix the spices and when to add the meat, which had to be simmered for hours on the charcoal braziers. I also learnt the difference between the curries of the different regions.

The hotel staff were always friendly and kind-hearted. They were delighted that I could speak to them in Hindustani, of which I had a good colloquial grasp. On their invitation I would stand about puffing on the Indian cigarettes they gave me. We would all laugh and chat while the chefs prepared elaborate Indian feasts for the British guests, many of whom were soldiers on leave.

Years later, when I was married, living in Australia and raising my own children, I never interfered with the plain diet that was typical of the so-called White Australia of the 1950s and early 1960s. Indian food was virtually unheard of and anything spicy was considered bad for children's digestion, especially among the ordinary people of Anglo heritage. But sometimes I would slip into the kitchen later in the evening, when my wife, Laurel, had gone off to work at the Bowral Empire picture theatre, and cook myself a curry — a Burmese dish or an Indian one, with heaps of rice. The smells and the flavours always took me back to my earlier life as they wafted and curled about the house.

When they were grown up and had developed their own love of Asian and Indian food, my children would complain.

'Dad, why didn't you ever cook us curries? They always smelled so yummy. We used to lie awake sniffing them. It's not fair.'

I would shrug and laugh. The truth was, I didn't want them to be torn between cultures.

I had never in my wildest dreams imagined that anybody, least of all a servant at school, had observed me at vacation time. So when the Indian servant began to ask questions, I tried to look casual.

'As a matter of fact, I do not have a home in India.'

'No family?'

'None in India, no.'

He seemed quite sad. I brushed aside his concern.

'I will be happy to travel as usual to a city in some part of India to savour the lifestyle,' I said with my chin up, but he was not fooled.

He followed me for a moment and, with his head on one side, looked up.

'Would Sir be kind enough to consider visiting my family in a village outside the city of Mysore?' he asked. 'It is about four hours' drive from Ootacamund.'

In a typical Oriental fashion he directed his appeal to my heart and not my head.

'You would be doing me a great favour by visiting my humble home with gifts I would send for the family,' he said, bowing his head in a gesture of respect.

I fell for it, but said, 'I can only accept the invitation if I may pay your wife and family the money I would otherwise spend in a hotel.'

'Thank you for your generosity, but I could not accept. It would be demeaning for me to do so.'

I could hardly believe my ears. Here was a poor native, who could probably provide for his family for a year on what I was offering, refusing money!

'It would be an honour to have you as a guest,' he said, adding, 'and it would raise my standing and that of my family with the other servants.'

Frankly, I was overjoyed with the offer.

I presented myself at the principal's office and told him of my decision. He appeared happy, but warned, 'It may be quite a culture shock, roughing it with a family in a village.'

Flora was thrilled for me.

'Colin, that is wonderful. Mother and I were going to ask you to spend the holidays with us in Central India. Perhaps we can do that another time.'

I packed my bag and, with a parcel of fruit and vegetables provided by the servant for his family, caught the bus. Public transport in India is always taxed to the limit but the buses take the cake in terms of the number of people to a given area.

For the next four hours I was to experience it all — a hot, crowded bus, being squeezed up against other passengers, and a driver who not only thought he owned the stretch of road but believed it was his mission to demonstrate to all around that he was the master, the pilot of this lethal projectile with its human cargo.

As we drove down the steep mountain road he constantly blew the horn, stuck his head out of the window and abused anybody who dared get in his way. Approaching the plains, the heat and smell in the bus became unbearable. We stopped often to check the overloaded goods on the roof rack.

The fact that the bus was top-heavy caused no alarm to the pilot, who strutted about at each stop as if to impress upon the passengers that he was the boss. It appeared that the travellers considered themselves subordinate to the man with the wheel, a strange outlook born of years of suffering under warlords and, in recent times, subservience to the British Raj, with its superior airs. During the journey I became frustrated at the number of 'pit stops'. But this was India, a place where time meant nothing and where process was more important than destination.

Finally we entered the busy streets of the ancient city of Mysore and pulled in abruptly at the bus terminal. As the only non-Indian alighting from the leaning bus, I was easily identified and was approached by a woman and a tribe of children, all smiling and with clasped palms. My vacation had begun.

The family home was on the outskirts of town, in a cluster of wooden huts. It was a tiny home by any standards but the woman was a proud housekeeper and the place was spotless. The younger ones were always cleaning and sweeping the floor.

For the next 12 days I became part of the family. We played together and ate as a family. The food was very much to my liking and surprisingly there was always sufficient rice to go around. I realised that the family belonged to a class somewhere on the middle rungs of the Indian worker.

It was cruelly hot, yet nobody made any mention of the weather. The Indian, unlike the Anglo, accepts whatever nature serves up, be it soaring temperatures, floods or cold winds, without talking about it.

I began to feel part of the family. I shopped with the older children as they went about the markets buying provisions for the day's meal. As in most Oriental countries, they purchased fresh food daily.

The day to catch the bus back up the mountain arrived too soon. The whole family accompanied me to the bus terminal. We shook hands and the lady handed me a small cotton bag. I assumed it was a gift and tucked it into my trouser pocket.

The trip up the mountain was not as hair-raising as the trip down, although the bus groaned under the weight of excess baggage and there were frequent stops to fill the radiator with water. The manservant from school was at the bus terminal to greet me. He pushed his way through the crowd with a beaming smile.

'How are you? How was your holiday?'

'Really well. I had a wonderful time with your family.'

We chatted all the way to the boarding house and he understood that I had genuinely enjoyed myself. It was a privilege to share in the joy of such a kind man and the family who had taken me in as one of their own.

I unpacked my bag, reached into my pocket and untied the cloth bag. It contained the rupees that I had given the lady of the house on my arrival. I did not pursue the matter, accepting that it was better to receive the family's hospitality and generosity without question.

As usual, everybody bragged about their holidays. When I told my friends about my extraordinary stay with the Indian family they looked at me with disbelief.

'If you continue to fraternise with the natives, you may find yourself with a ready-made wife!' said Turley, a reference to the Indian custom of arranged child brides.

I told Flora all about it. She was happy for me.

'You know, Colin, in the course of Mother's missionary work we have spent a lot of time in remote villages and we have always found the people to be lovely.'

I reflected on my other school term breaks, spent in hotels in one or other of the cities. I recalled wasted weeks when I had indulged in the high life of movies and restaurants, mixing with people much older than myself whose conversations focused on the war in which they were involved. I regretted that I had not taken the opportunity to learn more about the people in this great country where there is a sense of timelessness about everything.

During this new term Flora fell ill with one of the many exotic diseases that abound on the sub-continent. She was rushed to the local hospital and it saddened me to see my friend so sick and fighting for life. Her mother and I spent long hours at her bedside hoping and praying that she recover. She died in a matter of days. I had lost another of the people I loved.

I was asked to lead the pallbearers at the funeral and it was a devastating experience. We assembled at the boarding house and were marched to the church downtown.

'Wait here, outside, until the other boys have taken their seats,' the pastor said.

In due course we received a signal. I walked into the church with the other pallbearers and was led to the front of the hall.

All heads were bowed, for which I was grateful. I did not want my fellow students to see me grieving. We sat beside the coffin, a plain, dark-stained casket covered with just a few flowers, a simple bunch of white lilies. Visions of funerals I had seen in Burma and India danced before my eyes.

My eyes were fixed on the coffin and I took in every detail of the white flowers.

They called to mind funerals in Burma where, in contrast, the coffins would be covered in multi-coloured flowers. In Calcutta, funerals I had seen were always distinguished by a huge mound of red and orange flowers on top of the body, whose face was always exposed. The popular zinnia appeared to be the flower of choice in Calcutta.

Funerals in India are an everyday occurrence, but they are always a sad spectacle. I always thought of those left behind and wondered how they would cope, just as I had wondered how I would cope when my mother asked me to leave her in the jungle.

The organist stopped playing and the pastor took his stand at the pulpit. There was a moment of silence and the service began when the pastor in a booming voice asked the gathering to bow their heads in prayer.

I had expected to hear some soft words of comfort, but he looked down at the congregation and preached a sermon of fire and brimstone, with lessons from the New Testament that emphasised repentance.

'The wages of sin are death,' he kept repeating. 'Each of us has been born in sin and the only path to salvation is through Jesus Christ. Repent, sinners! Repent of your sins so that you may enter the house of the Lord.'

I felt uneasy. My Saturday visits to the Buddhist monastery as a child had taught me that birth was pure and that unskilled thoughts were learnt or unlearnt along life's journey by oneself.

'Praise the merciful Lord who has ended Flora's suffering!' the pastor exhorted us.

I wondered why, if the Lord was merciful, he was putting Flora's mother and me through this sadness. Why, also, did my own family have to suffer before they too were called by the Lord?

At the end of his sermon we sang a rousing hymn. After a few more words directed at Flora's mother we were called upon to lift the casket and head out of the church. It was a dreadful moment in my life. Everybody's eyes appeared to be on me. There was nothing I could do to stop the tears running down my face.

I pulled myself together during the short walk to the cemetery in the woods outside the town. Flora's mother broke down when the coffin was lowered into the grave. My heart went out to her and my thoughts fled to the jungle in Burma.

I wished my family could have had a decent burial; the picture remained of my mother leaning against a tree, my sister dead in a remote army hut and my brother and good friend lying in the tropical mud, his body covered with a blanket and a few sticks.

There were no white butterflies at Flora's gravesite, just the white flowers.

At the end of the burial service, the boarders drifted back to the house. For once, nobody had to march in file. Mr Subramanium, as a Brahmin, had not attended the church service but came to the graveside and walked back with me. It was comforting to have him with me.

'I am quite concerned that you have been put through the ordeal of carrying the casket,' he said after a few minutes.

I explained that Flora's mother had requested it.

'Our custom,' he said gently, 'is to engage professional mourners.'

As we walked past the stone Hindu temple, he touched me.

'Would you mind waiting a moment while I enter the building?'

'Not at all. I'm in no hurry.'

'Just let your mind float for a little while. Remove your shoes and let the cool marble floor at the entrance soothe your whole body.'

I did feel calmed by the cool stone beneath the soles of my feet.

In due course he emerged. We walked along to a tea shop that catered for those of his caste, and he bought me the sweetest cup of tea that I had ever tasted. When we had drunk, we did the customary breaking of the earthen cup on the footpath before heading back to the boarding house.

Some time later I discovered that this kind man had raised his concern with the principal about the burden that had been put upon me.

For days I wondered what I had done to deserve this tragedy. It brought back the dark days of the trek. I also grieved for Flora's poor mother, left to carry on without the daughter she had so cherished. There was nobody with whom I could talk over my feelings. Where were the good things in life? I was searching for answers. I did not want to believe that the scripture lessons that my mother had taught me were wrong. Yet I had just experienced a funeral service in a Christian church that did nothing to ease the pain of losing a friend. Indeed, the brief moment with Mr Subramanium after the burial service and his kind words contrasted starkly with those delivered from the pulpit. I could feel myself drifting away from all I had been taught to be true about Christianity, and yet I would not accept, completely, that my mother could be wrong.

I began to develop a cynical view of life and religion and disbelief in the assurances that good things come of good deeds. It was almost four years since

I had lost my own mother, brother and sister. Flora's death brought memories of Ethel flooding into my mind. To me, Flora had become the sister I had lost in the jungle. My mind conjured up the moments when Ethel had hugged and comforted me as a small boy when I had hurt myself. Incidents that had completely left me in the previous years returned to haunt me and I was moved to tears whenever I pictured the smiling face of my sister, the bubbly person who as far as I could remember had never shed a tear in all the time we grew up together, until the day our father had banished her sweetheart.

I remembered her quietness on the trek, how she never complained and always tried to support our mother. I recalled vividly the night she was left on the other bank of the flooded creek, alone, and the first whispered news of her death in the army camp on the border of Burma and India.

Chapter 23

OUT OF INDIA

*I*t was heads down for the finals. I had to try to put all the sadness out of my mind, otherwise I would never have done any schoolwork at all.

I had taken Mr Subramanium's advice and had chosen six subjects that I felt would guarantee me a place in an Indian university at least.

They were biology, maths, English, history, geography and French. The first five were not a problem but I had my doubts about French. A second language was compulsory and I had only begun it that year.

My French teacher had said, 'It will be difficult to catch up on three years' work. But with your cooperation and hard work I believe I can teach you enough to pass.'

We did it. I just scraped through.

The papers were sent to England for marking, so the results would not be known for months. The break-up party was a moving moment for everybody. It was held in the school assembly hall for the boys and girls of both schools and was an emotional occasion. We would all be moving on, some of us to different places in India and others to their own countries, now that the war was over.

I lost track of Turley after we said our goodbyes at school. I often wondered what had happened to him, but I heard nothing more until that meeting with William Beer at Sydney airport in 1999.

During our discussions about India, William asked me about Ootacamund.

'What was your school like? I always wondered whether you liked it.'

It had been a far remove from the family life he had led in Bangalore and he was fascinated to hear about it, just as he had listened all those years ago to my tales of my childhood in Burma. In passing, I mentioned the names of some of the students at Breeks. Peter Turley was one of them.

'I knew him!' William said, amazed. 'I met him in the missionary field in India years ago. We became friends. I had no idea that he was a friend of yours.'

'Oh, yes. But I never heard anything more about him after we left school. Where is he now?'

'I'm sorry to have to tell you, but he became ill and he passed away in India in the missionary field. His wife lives in England. When I get home I will contact her and tell her I have met up with you. She'll be very interested.'

William went on to explain that Turley's family and the Beers had been quite close. After leaving Breeks, Turley had enrolled in Madras University and had gone on to theological college. He had become a missionary.

I had known that he came from Hyderabad, the capital of Mysore, where I think his father had been in the Civil Service. Apart from that, I had never learnt anything about his family origins, although from his appearance I had always assumed he was part-Indian or Asian.

It had never occurred to me that Turley would become a missionary. He didn't seem the type somehow. He had been a pretty robust chap and if anyone had asked me where his future lay, I would have said, 'In the army'.

———————

I stayed on at Breeks Memorial for a few days after all the other boarders left, while plans for my future were being set in motion.

Then I caught a train to Madras. I was going to spend some months with a missionary who held the Chair of English Studies at Madras University.

Even before the results of my exams had come through, the professor had enrolled me in the university to begin an Arts course. He was an influential man. But I was not in the right frame of mind. After a few weeks I decided I was not prepared to continue. I said so one morning.

'Sir, I really don't think this is the right course for me. I can't focus on studying just now. My priority is to return to Burma.'

After thinking about it, he partly accepted my decision.

'You are probably right. There is no point beginning a university degree and failing it for want of concentration. However, a return to Burma is out of the question. The situation there is still chaotic. The nationalists have begun a political war with the British rulers and are impatient for independence. British and Anglo-Burmans, such as yourself, are still at risk from radical nationalists. Dreadful things have been happening.'

I was disappointed, but in my heart I knew that what he said was true, at least for the moment.

'Besides, your father would never countenance your return to Burma at this time.'

I was sent off to Bombay.

'When a passage becomes available you will travel by ship to the United Kingdom, where you will be able to link up with your father in due course.'

I knew my father was still working in Abadan but the usual pattern was for expatriates to return to England on furlough every few years. I would catch up with him sooner or later.

Bombay was less crowded than my beloved Calcutta but it did not have the same appeal.

I was met at the station by a Mr McNeil, another good friend of my father's from Burma days. He was the chief of Thomas Cook and was the person who had directed and financed all my travel in India, although I had never known this. Nor had I realised there had been any personal connection with my family.

Mr McNeil was a jovial fellow with a fondness for children. For the first time, so far as I knew, I had met a family friend who was not bound to a church.

He booked me into the Grand Hotel, on the harbour side of Bombay. The area around the dockside had been destroyed a couple of years earlier. The docks had been cluttered with ships carrying all manner of cargo bound for the war zone. A fire had started in the hold of an American freighter loaded with bombs and ammunition and the ship had blown up. Many other cargo ships had also caught on fire and exploded.

Witnesses had described the chain reaction as the worst disaster they had ever seen. More damage had been done to ships and the docks than any enemy planes could have possibly done. Thousands of Indian labourers died and one cargo of gold bullion was blown away. Days later, gold bars were turning up for miles around. The authorities issued a warning that anybody found in possession of a missing bar would be sentenced to death — a harsh penalty, but this was war-time and lives came cheap.

So here I was. The train trip from Madras had been slow and tedious, with many changes. Bombay was cleaner than Calcutta and the people appeared better off. However, there was a blandness about the place. I liked its amenities but missed the excitement and colour of the city on the opposite side of the continent.

I asked one of the hotel staff what would be a good way to spend a day.

'Perhaps you would like to take a ferry ride to the Elephanta Caves across the water. You would have a close-up view of the wrecks destroyed during the disaster.'

I thought that was a good idea, so off I went.

It was an eerie ride, skirting close to the rusting, burnt-out wrecks that had been towed out to this graveyard. But it was also exciting to see the results of one of the war's greatest disasters.

The Elephanta Caves formed part of a Hindu temple, once guarded by tigers chained to large pillars. The tigers were long gone, and in their place monkeys had taken up residence. The brazen beasts would snatch anything, given half a chance.

One day I went to see Mr McNeil.

'Would it be possible, please, to move to a smaller hotel?'

'Why, certainly, Colin, if you wish. What is the problem with the Grand?'

'Nothing at all,' I said hastily. 'It's just that it's very formal and I would like to be in the middle of the city.'

The Grand Hotel was old-fashioned and strictly regulated and was located in the dull business district. I moved to a guesthouse nearer the city centre, where most of the action took place. It was a quaint, well-run place. I liked both it and the manager, a Goanese man who was deeply religious. Many of the guests were retired British ladies and their elderly husbands. Others, who came and went, were mostly American servicemen waiting to be shipped home.

As I toured the city I was aware of the same unrest I had experienced in Calcutta. The Indians were pushing hard for self-government.

It reminded me of all the unrest in Burma just before the war. Then it had been Burmese nationalists protesting against rich Indian landlords as well as against the British colonialists. There had been some bloodshed, though I had been too young to be really aware of what was going on.

As I became acquainted with Bombay, I grew to like it more. The slower pace suited me after the madness of my last visit to Calcutta. My host directed me to the must-see places and the famous Taj Mahal Hotel was one of my favourite haunts. I loved the Indian curries served for tiffin. Across the road was one of India's famous landmarks, the Gateway. It was a huge concrete structure facing the Arabian Sea, a famous meeting place for young lovers and the elderly upper class, who strolled along the embankment.

One infamous spot I visited was the red light district of Bombay, the notorious Grant Road. It was not difficult to find; everybody knew where it was. Here the prostitutes of the city hung out. The seamy street ran for a couple of hundred yards and the dilapidated buildings housed the women in cages all along the way. On that day a lot of servicemen were haggling with the women who displayed their bodies from behind the bars. As I walked along, I wondered what lay behind the bars fronting the street. Perhaps, I thought, it was like something straight out of the Arabian Nights, where the Sultans kept their women. I never did find out.

The cricket season was in full swing and not far from the guesthouse stood the famous Brabourne Stadium, a first-class cricket oval where the game was played every weekend. I enjoyed watching some of the visiting service teams play.

On one of my first trips to the beach at Juhu, some miles from the city, I met an English WAAF officer who, like me, loved the sand and sea. She was good-looking and very friendly.

'I'm waiting to catch a ship home too,' she said. 'Why don't we link up and go sightseeing together?'

'I'd love to. Shall we meet at my guesthouse? It's very central.'

'All right. Ten o'clock tomorrow.'

So for the following few days we went sightseeing together. Despite the difference in our ages we got along well. She was like a big sister to me and said, 'It's lovely to have you around, Colin, especially since your presence deters other men from harassing me!'

Then one day she called at the guesthouse unexpectedly.

'Would you like to come for a walk to the coffee house?'

Along the way she called over a street photographer.

'Here, take a photograph of the two of us together!'

As we sat in the coffee house she said, 'Well, Colin, I'll be leaving tomorrow. I received the news last night.'

She gave me her family address somewhere in Suffolk and we said our goodbyes over a cup of coffee. She thanked me for a marvellous time and said, 'Colin, you will have many friends to see you through life. You're that type.' I felt good.

Back at the guesthouse, I shared a table for high tea with an Indian lady and her daughter. The mother was dressed in her native costume, and obviously belonged to the upper class of Bombay citizenry. She was immaculately attired and stunningly groomed. The Goanese manager introduced me, as was customary.

She was the wife of an executive of the Bombay Tramway Company, of Parsee stock, and she and her daughter were celebrating the end of the girl's schooling.

'We are awaiting news of my daughter's entrance to a university,' the mother explained.

I told them of my family background and the reason for my presence in Bombay.

'I can't believe you're Burmese,' the lady said. 'You don't look like it.'

'But I am, truly I am. My mother was Daw Ni and I was raised in Maymyo.'

I still had to convince her of my nationality. She was well educated and her knowledge of Burma was extensive. So I mentioned the names of some Parsee friends in Burma who had held positions in the commercial sector, and she was then convinced.

Before we had finished high tea, I had learnt a lot about the Parsees and their migration into India and further on into Burma. They had originated in Persia (Iran), hence their fairer complexion.

'Many chose their names in their new countries from their occupations. Hence, Merchants, Contractors, Engineers etc,' the lady told me.

We got along famously and they invited me to their home just up the road. Colaba Causeway was so named because it stretches out into the Arabian Sea. It was a busy end of the city, occupied mostly by merchants running export and import businesses.

The family lived in a unit in one of the better buildings and to my surprise it was furnished like a European home. I became a frequent visitor and the daughter and I became close friends. Her parents trusted her to go out with me whenever she pleased. She was very attractive, with long black hair and hazel eyes. She could quite easily be mistaken for a European. Her teeth too were unblemished.

Bombay thronged with troops awaiting embarkation for the trip home. The guesthouse filled with officers. Among a group of American servicemen and women was an officer from Ann Arbor in Michigan. His name was Paul Tomkin and he was a musical director who had been touring the Eastern front with the US Army. He and a well-known Hollywood actor, Melvyn Douglas, shared my table.

'What's a young fellow like you doing here, travelling alone?' they asked and were astounded to hear a brief summary of my life so far.

'You're welcome to come along with us, son. We want to make the most of our time in Bombay.'

So they included me in their tours of the city. I took along my Parsee friend. Paul was a talented pianist and, wherever there was a piano in a restaurant, he could not resist playing it. He had been in Hollywood before the war and had directed many musicals. One of them was playing in Bombay. It was titled *Anchors Away*. The four of us booked in to see it one night.

My Parsee friend was beside herself and could not get home quickly enough to tell her parents.

'You'll never guess where Colin and I are going tonight!' she told her mother in excitement.

The two Americans were addicted coffee drinkers and delighted in the famous coffee houses of Bombay.

When the time came to catch their transport home, they both gave me their addresses and said, 'Be sure to call on us if you ever visit the States.'

One day, soon after Christmas, I received a message to call Thomas Cook. I knew what to expect — a berth on a ship to the UK. My pleasurable stay in Bombay, which had lasted several weeks, was to be abruptly curtailed. I was saddened at the prospect of leaving India for another foreign country. India had become my de facto home. During my years on the sub-continent I had developed an enduring affection for the people. I shall always remember their generosity, no matter what their own circumstances were.

Mr McNeil ushered me into his office, presented me with documents and outlined the plans made for the voyage and my arrival in England.

'Your plans have been set in motion this time by your father,' he said.

If he expected me to be pleased, he must have been a little disappointed. I resented being treated as a child once again, but I returned to the guesthouse to prepare to board the ship the next day.

After dinner, I went to say goodbye to my Parsee friends. They appeared happy for me. The mother said, 'You will be thrilled to meet relatives whom you have never seen, and a whole new life will begin.'

Her words made me recall the old monk in the Buddhist monastery in Maymyo talking about rebirth.

'A good previous life gives one a better life on rebirth,' he had said.

I began to wonder if I had been let down in my previous life.

My Parsee friends came to see me board the ship, the P&O liner, the *Strathmore*. It was about 28,000 tons. On board I was introduced to my chaperone. She was an entertainer who had been touring the front lines keeping up the spirits of the Allied troops. I was struck by her delightful smile.

'Don't worry, Mr McNeil. I will take good care of him,' she promised, and she smiled at me warmly. I soon felt more at ease. She showed me to my cabin.

'I'll leave you here for now,' she said. 'Enjoy the trip and don't do anything silly! If you need me, you know where to find me.'

She gave me a free hand and I appreciated her consideration. When the ship stopped at the southern end of the Suez Canal she came to find me.

'Would you like to join our group on an overland drive to see the pyramids and catch the ship at Port Said?' she asked.

'I'd love to,' I said.

I had a lovely time. Everyone in her group was very kind to me. To this day, I don't know how or why she became my chaperone.

Voyages can be fun. They can also be boring if you are alone, but when I was not involved in deck sports, I was happy to sit in a deck chair and ponder.

I knew very little about life in England. One certainty was that it would not be as warm as the tropics. I spent hours filling my mind's screen with the events of the last four years. It had been a life of adventure, of getting to know people and enjoying their cultures and traditions. There had been moments when I had been desperately sad and grief-stricken. Yet the good times had leavened the moments when I slipped into sorrow.

I had a lot of time to think, especially when the ship was sailing up the Mediterranean Sea. The weather was warm and the sea calm, just the way I liked it. Every day took me further away from Burma and I began to accept it, although I was still determined to return one day.

My stay at the hospital in Tinsukia had almost faded from my mind. The improvement in my health when I left the hospital at Digboi, however, was still fresh in my memory. It had probably been the turning point on my road to recovery. Lying back on my deck chair, I thought about the people who had contributed to my convalescence. There were also those who had helped me through my adolescence, particularly the boys and girls who had accepted me as their friend. Above all, there was India, which had embraced me.

I knew I had been lucky in many respects. I had travelled far and wide, from Assam in the east right across the sub-continent to Bombay, and from towns like Darjeeling and Simla in the Himalayas up north down to Ootacamund in the far south. It had been a lifetime's experience crammed into a few short years. I had met some outstanding people. Each and every one of them had had something to teach me.

III

EAST TO WEST

Chapter 24

FATHER'S LAND

The ship entered the Bay of Biscay on its final run to the port of Liverpool. It was late January 1947, and I, at 16, was confronted with a new chapter in my life. The skies turned grey and the little I knew of England signalled that this was going to be an entirely new experience. On the final night I thanked my chaperone sincerely.

'Remember to call on me if ever you need to,' she said kindly, and gave me her home address.

The dining room was only half full for breakfast in the morning. Passengers were too busy gathering their possessions, I supposed, to worry about food. I decided to walk outside to get my first look at this new country. I went up to the promenade deck, opened the heavy door and stepped out on to inches of snow. I had never touched snow before; I had only seen it on the distant Himalayas. I felt frozen, but stood my ground and looked beyond at the buildings also covered in a carpet of white, with a backdrop of dull grey skies. I wished I could stay aboard and return to a place where the sun shone in mid-morning. I could not believe anybody could call such a depressing place 'home'.

I trudged off the ship with my worldly possessions in one small suitcase and followed the other passengers to the terminal building. I began to wonder where all the locals were. I had been used to milling hordes in India and here

I was, in a fairly heavily populated city, and very few people were about. I supposed the weather had something to do with it. Who in their right mind would venture out in such atrocious conditions? It was slightly warmer inside the building, and orderly queues formed. Customs officers had already begun searching the luggage; it was a slow and tedious process and, for some, very embarrassing.

One passenger ahead of me seemed to be having great trouble. I gathered that he was none too pleased with the Customs officer. There appeared to be a mountain of clothes on the table and among them some bottles of liquor. Suddenly the passenger gathered the bottles, walked out on to the wharf and emptied the contents into the water. All eyes were trained on the poor fellow. I glanced at his large trunk and noticed a yellow stain on the garments.

When my turn came, the Customs officer nodded his head at the departing passenger and said, 'The gent packed a jar of mango pickle in his trunk, and the lid worked loose. It spread right through his luggage!'

The officer was very sympathetic to me.

'I doubt whether you'd be carrying any contraband,' he said in a friendly voice.

He must have believed I was too poor to own anything but my few clothes. He smiled and I was quite taken aback by the greeting. I could not believe anybody could find anything to smile about in this frigid climate. We talked for a while and he mentioned again the poor fellow in front of me.

'I've encountered many of his type before in my job,' he said confidentially. 'They come home, and because they have had servants in the colonies, they think they can order us about. We bring them down to earth with a bang.'

He wished me good luck.

I walked out onto the street into an adjoining railway station. I knew I had to catch a train to Manchester, but how and when, I had no clue. I walked around gaping and a friendly wharfie stopped me.

'Are you lost?' he asked.

I told him I was trying to find where to catch the train to Manchester.

'Further down the street,' he said. 'You can't miss 'em.'

On the platform I discovered the timetable and looked for a phone booth. I had the number of a family friend, a Mr Morrison, who had offered to take care of me for a while. I read the instructions and as I pressed the button for the connection, out poured a stream of coins. They fell and rolled around my feet and the noise drew the attention of passers-by. I bent down and sheepishly picked up some of the coins. I was embarrassed, but a friendly old lady helped me scoop them up and told me not to worry.

'It happens when the box gets filled,' she said.

I pushed what I could back into the slot and went to another booth. I arrived at Manchester late in the evening, cold and hungry. There did not seem to be anywhere to get a meal. I sat on a bench and waited. Mr Morrison arrived shortly afterwards and welcomed me warmly.

'I do apologise for the terrible weather,' he said. 'It is the worst winter in years and the transport system is in chaos.'

We had to travel a few miles out of Manchester to the suburb of Denton. Along the way I saw machines clearing roadways, the snow banked high on either side. It was a slow journey and when we arrived at the right stop we stepped off the bus into deep snow to walk the few yards to his house. My feet were frozen. I wished somebody in India had forewarned me of the European winter.

I was introduced to Mrs Morrison and their daughter. She was about my age and was in her final year at school.

'Come in, Colin, and stand by the fire. You'll soon get warm.'

I stood by the coal-burning fireplace and, as my body began to thaw, I ached all over.

'Would you like a cup of tea and something to eat?'

Despite the fact that it was hours since I had eaten, I was by now too exhausted and depressed to cope with the thought.

'No, thank you. Might I be taken to my room?' I asked.

Their home was a terrace house and my bedroom was upstairs. The room was like an ice-box and I hurried into bed.

Mrs Morrison had said, 'You'll find a hot-water bottle between the sheets.'

I had had no idea what she was talking about. I felt under the covers and found a warm, hard pottery bottle. I had never experienced anything like this. Bed warming, where I came from, was unheard of. I laid the bottle on the floor, found a warm spot to put my feet on and lay back. I had spent less than 24 hours in the country, and I had hated every moment of it. I knew I could never love it.

I was a stranger in a strange place and I lay in bed and cried. It was still dark when I awoke, and I peered out of the small window. The glass was frosted over and there was a greyness, something jail-like, about the limited view. Even today, when anyone talks of England, that image springs to my mind.

Mr Morrison had confirmed that my father was back in Abadan as an employee of the Anglo–Iranian Oil Company, which was part of the Shell conglomerate.

'He is not due for another stint of furlough for quite some time. When you have settled in, you will need to start thinking about what you want to do here in England. Your father did not leave any instructions.'

After a few weeks Mr Morrison invited me to lunch at a restaurant in the city.

'Meat is still rationed in England, so you will have to bring your ration card,' he said.

The card had been issued on my arrival. At this point I suddenly realised what a hard time the English had been forced to endure during the war. We queued for our lunch.

'Have you made any plans yet for the future?' Mr Morrison asked, as we got down to eating the tiny morsel of meat and a few boiled vegetables.

I could see I should have something mapped out, but I didn't know what. So I said quickly, 'I would like to visit my Scottish relatives, if that could be arranged.'

Privately, I made up my mind that, from now on, I would be the person who would make the decisions about my life.

Mr Morrison's body language indicated that he was pleased with my choice.

'I have no qualms whatsoever about your ability to get around the country on your own,' he said with a smile. 'Despite what you have been through, Colin, you have handled the big step into manhood well.'

I felt good. Then I wondered how anybody else, in the same situation, would have handled the task of living.

So I said goodbye to the Morrisons and caught the train to Glasgow. There was not much to see, save acres of land covered in snow. I spent the night in a cheap hotel in the city and the next day found my father's relatives.

They lived in Bishopbriggs, some miles out of the city. I arrived to an unexpectedly warm and teary welcome. My two female cousins, who were years older than I, were thrilled.

'We're so happy to meet you! It's wonderful that you could come,' they said, wiping their eyes.

I bonded with them immediately. My uncle, their father, was a delightful Scot. He was short and spoke with a broad Glasgow accent. The first thing he said was, 'I thought I would see a wee black boy!'

We all laughed. My aunt, to whom I was also introduced, had recently suffered a stroke. As she sat motionless in her chair, I detected a tiny smile. I kissed her and tears formed in her eyes too.

'We told her about you and she was overjoyed with the news that you would be visiting us,' one of my cousins explained.

My father, it seemed, had been her favourite brother, but it appeared that they had fallen out. Nobody seemed to be prepared to talk about why. It wasn't until years later that I discovered she had taken a dim view of how he had conducted himself in relation to his family.

My cousins, the Mackies, were devout Christians like my father and also belonged to the Plymouth Brethren, but they were more broad-minded than he. They took me on tours of their favourite Scottish places. I toured the engineering works where my father had started his apprenticeship and the shipyard on the Clyde where my uncle worked as a boilermaker. There he showed me first-hand the birth of an ocean liner.

There was hardly a moment when I had time to think about myself or the years since we had set out on that fateful walk. I loved the friendliness of the Scottish people, but I thought they had a lot to learn about good food. Perhaps, I thought naively, it was the restricted rations.

I stayed with my cousins on and off for more than a year. During that time my uncle retired from the shipyard and the younger of my cousins married a man from the church. He was a salesman for the Caledonian Oat Cake Company, a Scottish institution that made biscuits. He was a go-getter and wasted no time in talking the family into buying a guesthouse in the English town of Ilfracombe, in the county of Devon. I travelled down with the couple to inspect the property, a well-established business in a popular seaside resort.

The whole family moved down to Devon some months later, and I went along to help. They knew little about the hospitality business, but they worked hard and provided a good service. The girls did all the cooking, serving and housework for 20 guests; their father too lent a hand. But my cousin's husband took life easily.

'My job,' he always said, 'is to look after the finances.'

My invalid aunt's health deteriorated with the move, and she passed away. It was the first time since losing my mother, brother and sister that a close family member had died. I was saddened, because I felt she would have given me the love that I had craved since the loss of my own mother.

Once again I wanted to run away from the grief and sadness that death brings. I made plans to move on.

I applied for a place in a forestry college at Glenmore in Argyllshire. I was accepted and off I went back to Scotland, alone again. What had prompted me to enrol in the three-year course was the dream that I could one day apply for a job in a timber company with interests in Burma. I joined 15 other new students at the hostel in a tiny village, Kilmun, on the shores of the Holy Loch in the west of Scotland. The nearest town was Dunoon, an hour away.

The move did not turn out as I had hoped. I certainly met some great Scottish characters and made good friends among the kindly locals and the other students, including a madcap from Rhodesia who first put the idea into my mind of emigrating. I even fell in love for a while with a Scottish girl whose father was a ship designer. But the forestry training was not what I had been led to believe it would be. Instead of receiving an education, we were used for the most part as labouring fodder. I stayed for a year, but could see it was getting me nowhere.

During my year in Scotland I met Donald again. He took a job with the Scottish Forestry Commission, and for a while we worked near one another.

Donald had gone back to Burma after the war with his wife and, by then, two children, his son Robert whom I had seen as a baby in Madras, and his daughter Bettine, who was born in 1947 in Burma. Bettine was named after her mother's sister who had perished in the internment camp at Myitkyina. Her second name is Ethel, after our own sister. Robert now lives in Canada, while Bettine lives in Melbourne. My children and I are all exceedingly fond of Bettine and her family.

According to Donald's record of events, the marriage had become rocky and he had come to Britain in the hope that Pamela and the children would all join him to start a new life as soon as he found the money for their fares. Unfortunately, the marriage did not last, but eventually the children did come to live with him in England, as he had custody of them and their mother had moved on.

His main memory of me during that time in Scotland is my continuing obsession with finding out what had happened to our mother.

As soon as I had made the decision to leave forestry college, I packed my few belongings and set off for England. It took me months to make my way back to London. I gave into my gypsy spirit and pottered all over the country, stopping in any place that took my fancy, doing odd jobs here and there, and meeting good people wherever I travelled. It was easy to lose track of time in such a rootless existence. The experience almost had me convinced that England, after all, was not such a bad place.

It could not last. After a stint in Kent, I found a room in a cheap guesthouse in London's Russell Square. It was all I could afford and the tiny room and sparse fittings depressed me.

I had heard a lot about the Madame Tussaud waxworks gallery, and one day I decided to go there. It was a quiet day and very few people were about. I walked down into the Chamber of Horrors and stood before the figure of one of England's most notorious murderers. A young woman came up and struck up a conversation. We chatted for a while and decided to go for a walk.

'What are you doing in London?' I asked.

'Well, as a matter of fact, I am working as a prostitute,' she said candidly, giving me a sideways glance to see how I reacted. 'I use the art galleries to pick up clients.'

I was momentarily lost for words. She seemed to be a decent person, well dressed and well spoken. I conjured up visions of my new-found friend displaying herself with the other girls in Grant Street, the brothel strip in Bombay.

'I come from the Midlands,' she explained as we walked along. 'I moved down to the big city with my boyfriend, but he ditched me. I couldn't go home. My father would have killed me. In the end, this was the only way I could survive.'

She was a nice person and we became friends. Whenever she made a pick-up she would joke, 'I have to make some money to pay the rent. If I relied on you, I would be thrown out of my digs!'

After a good week, we often took a train into the country. We liked the pubs in Kent best. Then, one day, she made an announcement.

'I've decided that I'm going across to the Continent.' she said. 'The work will be better over there.'

I too had been thinking it was time to move on. That night I returned to my room, had a quick wash, lay down and fell asleep.

I was awakened by loud banging on my door and jumped up, to see a distressed old lady in the corridor.

'There's water seeping through my ceiling under your room! Something's leaking!'

After I shut the door I discovered that my washbasin was overflowing. I had left the plug in and had not turned off the tap.

At breakfast I confessed my wrongdoing to the landlady, a generous Londoner.

'I'm dreadfully sorry,' I said. 'I'll make sure it won't happen again.'

'I'm sorry, but I'm going to have to ask you to leave.'

'I understand,' I said, but I had reached the end of the road. The mishap and the parlous state of my finances made me realise that I had little choice but to eat humble pie and seek help from my father's associates.

Chapter 25

MY FATHER'S OTHER LIFE

My father was an executive with one of the Shell oil companies and I figured that somebody at their head office would tell me whether he was still in Persia. It was quite possible that he had returned to England. He wouldn't have known my whereabouts, because I had deliberately dropped out of sight.

It was mid-afternoon when I walked into the offices.

'My name is Colin McPhedran,' I said. 'My father is Archibald McPhedran, and I understand he holds a position in your company. I wonder if you know of his whereabouts?'

'Please wait here,' I was told.

A man presently arrived.

'Your father is in London,' he said. 'He is not at the office today, but he will be here tomorrow.'

He gave me an address in the north London suburb of Neasden.

'You will have no difficulty locating the house,' he said.

Great, I thought. If I was in India, he would have delighted in personally escorting me to the address.

It was dark and cold when I left to catch the train. By now it was late autumn. I arrived at the street and made enquiries. I drew a blank on every occasion until I spoke to a milkman, who pointed to a house.

'There are new people in that house, foreigners,' he said.

I hadn't a clue what he was talking about.

'It can't be the right place, because my father is no foreigner,' I said. He shrugged and went back to his deliveries.

I walked up to the door anyway, and knocked. A small woman opened the door and I knew I was at the right address. She was Burmese. She looked at me quizzically, saying, 'Yes?'

In Burmese, I said, 'I have come to see Mr McPhedran.'

She invited me in and called out to my father. It was an emotional meeting. He enveloped me tightly in a big bear hug. It was the only time I can remember his hugging me.

'Ah! Here you are, lad. The last I heard, you were in Scotland! Donald said you left and he hadn't heard anything since. Where have you been?'

'Oh, just here, there and everywhere. I only found out you were here yesterday.'

My father was never known to display his emotions, but he was obviously happy to see me once again. He sat me down in the sitting room and asked the Burmese lady to make some tea.

'You've grown a lot since India. Where are you staying?'

Many thoughts went through my mind. I wondered why he had brought a servant woman from Burma to keep house. I thought he must have grown used to having servants in Burma, and was continuing the lifestyle. But then he said something that shocked me:

'Colin, I'd like you to meet your brothers and sisters.'

My immediate reply was, 'But my family died on the trek out of Burma!'

He then said to the lady, 'Please call the children down from their rooms.'

Two girls and two boys entered.

My father said, 'Meet your new family — Eddie, Mary, George and Daisy. Children, this is your brother, Colin.'

I had barely recovered from the shock when he gestured towards the Burmese lady and said, 'Ma Taw Tin May is my wife and the mother of these four.'

My initial reaction was not anger but thudding disappointment. I made quick mental calculations and realised he must have fathered these children while still married to my mother.

We began to talk. The four were a fine bunch and well behaved. Eddie, born in 1936, was six years younger than me. Next came Mary, born in 1938, George, born in 1940, and Daisy in 1941.

They had arrived in England quite some time ago, and were already settled in schools, as my father had bought the house in Neasden after he arrived.

We chatted for a long time and I realised that they knew a great deal about my family. Mary confided, 'I've always wanted to meet you.'

They seemed well informed about my mother. While my father was out of the room, Mary said, 'In Burma, your mother was held in high regard.'

She mentioned my mother's relationship to the Prime Minister of Burma, Dr Ba Maw.

'I even heard it said that your mother had guided the doctor before he became Prime Minister.'

I felt a glow of pride, even though I knew my mother had had her doubts about Uncle Ba Maw. I had always believed that she was a great person, a compassionate soul who cared not only for her family but for every living person, and it was wonderful to hear her praised after all these years.

My father had his wife prepare a bed for me for the night. I resisted initially, but my new-found brothers and sisters pleaded.

'You can't go. We've only just met you.'

Somehow, I was talked into moving in with the family.

Weeks went by and, despite the extraordinary circumstances, I grew to love my brothers and sisters. I also grew very fond of their mother, who, I know, loved me as her own. She was a gentle woman and seemed out of place in this cold, sunless country. We talked a lot while my father was at work and I enjoyed the shopping trips for the groceries. We communicated in Burmese and other customers would look at us strangely as we chatted away. Whenever the opportunity arose, she would invite me into the boiler room to share a cigarette.

––––––––––

I discovered years later from Donald in Canada that he had known for years about my father's second family. He had found out not long before Burma was invaded. This is how he described what must have been a terrible burden of knowledge for a young man of his age.

After my first year in college a few drastic changes took place in my family's life. I became aware that my father had acquired a second family and that it consisted of two boys and two girls. This was most disconcerting to me ...

My mother had done an excellent job of concealing the facts from us. When she did disclose the facts to me, I was so incensed that I wrote my father a stinking letter. This was a very bitter pill that I and my siblings had now to swallow and out of righteous indignation, combined with the confidence of a person on the threshold of young manhood, I wrote to my father letting him know exactly how I felt, and predictably, he wrote back to say, in no uncertain terms, that I had better mind my own business and that what he expected of me was complete obedience and no criticism.

Since he was the fount from whom would flow the wherewithal to continue my higher education, I did, with the pleadings of my mother, acquiesce and behaved as a 'dutiful son' should. These days it would not be unheard of to hear a person wonder why I had not stuck to my guns and weathered the storm, come what may. Regrettably, I was not equipped to do otherwise. One must try to understand that we were reared in the lap of luxury and we were sheltered from any extraneous influences that may have tended to harm us…

When my mother was having her problems with my father, she was not without relatives who made it quite clear to her that she could expect their entire support and that this was not just lip-service. My mother, I am very glad to say, only replied that she was not about to disgrace the father of her children by any legal action that would eventually reach our ears. She was happy to be with us and enjoy, with a feeling of satisfaction and pride, our flowering into manhood and womanhood.

Sadly, she was deprived of this because my father took my siblings away from her and had them enrolled in schools in Rangoon, miles away from her. None of them were happy with the move and when I visited Bobby and Colin at St Paul's School in Rangoon, the change that had come over them was patently obvious. I carried a heavy heart within me from then on and when I went up to Maymyo during a college break, I saw the abject misery and heartrending descent into the depths of loneliness that this deprivation of the company of her children had left my mother.

When Burma was brought face to face with war by the Japanese, all the schools were closed and my father, not being able to have my brothers and sister with him in Syriam, sent them to Maymyo to my mother. In retrospect, although it would seem quite unlikely to be called a blessing by anyone who was affected by the war, it actually was, to my mother. It enabled her to have her children with her, albeit for a very short time. Nevertheless she did have us with her and to her that was all that mattered.

In many ways my father's second wife was similar to my mother, even though they came from completely different walks of life. She was a typical Burmese woman, a caring person who was willing to share one's burdens and joys. We talked about her own people and how she missed the warm weather and the family gatherings that are part of Burmese life.

'When we were still in Burma I tried to find out more about your mother,' she confided one day.

Although she had never met my relations she knew of their backgrounds, their social positions and their connections with the University of Rangoon.

Perhaps surprisingly, the whole family got along famously, but I was concerned that the children were not encouraged to get out and about. Their social life was sadly lacking. I got around as much as I could, catching up with friends from Burma who had arrived in England.

Among them was the Van Bock family, who were also Eurasians. Diane, one of the daughters, was my age and I became sweet on her. They lived on the other side of London in Ealing. I was invariably late home from my visits and my father took to staying up until I arrived, sometimes at 2 o'clock in the morning.

'You should not be associating with a Roman Catholic family. They are not in our class.'

'What do you mean by that?' I asked. 'They are very nice people.'

It was becoming obvious to me that I needed a break. One day I was glancing through a newspaper.

'Oh, look, here's an advertisement for a seasonal assistant on a farm in Devon. I've a mind to apply for it.'

My father seemed rather disappointed, but said, 'It's a pretty part of the country and it will keep you busy.'

I wrote away and was accepted, to begin work immediately.

My stepmother was unhappy that I was leaving, but I had made up my mind. I hopped on a train and was met by my new employer at Holsworthy.

The farmer, a retired officer of the Royal Navy, owned a small-holding a few miles out of town. The farmhouse was a delightful old place, rather like a manor. I spent the best part of eight months there and learned a lot about dairy farming. When the work finished I headed back to London.

'Well, Colin,' my father said. 'You've been working hard at the farm. How would you like a holiday in Glasgow?'

I was always open to suggestions of travel, and said so.

'I would very much like you to visit a friend of mine who owns a guesthouse in Kelvingrove, which is one of the better suburbs,' he went on. 'Mrs Millar's guesthouse is a well-run establishment where the clients are mostly businessmen seeking a short break.'

Off I went.

Mrs Millar was a lovely person, very attractive and rather refined, not in the line of the usual proprietresses of the day. She had a daughter my age who was given the duty of showing me the sights of Glasgow. I was treated royally. Glasgow in those days was a centre of live shows and boasted many theatres.

We were beginning to become rather amorous when a fleeting thought went through my mind. I began to wonder about my father and his friendships with women. I remembered Miss Coutts in Kalimpong, and he often mentioned other ladies.

I took a good close look at the Millar girl. She had dark hair and light brown eyes; she bore a striking resemblance to my Scottish cousins. There had never been any mention of Mrs Millar's husband, so I began to conjure up all sorts of connections. Could she be another half-sister? I was probably way off the mark; nonetheless it put a damper on our brief relationship.

I returned to London. Father, who now seemed eager to have me around, said one day, 'There is an opportunity for you to join the oil company as a filing clerk.'

It was a fancy title for a messenger boy, but I did not mind. It was a job and a source of income. My stepmother was delighted to have me back and we carried on where we had left off.

However, after some months the novelty wore off. The nine-to-five routine was not for me. One morning, I had to take a document up to my father's office. I had never had the privilege of climbing the stairs to his office before. I entered and walked over to his desk. There were two men with him and, rather than hang about, I handed him the papers and said, rather innocently, 'Is this what you wanted, Pop?'

He looked at me through his horn-rimmed spectacles.

'Are you aware of office protocol?' he asked.

'I don't know what you are talking about,' I said.

'Well, protocol demands that you address me as "Sir".'

I looked down at him and said, 'What are you talking about? You're my father!'

I walked out of the room. One of his staff followed me down the stairs and, stopping me at my desk, repeated what my father had just said.

'You must call Mr McPhedran "Sir" whether he is your father or not.'

'I'm not in the mood to take this rubbish,' I told him.

'You had better think about changing your ways,' he muttered, but I had had enough.

'Please instruct the paymaster to have my wages made up until 5 pm today,' I said.

He mumbled something further, about informing my father.

'Don't worry, I shall tell him myself when he gets home tonight.'

I wandered out into the streets of London. It was my lunch break. It was a dreary day, and cold, and I looked for a tea-house. As I walked along, anger welled up and I wished I could get out of this country.

I stopped before a shop window that had on display a model of a passenger liner. Always interested in ships, I studied the name *Largs Bay* on the bow. I walked into the shop and approached a young lady at the long desk.

She was pretty and, in an Australian accent, said, 'Can I help you?'

'Thank you. Is this a travel agency?'

'Yes, a travel agency and a trading house,' she said cheerfully.

I looked at the wall behind the counter and saw the name Dalgety and Company (Australia).

'How much is the fare to Australia?'

'British migrants are going out on a £5 fare and other visitors have to pay £75,' she said.

'That will be fine. When can I get a berth?'

She laughed. 'Maybe in five years if you're lucky!'

'But I am prepared to pay the full fare,' I repeated. She laughed again.

'It makes no difference,' she said. 'All the ships to Australia are booked out. But I will put your name on the waiting list if you like.'

'No, thanks,' I said. Five years was a long time.

Out of the blue, I said, 'I wonder whether you would have dinner with me this evening?'

She hesitated for a moment, then said, 'Yes!'

I collected her after work and we walked to a Lyons Cafe. Over the meal I told her of my circumstances at the office and I learnt that she had only recently arrived.

'I'm already missing the warm weather. It's summer at home and I'd be at the beach instead of freezing here in London. Have you heard of Bondi Beach? It's beautiful.'

She raved about the country and the prospects. My mind was filled with vivid images of a happy, sunny place full of cheery people just like her. I made up my mind to get there one day. Just before she left, she asked for my address and phone number.

'If anything crops up during the next 12 months, I'll get in touch with you,' she said.

'I appreciate your gesture,' I said. 'And I hope to see you again.'

The following day a message was left at our house.

'Would Mr McPhedran please call into the office of Dalgety and Company as soon as possible.'

It was midday when I walked in, to be greeted by my new-found Australian friend. First, she gave me the sad news that an Australian booked to return home had passed away.

Then she said, 'You can have his berth if you can find the fare and a permit from the Australian authorities.'

I was overjoyed.

'Thank you! It's very kind of you. I'd love to go. Please get the papers in order. I'll be back before the end of the day,' I said.

I hurried down to my father's office and was shown in.

'Father, I have secured a berth on a ship to Australia, leaving tomorrow. The only drawback is money. Would you lend me £100?'

He stalled for a moment and began to preach about going out into the world and getting caught up with the wrong types.

'Father, I have travelled around half the world without falling victim to the work of the devil.'

'I visited Australia in 1939 and found nothing attractive about the place whatsoever. The Australians are a lot of gamblers with the curse of the evil drink. Why don't you go to Canada?'

'Canada's too cold. Australia sounds good. Who knows, I might even contribute to a change in their ways!'

He was in no mood for fun, but he did produce a cheque for £100 and said dourly, 'Well, lad, I hope you're doing the right thing by yourself and the family.'

I rushed off to the Inland Revenue Bureau for a tax clearance.

The next stop was Australia House to apply for an entry permit. The man there was most helpful.

'Australia is a wonderful country and it is full of opportunities for people who are prepared to work hard,' he said. He studied my passport.

'I see you were born in Rangoon, in Burma. What is your nationality?'

'My mother was Burmese and my father is a Scot.'

'Oh! You don't look like a Eurasian,' he said.

He went on to tell me of the country's White Australia Policy. I was not concerned. All I wanted was to get out of this cold, dreary place. I had visions of golden beaches and warm seas.

With all my documents in place I walked down to Dalgety's, paid my fare and again thanked the young woman.

'I'll see you in Sydney,' I told her.

Back home, I packed my small suitcase and waited for my father to return home from work for a further lecture.

Unbeknownst to me, he had invited a woman friend for dinner. I had hoped to spend a a quiet evening with the family. Instead, I was subjected to a lot of questioning about my sudden decision.

The evening got off to a bad start, even though the woman had brought an expensive bottle of champagne and presented me with the cork to remind me of my last dinner.

'Where is your wife?' I asked my father. 'Shouldn't she be at the table with us?'

'She is busy in the kitchen,' was all he would say. I was furious. How dare he bring a girlfriend home and flaunt her like this?

My father kept on about my move to Australia.

'The Australians are a bunch of heathens, penal settlers without a spiritual base. You will find it a friendless country.'

I could hardly believe what I was hearing. As soon as his guest left I said, 'Speaking of Christianity, having another woman over for dinner while your wife acts as a servant is hardly a Christian thing to do.'

He did not respond.

Before he retired for the night, however, he said, 'I will accompany you to Southampton tomorrow.'

I joined my stepmother in the kitchen. We walked out into the cold night, lit our cigarettes and talked about many things. She talked about the years the family had spent at their farm in Syriam during the Japanese occupation of Burma.

Unlike many people, they had fared reasonably well, although food had been scarce.

'As you can see, the children all look very Burmese and so the Japanese left us more or less alone,' she said.

After the war ended, my father had returned to Burma and had brought them to Britain.

'I wish your mother had decided to stay in Burma rather than face the long trek,' she added. I believe she was genuinely sad at the loss of my family.

Going back into the house, we had a long talk with her children about my imminent departure. I was desperately sad about leaving them to such a stern person as our father.

'Your presence has been appreciated by all of us,' my stepmother said.

I was gratified, but once again I was beginning to feel guilty about walking away from people I had grown to love.

Chapter 26
BOUND FOR BOTANY BAY

I said goodbye to my step-family and boarded the train with my father for the short journey to Southampton. We did not have much to say along the route, but I realised he was sad that I was leaving, despite our poor relationship.

It is only a hop, step and a jump from London to Southampton but I felt as if we had been in the train for hours. My father, like all British travellers, had his head buried in the newspaper while I gazed out and took in the scenery of a country in which, I suddenly realised, I had lived about as long as I had lived in India. I vowed I would never return. Hopes flashed through my mind of a brighter future in a sun-drenched country. Then I thought of my step-family left behind in London and a pang went through me.

I was concerned for my stepmother. She was a gentle Burmese woman who had been taken away from her country into a world for which she was not prepared and which she did not like. I never blamed her for the strange family set-up in which we had found ourselves, due to my father's double life. I never discovered what my father had told her about his first family. Perhaps she thought he had divorced my mother. I could not bear to distress this gentle woman by asking brutal questions; better to let things lie. Nothing was going to change the past.

I thought of my half-brothers and sisters and wondered how they would fare under the authoritarian stewardship of the man beside me in the train. At the same time, I took comfort from knowing my father would have some companionship with his second family.

The train pulled into the city. It was a short distance to the dockside.

My love for ships went back a long way and I was overawed with the tonnage at anchor and dockside in Southampton. There were ships from all around the world. My father pointed to a small vessel and said, 'There is your home for the next month or so.'

No fancy liner for me! We walked up the gangway and joined a few passengers who were also saying their farewells. We hugged one another and we both cried.

His last remarks were, 'Colin, if you ever feel you want to return to England, cable me and I shall forward the fare.'

He retired to the first deck of the terminal building and waited until the ship pulled out. The last I saw of him was a solitary figure, dressed in his customary overcoat, felt hat and tartan scarf, waving an arm as we moved off slowly.

I was desperately saddened. I wondered if I could have handled things differently. Perhaps I had interpreted his feelings towards me wrongly. Maybe he did love me deeply. Perhaps his way of showing his love for me was to provide generously and let me have a free hand to move about like an unfettered spirit.

Many years later my half-sister Mary told me what I wanted to hear. It was during one of the many moments when I was being critical and judgmental of our father.

She said, 'Colin, you should not speak like that about your father.'

She went on to tell me that, after I set sail for Australia, he had spoken a lot about me.

'He always told the family he was confident you would get along fine in Australia.'

She also said that, following my trek out of Burma and the loss of my family, he had gone to extraordinary lengths to find out more about the refugee trail through the Hukawng Valley. Apparently he had been told of the huge death toll and the conditions endured by those who had survived.

'He appreciated that you had been to hell and back. He never tired of telling his friends that one member of his family had survived a walk where thousands had died.'

It was in this context that he apparently expressed his belief that I would get along fine in Australia.

'He constantly referred to the fact that you had asked nothing of him save the £100 for your fare.'

In his later years, he had told the other members of the family that he admired me for speaking out for what I thought was right.

'He loved you, and he was saddened when you returned the fare from Australia. You should have learnt during those visits to the Buddhist monastery as a young boy that receiving a gift from a person creates a circumstance for that person to gain a merit in life. You should have accepted the money graciously.'

Perhaps I was unkind at times in my criticisms of him. Certainly, he provided for me. But rightly or wrongly, I had come to lay the blame for my family's death squarely at his door. I will never know the circumstances of my parents' relationship, but I am sure that my father had had the means to get us safely to India long before we were forced to undertake the trek.

Perhaps he simply did not believe the Japanese would succeed in invading Burma. Or perhaps my mother dug in her heels and insisted that she would not let the children go without her. I will never know. I have learnt to accept that whatever occurred was preordained. I gain comfort in the knowledge that those members of my family will, in the cycle of rebirth, return as better people.

Many years later, while browsing through some magazines in a doctor's surgery, I picked up a publication called *In Britain*. There on the front cover was a picture of a man in an overcoat, tartan scarf and hat, inspecting some vintage cars during the annual London to Brighton run. It was a picture of my father, taken a few months earlier.

In 1967 I received a cablegram from Barclay's in London informing me of my father's death. They had been appointed trustees of his affairs. My father had not forgotten me.

————

The ship rounded the tip of Portugal and sailed into the calmer waters of the Mediterranean Sea. Since my childhood days, I had been fascinated by ships and had once even contemplated a life aboard one of these vessels. But a sailor I was not, and the slightest pitching and rolling of the ship started me heaving. I soon linked up with other young people on board, mostly Australians returning home. I found them to be an exuberant and friendly bunch, with a love of socialising and a deep commitment to drinking the ship's bar dry.

The Mediterranean was fine and the weather was balmy. We pulled into Valetta harbour on the island of Malta. The ship dropped anchor and the passengers were ferried ashore for a visit to this famous island. Malta had sustained the heaviest of the bombing by the Germans during the war. The onslaught had forced the islanders to live underground for most of the duration. They had been awarded the George Cross for their bravery.

Malta was an uninteresting, treeless outcrop of rock. Yet the inhabitants were cheerful. We were bundled into large lifts that carried us to the top of the island and the main city centre.

I was anxious to get my land legs back and joined a group of youngsters in a game of football.

'Why don't you come with us to find a drinking hole?' chorused my new Australian friends.

'You go, I'll join you later.'

Half an hour later, sweaty, dirty and hot from the game with the local youth, I went in search of my friends. Sure enough, they were already well intoxicated. The local bartender was also in a jovial mood, not, I guessed, from any liquor he himself had consumed, but from the money he was extracting from my drunken friends. I gathered them up.

'Come on, you lot. It's time to get back to the wharf to catch the ferry back to the ship.'

Grumbling, but in good spirits, they allowed me to lead them out of the bar.

The next stop was the city of Port Said on the northern end of the Suez Canal. I passed on my knowledge of Muslim customs our party would have to observe in the port city.

'Be careful, everyone. The locals won't take kindly to people consuming liquor.'

'What are they? Miserable bastards?' They were incorrigible.

We arrived at night and went ashore to buy some artifacts of old Egypt. It was a pleasant excursion and everywhere we were besieged by hawkers. Pimps too followed us around despite the presence of some wives.

One woman in our party, the English wife of an Australian air force pilot, tried to get me to take up the offer of a particular pimp who seemed happy to pester us all night.

'Go on, Colin, I dare you.'

'No, thanks. I was reared in the East and I know all about their game,' I said. I didn't really!

Port Said was one of our better stops. Next was the ancient city of Aden, a British protectorate garrisoned by British troops.

The women were thrilled.

'Ooh! Silk and nylon stockings! Let's stock up!'

As far as I was concerned, it was a desolate place and the buildings were uniformly constructed from mud bricks. Most of the traders were Indians and I did my part in bargaining with them to get the best price for my friends. Some of the more cunning vendors tried to bribe me with a kick-back.

The journey across the Arabian Sea to our next port of call, Colombo, was along the route the ancient traders had taken and, indeed, the present traders took, back and forth to India. The weather was stifling and most of the passengers slept on deck. The night was full of the sound of the foghorn blowing constantly as we passed the Arab dhows that plied the sea. It was a miracle that we did not run down any of these craft, which had just a few kerosene lamps to identify their location.

Colombo was a fine city. There was something about it that made me feel comfortable. Again, we were ferried ashore.

'I might leave you for a while,' I told my companions. 'I'm thinking of looking up some school friends from Ootacamund.'

'Where?'

'Ootacamund. It's in India, where I went to boarding school. Their parents own tea plantations here, on the island.'

'Oh, good, we'll come too,' the Australians insisted. I was not about to take this exuberant mob along to meet some of Ceylon's most distinguished families. Abandoning the idea, since I could not bear to offend these kindly if noisy people, I suggested we visit the renowned Galle Face Hotel for afternoon tea and a swim at the private beach.

I had gathered that most Australians loved the ocean and they took up the suggestion with enthusiasm.

'Great idea. Let's go!'

Away we went in a motorcade to this magnificent hotel. The white building was strikingly beautiful and we sat on the verandah and enjoyed the view of the palm trees growing along the curve of a sandy beach.

'Would anyone like some afternoon tea?'

'Fair go, mate. Beer, anyone?'

I sat with them for a while but when they changed to spirits, I knew I was in for trouble. Some of the local gentry seemed none too pleased to have to share the verandah with my shipmates. I tried to turn their attention to food, but they would have none of it.

'We're having lunch. Liquid lunch.'

I was hungry, so I excused myself and walked down the road leading to the hotel, along which I had spotted some foodstalls on the way in. I enjoyed a feast of Indian curries at the fraction of the cost I would have paid in any restaurant.

I returned to the hotel and asked the taxi drivers to get ready to escort us back to the pier. It was dusk when I finally got my friends to join me. They grumbled about having to leave, but eventually I rounded them up.

Back on board, at dinner that night, they spoke glowingly of the fine time they had spent, on my recommendation, at one of the great hotels of the Orient. The other less adventurous passengers were very impressed with this migrant boy's knowledge of the Orient.

The next leg was the long haul across the Indian Ocean to Fremantle in Western Australia. With nothing but expanses of water to bore the passengers, entertainment had to be arranged. Deck sports were popular during the day and amateur entertainment at night. Of course there was plentiful alcohol, at very cheap prices, so my friends' priority was as always to drink the night away.

On this leg of the journey I became acquainted with a blonde Australian woman. I had seen her during the trip and she always seemed to be hanging off the arm of some male or another. Since she was some years older than myself, I never gave her much thought. Besides, the excitement of the journey and my mind focused on a new country had left little room for shipboard frolicking.

One evening when I joined my group for dinner, Madge, the wife of my Australian air force friend, took me aside.

'Colin, there's someone who wants to meet you. I've invited her to join our table tonight. Her name is Shirley. You've probably seen her around.'

Indeed, I had. She was a young blonde-haired lady, a dress designer who had completed a stint in the UK. She was attractive and knew it.

The dining room was quite luxurious and the passengers had to enter by walking down a wide stairway that was mirrored at the head of the stairs. I had noticed that Shirley always made a late entrance. This night was no exception. She walked down the stairs in style and came straight over to sit down beside me.

We went through the usual pleasantries and Ian, Madge's husband, said, 'Why don't we retire to the bar after dinner?'

Everyone nodded.

'Good idea.'

Madge, who was quite a character, whispered in my ear, 'You're set for the rest of the trip!'

I was embarrassed; nonetheless I went along with it. The long leg from the last port was becoming boring. Our group sang a bit, laughed a lot and as usual consumed a lot. I even had a drink or two of gin and lime, which I had first tasted in Calcutta the night the war had ended.

Shirley and I got on famously. She told me of life in Sydney and her parents' home in Randwick. She was travelling in a four-berth cabin and her fellow travellers came over to join our group. I noticed her speaking to a couple of her friends and thought nothing of it.

She then got up, stretched and announced, 'I need some fresh air. How about a walk on the deck, Colin?'

She led me up the stairs, along a passageway and down to her cabin.

I looked at the other bunks and said, 'We may have some visitors while we are here.'

She just looked at me and said, 'I've taken care of that. We'll be alone for some time.' I realised what she had been up to in the bar.

We entered the rather cramped cabin and I sat on the lower bunk and began a conversation. She shut the door and peeled off her dress and stood before me unclothed. I was taken aback. She had not worn any underwear beneath the stunning dress. I couldn't believe it.

Afterwards, we rejoined our friends.

Madge raised her eyebrows and commented archly, 'Something on deck must have kept you, you were such a long time.'

As the ship sailed towards Australia on that last leg, a strange feeling that I was leaving my Oriental ties to begin a new life came over me. Nothing seemed to take my fancy. Yet the uninhibited Shirley was set upon making this trip memorable for both herself and me. Certainly she did so, providing me with quite an education in the process, but on the last night before we arrived at Fremantle I summoned enough courage to tell her we should make it the final chapter of fun.

'You're right, Colin, but it's been terrific. We must catch up in Sydney. Don't forget to come and see me.'

Traditionally, the night before arriving at the ship's destination was a time for frolicking and partying. I had had no idea what to expect from my Australian friends, but I had an inkling that alcohol would flow freely and the pranksters would take over. I had grown to expect boisterous behaviour but it seemed my shipmates knew no limits. The ship was like a fairground. Litter was everywhere, tables and chairs were upturned, people danced and sang and generally carried on like a lot of hooligans.

I must admit, I was privately a little shocked, especially when I had to carry an unconscious Shirley down to her cabin. I could hear my father's censorious voice in the back of my mind. Perhaps he had been right!

At breakfast the next morning all the conversation was about the terrific night before. I reminded my table companions of their drunken behaviour.

'How on earth can you even remember anything about it?'

'Get away. It was a great night.'

'But you were so drunk!'

'Yeah, legless. It was good, though.'

They were sweet-natured people who laughed at themselves as much as at others and took my criticisms in good spirit. Shirley was not the least bit fazed.

'Who needs legs when you've got someone to carry you?'

She gave me her address and a token of the time together on board the *Moreton Bay*. It was the knickers she had worn on the last night, a skimpy pair of polka-dotted panties.

As we headed into Fremantle, however, my Australian companions were suddenly on their best behaviour. It seemed that they were determined to present sober and alert when they touched home, rather like a child who, arriving home from school covered in dirt, brushes himself down before fronting up to his parents.

Chapter 27
AUSTRALIA

$\mathcal{I}$ awoke early to find the ship inching its way up to the dock in Fremantle. Already, despite the newness of the day, it was hot. It was January 1951, in the middle of the Australian summer. On the dockside a group of men in singlets and shorts lounged around smoking cigarettes.

'Who are those fellows?'

'Oh, they're wharfies. They'll be coming aboard soon to unload the vessel.'

I was astounded.

'But they seem such a bunch of layabouts!'

'You're telling me!'

We tied up and the ship's speakers announced that we would be spending two days in harbour before setting off for Adelaide. I was thrilled. I would be visiting the main cities of my new country before I disembarked in Sydney. I planned to get a good look, knowing I might never get another chance to see them.

My RAAF friend, Ian, was as keen as ever to introduce me to the Australian culture.

'I'm going to show you all around Perth and the beaches,' he said.

We caught the train from the dockside and got out at the beachside suburb of Cottesloe. With towels borrowed from the shipping company we headed to the beach for that great Aussie experience, a surf. The sand underfoot was as hot as live coals, but that did not deter the locals from frolicking and lying about exposed to the sun.

Now, a 20 year old and in a new country, I loved every moment of it and recalled the tales told by the young Australian woman who had found me the berth on the *Moreton Bay*. If Bondi Beach is anything like this, I thought, I have made the right choice.

'Watch out for sharks,' Ian said. 'If you see a fin sticking out of the water beyond the breakers, swim like hell!'

He also put me wise to picking a rip, a dangerous current of water that often swept bathers out to sea.

It was a delightful way to spend a hot summer's day. We retreated to a kiosk nearby and Ian introduced me to the other Aussie favourites — a pie, a lamington and a milkshake.

'Great national food, mate.'

We boarded the train for Perth. I liked the city. There were no high-rise buildings. If anything, it looked like a large provincial town. True to form, our little group ended up in one of the city's pubs.

'Geez, it's good to drink local brew,' they said.

'But surely, beer is beer. I think you chaps would enjoy any fluid that resembled it, no matter where it originated.'

'Give us a break, McPhedran. It's holy water, mate.'

The following day I kept more or less to myself and wandered about the Port of Fremantle. There was not much to see. The buildings resembled large sheds and most of them were piled high with bales of wool.

Back on board, I chatted to a group of wharfies who seemed quite relaxed, unloading cargo. Occasionally, a box would fall in the ship's hold and the contents would scatter. The wharfies were none too shy in helping themselves to an odd tin of biscuits or a bottle of spirits.

I loved Adelaide. Once again we berthed with temperatures over the century. A middle-aged couple, who had travelled from England, were due to disembark there. They were well-to-do and had sometimes chatted to me about their sheep property out in the Adelaide hills.

One day, the man had asked me what my plans were on arrival.

'My wife and I have noticed that you're a non-drinker. You seem bent on keeping your friends sober. Now there's a task!'

We laughed.

'Not all Australians carry on the way these fellows do,' he had said. I had been relieved to hear it.

When we docked in Adelaide he sought me out to say goodbye and handed me his address.

'I'd be happy to give you a job if ever you choose life on a farm,' he said.

'Thank you very much, sir. I'll keep it in mind.'

The ship stayed in Adelaide for two days. We mustered a cricket team and challenged the mostly Irish crew to a match on one of the public ovals. We scrounged around for a set of cricket gear and had a great day on a bitumen wicket. The heat of the day had almost melted the surface and every time a ball was bowled, it almost remained embedded in the tar.

The stop in Melbourne was a memorable one. As soon as the ship docked at Port Phillip I was singled out by some news reporters as one of a handful of new arrivals for an interview. My Australian friends insisted on getting in on the act.

'He's our protege. We'll screen your questions.'

The young reporter, I could see, was a bit embarrassed by their boisterous intrusion but continued to ask me a few questions.

'Can you tell me about your first impressions of Australia?'

'I haven't yet had the opportunity to see much of this beautiful land.'

I added that if this mob alongside me was any indication, what my father had warned me of the people was spot-on.

'That is, that most Australians indulge heavily in alcohol, gamble a lot and don't care two hoots for anybody in authority,' I said.

The young fellow kept writing.

'Ask him what he thinks about Australian women,' Madge said knowingly. 'He's already had an intimate relationship with an Australian blonde!'

I managed to brush that aside and went on to tell the newsman, 'I'm arriving in this country with nothing to offer but myself. I'll take up the first job offer that comes my way!'

'What brings you to Australia?'

'Oh, I just got the opportunity to get a berth on the ship,' I said, hoping he wouldn't ask about the war.

A few snapshots and away he went.

The port workers in Melbourne were on strike and we were told our stop could be extended for a few days. The English cricket team was on tour and my friend Ian had a good idea.

'How would you like to come with me to the match at the MCG?'

'The famous Melbourne Cricket Ground? I'd love to!'

We had a memorable day, watching a great cricket match on a typical Australian summer's day on one of the finest cricket ovals in the world.

I was looking forward to a hot bath on board and a dinner to top off the day. When we arrived at the wharf we were surprised to see a vacant space where our ship had berthed. I turned to my friend, who was now in a state of panic, and said, 'The ship's gone to Sydney without us!'

He was mortified.

'Geez, Madge'll kill me!'

She had stayed on board and I remembered her earlier attempts to dissuade us from attending the match. She had been none too pleased to see us traipsing off that morning. Ian was in trouble and he knew it.

We looked out into the grey bay as the sun began to set and saw the *Moreton Bay* anchored about a mile offshore. Ian rushed to the nearest phone and contacted the ship's agents.

He came back disappointed.

'They said there's nothing we can do but wait till the morning when we can catch a ferry out to the ship. What are we going to do?'

The poor fellow was nearly out of his mind as he contemplated facing a hostile spouse who would tear strips off him in front of the other passengers. Our more immediate worry was the total lack of funds to pay for a bed in a lodging house.

'A milkshake and a lamington is about our limit,' I said when we had turned out our pockets.

We sat down on a wooden bench on the wharf.

Ian was disconsolate. 'How are we going to fill in 12 hours doing nothing?'

'We could just curl up on the bench and sleep. That's what the natives do in India.'

My friend did not take kindly to this suggestion.

'I'm not a bloody blackfella!'

'Maybe not,' I said, 'but we are two whitefellas in the same boat as those blackfellas on the streets of Bombay.'

'Bloody port workers, they would pull a strike. The agents should have put on a ferry to get us on board.'

'Look, Ian, there's absolutely nothing we can do about it. We should make the best of it.'

'What is there to make the best of?'

'Well, if you're so desperate to get on board, why don't you swim out to it?'
That kept him quiet for a while.

Night was closing in. The city of Melbourne was lit up. Ian cheered up a little, and, pointing to a strip of light some distance away said, 'That's St Kilda, let's get over and mingle with the people.'

'Great idea.'

We set off in that direction and when we got there we entered a brightly lit milk bar and ordered a milkshake apiece.

I was not to know that this part of the city was renowned for its fun parlours and brothels. Some attractive women approached us.

'Hey, good looking. Want to have fun with us?'

I was embarrassed. Ian turned to me and said, 'Why don't you take up the offer? If they like you we might just score a bed for the night.'

'Sure, and get beaten up for not paying for the privilege — not on your life!'

We wandered about like a pair of tourists out for a bit of fun. It was past midnight and the crowds thinned out. I felt weary.

'Let's make tracks to the pier and rest until sunrise.'

Back to the bench on the pier we went, and sat and looked out at the *Moreton Bay* on the water, lit up from bow to stern. It was the middle of summer but the night was cold. Ian went around the nearby rubbish bins and returned with some newspapers.

'Tuck them into your shirt and they'll keep you warm,' he said. He was right. I awoke just as the grey turned into light. Stiff and sore from the wooden battens on the bench, I got up and walked to a tap and splashed my face with cold water. I felt awake.

We were joined by a few people from other vessels that stood anchored out in the bay. Our ship's doctor too joined us. He had been on the town all night and looked it. At the ship's side we had to climb aboard on a rope ladder. The poor doctor made heavy work of it, almost falling off a couple of times. A few passengers lined the rails and cheered us aboard.

Up there was Madge, and I had guessed right. Ian received a right royal welcome the moment he set foot on deck. I copped a bit of her tongue-lashing too, but laughed it off.

She was implacable.

'You two have been painting the town red with the city's whores!'

'We should be so lucky,' I said and wandered away to my cabin.

Day after day, we awaited news of the ship's movements. The passengers were getting restless and some decided to catch the train to Sydney.

Then, one afternoon, the ship was tugged alongside the pier again. Cargo was loaded and we sailed off on our last leg to Sydney.

It was a glorious summer's day when we entered the Sydney Heads. We moved slowly up the harbour and sailed under the magnificent Harbour Bridge and tied up at Dalgety's wharf in Walsh Bay.

We assembled in the Customs hall. I lifted my meagre possessions of one small zip bag on to the table.

'Is this all you have?' asked the Customs officer, showing very little interest. 'Please open your bag.'

As I did, the zipper broke off. The officer felt sorry for me.

'That's bad luck. Wait here, I'll get some string.'

He helped me wrap it around the canvas case and wished me luck. All my shipmates had gone. I stood on the footpath and counted the cash I had left. Five pounds and a few silver coins was all I could find.

Chapter 28

ANOTHER HILL STATION

A taxi pulled up alongside. I spoke to the driver.

'Are there any cheap lodging houses nearby?'

'Get in, mate. I'll drive you to one.'

'How much is the fare?'

'Don't worry about it,' he muttered, and off we went. It seemed rather a long drive when we finally pulled up in front of a cottage.

'Where are we?'

'Bondi Junction.'

'Is that near Bondi Beach?'

He looked at me.

'Yeah, it's just down the road.'

We entered the place together and he spoke to the landlady, who was obviously a friend.

'Have you got a spot where you can put this bloke up?'

'I certainly have.'

She was a kind person and showed me to a room I would share with four others.

'This is a bed-and-breakfast. It will cost two pounds 10 shillings for the week.'

I paid her in advance.

'I'm going to look for a job tomorrow. Would you mind if I paid you the second week's lodgings when I find one?'

'That will be fine,' she said. I was relieved.

The next few days were taken up with the search for a job. There was a slowdown in employment in the early 1950s and any job was hard to come by. I walked the miles into the city and returned to the dock area.

Across the harbour at Pyrmont, I noticed some construction work going on. I entered the site and asked the foreman for any position going.

'Can you rig?'

'I've had some experience in the timber industry in Scotland.'

'Okay then, I'll take you on for three months. You'll be working with an Irish crew building the chimney stacks for the Pyrmont power station.'

The wages were relatively good.

'There's a component of danger-money because of the height.'

I took the job.

The next day I snatched an early breakfast and caught the tram into the city to the building site. I did as I was told and got on with the task. My co-workers were good to me and showed me the ropes.

'Mind you don't kill yourself working too hard,' said one of them with a wink.

During the lunch break all the workers headed for the pub across the road for lunch. I had to conserve my money, so I found a hot food stall down the street and lunched on a pie. My finances were dwindling and I became quite concerned. The tram fare was not expensive but any penny saved would go towards a pie or a milkshake during the lunch break.

At the end of the day I walked home to Bondi Junction. It was much further than I had expected. I asked the landlady for an early breakfast the next morning. She obliged and so I fell into the pattern of rising at 4 am, grabbing some breakfast and taking off on the long walk to my job at Pyrmont.

The daily routine was getting to me. The long walk to my digs was becoming wearisome. I was constantly hungry and the smell of food cooking in the cafes along Oxford Street brought on pangs of hunger.

One night as I strolled along Moore Park a car stopped beside me.

A group of young people in the car asked me for directions.

'I'm sorry, I'm new to the area.'

Two of them got out of the car and set about me. I heard some women's voices from the car and another chap got out. They hit me about the head but

I got an opportunity to retaliate, so I raised my boot and kicked one of the assailants in the groin. He screamed and fell to the ground. His mates went to his assistance and bundled him into the car and took off.

I returned to the boarding house bleeding from my ear. I was greeted by my room-mates who appeared unconcerned.

'What've you been doing? Got in a shindig at the pub, didja?'

At the end of the week I lined up at the paymaster's office.

'I'm sorry, you won't get any pay until next Friday. We hold a week's wages in hand.'

I was mortified. I had been banking on some money to carry me through for the rest of the week. I was in a predicament.

I asked the landlady to carry me for another week, which she did quite happily. But I still had to eat. During my walks home from work I had seen a pawnbroker's shop along Oxford Street. There was not much I could pawn save a suit I had purchased in London from the 50 Shilling Tailors, the working men's mercers.

It was Saturday, my day off, when I set off to find the pawn shop. I wrapped the suit in brown paper and entered. The man at the counter was not overly impressed with doing a deal.

'I really need the money, because I've just started working and I need to get by until next payday.'

'All right then,' he said, grumbling, handing me one pound and 10 shillings.

'I'll be back next week to retrieve the suit,' I said. I never did.

With some money in my pocket I sat down in a park and mapped out my finances for the next six days. I budgeted for six Sargent's pies and an occasional lamington.

I began to feel that I had blundered in choosing this country to escape to. During my working hours atop the building at Pyrmont I had a grandstand view of the overseas ships pulling into the terminal.

Looking down on to the decks I felt an urge to stow away on one of the liners and head away to some other land.

But when Friday came around I felt good. I picked up my wages, had a quick shower in the toilet block and headed for a restaurant for a feast. I walked along George Street and noticed a sign advertising a Chinese restaurant called the Golden Hind.

I walked down into the basement, sat at a clean table and called the Chinese waiter over. As I scoured the menu, I asked for a glass of sauterne.

I ordered more than I could possibly put away and left the restaurant feeling on top of the world. I hailed a taxi and drove back to Bondi Junction in style.

With my debt to my landlady paid off and some money in my pocket, I was set to take on anything. I grew in confidence. Down the road from my lodgings I discovered a cheap eating-house run by a dear old lady who dished up home-made food for the workers in and around the area. As the weeks rolled by and the money kept coming in, I spent the weekends exploring the city. Yet every night I would return to the old lady's cafe and eat a home-made meal. We became good friends and there was always that bit extra set aside for me.

'You're my favourite customer,' she would say as she ladled an extra slice of meat on to my plate. God bless her.

Some time later when the job was completed I went along and told my dear old friend that I would be moving on.

'That's a terrible shame, dearie. I'll miss you. Mind you come and visit whenever you're in the area. You can have a meal on the house.'

My friends at the lodging house invited me down to the local pub for a farewell drink. I thanked them but declined the offer.

'I've already spent more than a month on board a ship with hard-drinking Australians! If I keep doing it, I just might fall into the trap of alcohol dependency myself!'

They laughed uproariously and wished me luck.

My wandering spirit lured me to the railway station. I wanted to visit the national capital, Canberra, but I looked about the platforms at Central station with an open mind, to see if any other destination caught my eye. In the end, I bought a return ticket to Canberra, intending to come back to Sydney at a later date to look for some more work. I was relatively flush with money and I intended to have a good time. Nothing was mapped out and I was prepared to take each day as it came along. I was a free agent and the *wanderlust* had reignited after my forced stay in Sydney.

Another train ride. In a moment I was clacketing along the outer suburbs of Sydney and heading for the highlands. How did I guess that? The train was called the Highlands Express. My travelling companions in the strange carriage were not very talkative. I was reminded of commuters in the suburban trains in London, who always preferred the newspaper to conversation. I thought, too, of my many travels on the Indian rail system which were exactly the opposite. There, I had sometimes wished for peace from an inquisitive and talkative group of fellow travellers.

As the train sped along I began to wonder where the highlands were and when we would start the climb. I had pictured scenes similar to photographs I had seen as a child of the Rocky Mountains, with huge plantations of pines and other cold weather trees and rocky outcrops.

It was not to be. The train did slow down a little as we started to take on the slopes ahead. Some timber appeared and the air become cooler. It was a gradual change from the city which was not very far away. The train negotiated a tunnel or two and we stopped at some very small stations that were empty of people. It was a complete contrast to the tiny villages where the Indian trains stopped and there were always more people than there was room to stand. Still, I enjoyed soaking in the scene.

The countryside was quite different from any I had experienced before in my journeys. The grass was not as green as the pasture in England and the trees carried a different shade of green from the trees in the tropics. Of course, I realised that this was a dry continent that lacked the lushness of growth of vegetation in the wetter regions.

The engine slowed again and I looked out of the window to catch the view ahead. I began to wonder if it would be anything like the climb up to my home town of Maymyo in Burma. The air became decidedly cooler. I was excited at the prospect of getting off at Canberra, which I knew from early geography was somewhere near the Australian Alps.

It was the end of April 1951. I pondered the nine years since I had set out on that fateful journey. Now I was a strapping young man, free once again, and the gypsy spirit was running in my veins. Farms appeared alongside the track. They seemed to be orchards of some description. Shades of autumn, I figured. The train stopped again at the town of Mittagong. Strange name for a town. Off again, and this time we entered a fairly long tunnel.

On emerging from the darkness I looked out at a landscape that seemed miraculously to have changed to a place I remembered dearly, my home town in Burma. The countryside was green and the trees had taken on a different shade. Some were changing colour with the season, and they were surely temperate trees. The train stopped and I alighted to stretch my legs and to admire the scene. I had occupied the last carriage on the train.

Now I stepped out on to the platform marked with a sign saying 'Bowral'. I was confronted by an older man, with newspapers tucked under his arm. He was a newspaper vendor. I bought a paper and while we chatted for a moment I looked about and my eyes caught the view of hills on either side of the track.

One of the hills appeared to have been quarried. It was as if the ghost of my home town had suddenly appeared before me. Maymyo, too, had a similar hill that had also been quarried and I remembered as a young lad playing rather dangerously there, among the gravel. Surely this must be another hill station.

As I looked about, absorbed in what I saw, the train took off without me. My earthly belongings, too, were being carried away. I waved to the guard but got no response. Nonetheless, I felt good. The place had a good Karma. Almost nine years to the day, I had arrived.

INDIA 1942

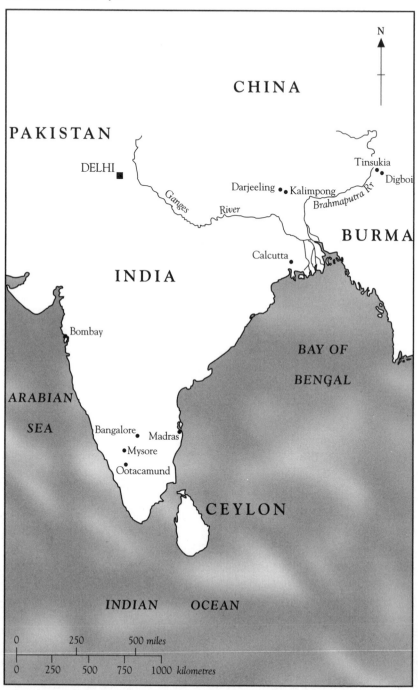

BURMA 1942

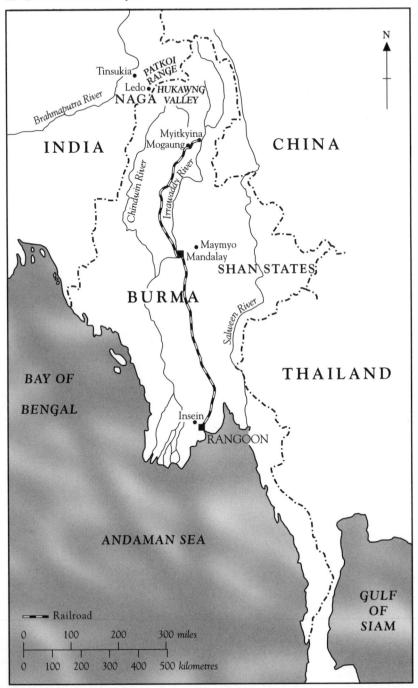

A SHORT BIOGRAPHY

 Colin McPhedran has lived in the Southern Highlands of New South Wales for more than 50 years. *White Butterflies* is an autobiographical account of his remarkable survival, as an 11 year old and beyond, of one of the most hazardous and tragic wartime refugee trails in the world.

Colin was born in 1930 in Burma to a Scottish father, an executive with Shell Burmah Oil in Rangoon, and a well-born Burmese mother.

With his mother, brother and sister, Colin fled the Japanese occupation of Burma in 1942, walking through the dreaded Hukawng Valley to India during the monsoon. Barely alive, and suffering malaria and dysentery, he was rescued on the border and spent months in hospital struggling back to life.

Having survived, he spent the next four years without his own family, but nurtured by the warmth and colour of the vast Indian culture. Completing his schooling in India, he spent several years in England before arriving in Australia in 1951.

Colin settled in Bowral, married an Australian girl, Laurel Hales, raised a family and worked in a variety of jobs, eventually owning two service stations, ironically pumping Shell fuel. He led an active community life, serving on the local council and the hospital board, but rarely mentioned his extraordinary tale, even to his family.